LEARNING WITHOUT CLASSROOMS

Visionary Designs for Secondary Schools

Frank Kelly & Ted McCain

FOREWORD BY **Jason Ohler**

Solution Tree | Press

Copyright © 2019 by Solution Tree Press

Materials appearing here are copyrighted. With one exception, all rights are reserved. Readers may reproduce only those pages marked "Reproducible." Otherwise, no part of this book may be reproduced or transmitted in any form or by any means (electronic, photocopying, recording, or otherwise) without prior written permission of the publisher.

555 North Morton Street
Bloomington, IN 47404
800.733.6786 (toll free) / 812.336.7700
FAX: 812.336.7790

email: info@SolutionTree.com
SolutionTree.com

Visit **go.SolutionTree.com/instruction** to download the free reproducibles in this book.

Printed in the United States of America

22 21 20 19 18   1 2 3 4 5

Library of Congress Cataloging-in-Publication Data

Names: Kelly, Frank S., 1941- author. | McCain, Ted D. E., author.
Title: Learning without classrooms : visionary designs for secondary schools / Frank Kelly and Ted McCain.
Description: Bloomington, IN : Solution Tree Press, [2018] | Includes bibliographical references and index.
Identifiers: LCCN 2018000332 | ISBN 9781945349904 (perfect bound)
Subjects: LCSH: Education--Effect of technological innovations on. | Educational change.
Classification: LCC LB1028.3 .K434 2018 | DDC 371.33--dc23 LC record available at https://lccn.loc.gov/2018000332

Solution Tree

Jeffrey C. Jones, CEO
Edmund M. Ackerman, President

Solution Tree Press

President and Publisher: Douglas M. Rife
Editorial Director: Sarah Payne-Mills
Art Director: Rian Anderson
Managing Production Editor: Kendra Slayton
Senior Production Editor: Todd Brakke
Senior Editor: Amy Rubenstein
Copy Editor: Ashante K. Thomas
Proofreader: Elisabeth Abrams
Text and Cover Designer: Abby Bowen

For Lynda, whose scholarship about all things French remains an inspiration—intellectually and culinarily.

—Frank Kelly

For Sarah and Joel (my daughter and son). Your fresh perspective on life and learning has continually challenged my thinking. You would thrive in the schools without classrooms that we describe in this book.

—Ted McCain

ACKNOWLEDGMENTS

We are grateful to a team of creative individuals at Stantec who supported Frank's time, provided travel expenses, and helped generate the graphics that contribute to explaining the concepts we explore in this book. Given the challenge of gathering information from diverse districts and getting it into a common format, it was a big, well-done job over many months with lots of changes. We would also like to thank the following.

- Liz Katz is an architect with a passion for education and a graduate of the Westside High School in Omaha, Nebraska. She had a major role in creating the plan diagrams for transforming existing high schools.

- Luis Ayala is an architect and skilled designer in both the United States and his native Paraguay. He has both practiced and taught and is an avid architectural photographer.

- As our manuscript and graphics progressed, we had the support of two architectural students: Will Crothers, a graduate student at Rice University, and Edgar Saucedo, who completed his studies at the University of Houston. Their expertise and perspectives were very helpful.

- With the major role our book prescribes for digital technology, Ramy Hanna's expertise in visualizing and animating our architectural concepts was an excellent resource. He made us mindful of the amazing things we can do to create a more engaging school environment for students and teachers.

- Lori Clifton and Kimberly Bow did amazing things with InDesign, helping us turn a huge collection of separate files into a plan for one cohesive book.

- An old friend and distinguished author and speaker, Ian Jukes, joined with Frank and Ted for some long weekends at the Best Western Maple Ridge, British Columbia, Canada, to explore many of the ideas we delineate in this book. We are grateful for his friendship and the lively conversations.

Solution Tree Press would like to thank the following reviewers:

Tura Bailey
Principal
Hackett Elementary School
Hackett, Arkansas

Melissa Barlow
Principal
Yukon High School
Yukon, Oklahoma

Dawna Buck
Principal
Muskogee High School
Muskogee, Oklahoma

Sandra Carmony
Principal
Washington Elementary School
Bountiful, Utah

Carri Eddy
Principal
V.R. Eaton High School
Fort Worth, Texas

Jane Garraux
Principal
Dr. Phinnize J. Fisher Middle School
Greenville, South Carolina

Philip McIntosh
Department of Science
Challenger Middle School
Colorado Springs, Colorado

Thomas Noonan
Principal
Catholic Memorial High School
Waukesha, Wisconsin

Gail Pletnick
Superintendent
Dysart Unified School District
Surprise, Arizona

Sheldon Russell
Vice Principal
Fort Herriman Middle School
Herriman, Utah

Lisa Sprague
Principal
Grandview High School
Greenwood Village, Colorado

Ruth Steidinger
Senior Director of Academic Programs
  and Support
Wake County Public Schools
Cary, North Carolina

Visit **go.SolutionTree.com/instruction** to download the free reproducibles in this book.

TABLE OF CONTENTS

Reproducible pages are in italics.

About the Authors xiii

Foreword xv
by Jason Ohler

Introduction 1
by Ted McCain and Frank Kelly

    The Elements of Schooling 3

    About This Book 6

PART 1

Understanding 21st Century Learning 9

Chapter 1
The Classroom Has Run Its Course 11
by Ted McCain

    See the Hidden Mindset 13

    Move Beyond Classroom Attachment 14

    Essential Questions 16

Chapter 2
Key Principles for Modern Schooling 17
by Ted McCain

    Technology Transforms Lives 18

    Technology Changes How Students Learn 21

    Focus on Individuals 22

    Build Flexibility Into Everything 24

  Rethink How We Use Time 25

  Develop Higher-Level-Thinking Skills 26

  Essential Questions 28

Chapter 3

Nine Essential Skills for the Modern World 29

by Ted McCain

  Intrapersonal Skills 31

  Interpersonal Skills 32

  Independent Problem-Solving Skills 32

  Interdependent Collaboration Skills 33

  Information Investigation Skills 33

  Information Presentation Skills 34

  Imagination Creativity Skills 34

  Innovation Creativity Skills 35

  Internet Citizenship Skills 36

  Essential Questions 38

Chapter 4

How Technology Will Change Education 39

by Ted McCain

  Debra Goes to an Advisory School 41

  Arthur Helps Plan a Career Fair 42

  Sarah Progresses to Project-Based Learning 44

  Brian and Virtual Learning Environments 45

  Bobby Partners With His Smart Personal Assistant 48

  Mr. Harrison Uses a Smart Assistant to Teach Differently 50

  Brenda Learns Sculpture From an International Expert 52

  Thomas Learns in a Global Work Group 54

  Essential Questions 58

PART 2

Designing 21st Century Schools 59

Chapter 5
Schooling for the Future 61
by Frank Kelly

    The Merit in Open-Plan Schools 62

    Schooling Without Classrooms..64

    Advisories as an Instructional Approach..................................66

    Technology Resources...75

    Use of Time..77

    Funding Resources 82

    Spatial Environments...83

    Community Context 84

    Transitions From Elementary Schools to Advisories........................84

    Staff Development in an Advisory..85

    Essential Questions..87

Chapter 6
How to Make It Happen 89
by Frank Kelly

    Gather Data and Establish a Vision 91

    Plan Options, Scope, Schedules, and Budgets 95

    Obtain Funds for Construction, Acquisitions, and Other Necessities 96

    Create Construction Documents 96

    Construct the School 97

    Obtain and Build Out Furniture, Fixtures, Equipment,
Technology, and Instruction Materials 97

    Occupy and Operate the Facility 98

    Develop Staff 98

    Understand the Big Picture 98

    Essential Questions..99

Chapter 7
Concepts for New Advisory-Based Schools..........101
by Frank Kelly

    The Comprehensive Advisory High School................................102

    The Academy Advisory High School.....................................104

The Project-Based Learning Advisory High School 104
The Advisory Middle School... 106
Essential Questions.. *108*

PART 3

Reimagining Schools for the 21st Century 109

Chapter 8
Additional Considerations for Transitioning to an Advisory Format 111
by Frank Kelly and Ted McCain

Minimum Thresholds for Effective Instruction 112
Challenges for Creating New Learning Environments 114
A Future for the Past 116
Essential Questions... *118*

Chapter 9
The Capital School:
A Historic High School Draws Inspiration From Its Rich Urban Context 119
by Frank Kelly

The Existing School 120
Our Proposal and Spatial Modifications 122
Cost and Time Implications 125
Observation 125
Essential Questions... *126*

Chapter 10
The Green School:
A School Built Before Air Conditioning or Computers Inspires New Teaching, Learning, and Sustainability......... 127
by Frank Kelly

The Existing School 128
Our Proposal and Spatial Modifications 129

Cost and Time Implications 131

Observation 132

Essential Questions. *133*

Chapter 11
The Connected School:
A Small Rural School Uses Sophisticated Teaching and Technology to Link to the World 135
by Frank Kelly

The Existing School 136

Our Proposal and Spatial Modifications 137

Cost and Time Implications 139

Observation 139

Essential Questions. *140*

Chapter 12
The Open School:
A Formerly Open-Plan High School Reconsiders Its Past 141
by Frank Kelly

The Existing School 142

Our Proposal and Spatial Modifications 144

Cost and Time Implications 148

Observation 148

Essential Questions. *149*

Chapter 13
The District School:
A Multicampus High School Provides Diverse Learning Opportunities 151
by Frank Kelly

The Existing School 152

Our Proposal and Spatial Modifications 157

Cost and Time Implications 160

Observation 161

Essential Questions. *162*

Chapter 14
The Tech School:
A Middle School That Paces Technology's Progress 163
by Frank Kelly

    The Existing School 164

    Our Proposal and Spatial Modifications 166

    Cost and Time Implications 169

    Observation 169

    Essential Questions. 170

Chapter 15
The Academy School:
A High School That Uses the Flexibility of an Office Building to Serve Teaching and Learning 171
by Frank Kelly

    The Former Building and Existing School 172

    Our Proposal and Spatial Modifications 174

    Cost and Time Implications 176

    Observation 178

    Essential Questions. 179

Epilogue
Concluding Thoughts 181
by Frank Kelly and Ted McCain

    Schools That Break the Mold 182

    The Path Forward. 187

References and Resources 189

Index 197

ABOUT THE AUTHORS

Frank Kelly is an architect and planner with Stantec in Houston, Texas. He has a deep interest in education and all the elements that comprise the environment teachers and students experience in our schools.

Frank often lectures at U.S. school conferences. The Texas Association of School Administrators and Texas Association of School Boards have recognized projects for which he provided planning and programming services with Caudill Awards in 2007 and 2008. His work also received the 2008 Council of Educational Facility Planners International's MacConnell Award. (This organization is now the Association for Learning Environments.) In 1984, he was elected to the American Institute of Architects' College of Fellows (Design) and in 2009, the Association for Learning Environments (then Council of Educational Facility Planners International) Southern Region named him planner of the year. He coauthored with Ted McCain and Ian Jukes *Teaching the Digital Generation: No More Cookie-Cutter High Schools*. He authored the paper "Artifacts of Schooling" for the *Journal of Applied Research on Children* for the CHILDREN AT RISK organization.

A graduate of Rice University, Frank has taught design in the school of architecture at the University of Tennessee and worked with architectural classes at Rice University and Texas A&M University.

Ted McCain, first and foremost, is an educator who has taught high school students at Maple Ridge Secondary School, British Columbia, Canada, for over thirty years. Although he has had several opportunities to take other jobs, both inside education and in the private sector, he has felt his primary calling is to prepare teenagers for success as they move into adult life. He is the coordinator of Digital Arts Academy for the Maple Ridge School District in Vancouver, British Columbia, and has taught computer networking, graphic design, and desktop publishing for Okanagan University.

In 1997, Ted received the Prime Minister's Award for Teaching Excellence. Ted received this prestigious Canadian national award for his work in developing a real-world technology curriculum for grade 11 and grade 12 students that prepares them for post-graduation employment in website design and computer networking. The Prime Minister's Award for Teaching Excellence recognized Ted's work in creating his innovative problems-first teaching strategy, his "4D" approach to solving problems, his unique use of role playing in the classroom, and his idea of progressive withdrawal as a way to foster independence in his students. Ted wrote or cowrote eleven books on the future, effective teaching strategies, educational technology, and graphic design.

Prior to entering the teaching profession, Ted worked for several years in the computer industry as a programmer, salesperson, and consultant. In addition to his work as a teacher, Ted has also consulted with school districts and businesses since the 1980s on effective teaching for the digital generation and the implementation of instructional technology. His clients have included Apple, Microsoft, Aldus, and Toyota, as well as many school districts and educational associations.

To book Frank Kelly or Ted McCain for professional development, contact pd@SolutionTree.com.

FOREWORD

by Jason Ohler

We will always want schools in some form. They may remind us of the patch of ground beneath the shade of the olive tree where Socrates and his students sat to debate truth and logic. They may consist of constellations of simple, satellite-connected rooms, distributed throughout the world, enhanced by augmented reality and robot mentors. They may consist of fabricated universes, shared by avatars or holographic projections, with multisensory capabilities that are so immersive and visceral that they are indistinguishable from real life. Depending upon how far into the future we want to look, they may well come to us in forms that we can't yet dream of.

Regardless of the form or what we call them, we will always want schools to develop collaborative learning environments, serve as hubs of community activity, and allow new generations of students to pursue individual passions. We will always want schools that allow us to work together, so we can share resources, tell stories to each other, and pass on skills, ideas, and what is most enduring about our cultures. We will always want our places of learning to model what is best in us and best for our children.

What has changed is *how* all of this can happen.

Our technological trajectory promises unfathomable, roller-coaster innovation with no braking system. It's a wild ride, full of panic and possibility, and it poses the following challenge to anyone interested in education: in an era of unbelievably powerful tools, embedded within the universal connectivity of the internet, we can have whatever we want. The question is: *What do we want?*

Until the late 20th century, that question had all the substance of asking how many angels dance on the head of a pin. But in an age when we can code, fabricate, and reinvent just about anything we can imagine, the question is not only real but also urgent. With a future that unfolds at the speed of thought, we need to be able to plan for change, rather than keep changing our plans.

That is why this book is so important. If we want to create schools that lead the way in a time of change, then we need to read this book seriously, with a mind focused on the big picture it presents, as well the practical details it provides. *Learning Without Classrooms: Visionary Designs for Secondary Schools* answers the question, What do we want? It also addresses not just what is going to happen, but what we could make happen. It goes on to ask, "How can we better design schools for maximum effectiveness in facilitating improved student and teacher interaction?" Above all, it puts the importance of student learning at the center of our efforts to reinvent schools, particularly in ways that are relevant to students and the times in which they live.

In the end, Frank and Ted provide a theoretically fascinating and practically based road map that connects education's changing nature with new possibilities that await us. All that is necessary to take advantage of their vision is leadership that is willing to seize the challenge. They leave that up to you.

INTRODUCTION

by Ted McCain and Frank Kelly

Do you realize that we teach the same way today that Aristotle taught Alexander the Great 2,000 years ago? It hasn't changed. That's got to change.

—Michio Kaku

The purpose of any education system is to help students learn. The key to student learning is effective interaction between a student and a teacher. Schools are the places best equipped to facilitate that interaction. This raises the question: How can we better design schools for maximum effectiveness in facilitating improved student and teacher interaction?

We immediately face a significant challenge when we ponder the answer to this question—the general look and nature of schools haven't changed much since the early 20th century. This is something that anyone who was raised in public schools, and then raised their own children or grandchildren in public schools, will recognize. Virtually everyone has a common picture in his or her mind for what a school is and how it operates, and that vision is consistent whether you are a teacher working directly with students in a classroom; a school administrator responsible for creating a timetable that determines when and where teachers and students meet; a facilities staff member for a school district responsible for determining the specifications for new or renovated school buildings; an architect tasked with designing a school facility; a parent of a school-age child; a schoolboard trustee charting the future course for the schools in your district; or a department of education official at the state (or province) or federal level involved in planning curriculum for secondary schools (grades 6–12). The list goes on, but the mindset persists that learning occurs in schools with classrooms. Communities have built schools this way for so long that it's difficult to conceive of any other way for them to look.

However, the foundation for why we organize schools this way is gone. The stable, predigital world for which we designed our school system no longer exists. A highly volatile, ever-changing, globally networked world of instantaneous information transmission is replacing it. The skills students need for success in this new environment are significantly different than those educators traditionally teach in the school system. This puts our schools in a precarious position because we are too often preparing our students for the wrong future. Instead, schools must serve and be a part of the world in which they exist. To do that, they must evolve with that world.

This is not to say that secondary educators, administrators, school architects, and district leaders are not giving their all to make schools work. There are many dedicated people working hard to make the education system the best it can be for students. The problem is that we educators can do an excellent job executing within existing systems, but we are often not doing the *right* job. The digital world does not need our modern school systems' obsolete picture of excellence.

Modern school systems are obsolete because technological innovation has disrupted the traditional ways the world outside of school works. This disruption brings radical new ways of accomplishing tasks into our lives. For example, knowledge workers in diverse fields like accounting, engineering, medicine, and financial planning can now reside anywhere in the world and digitally send their work to clients via the internet. North American workers must compete with highly qualified workers from around the globe. Automation in the form of both robots and software continues to replace many jobs humans traditionally performed. This is the new workplace reality. In contrast, and as we will explain in this book, the world inside schools looks much like it did throughout the 20th century. For the most part, the skills schools teach, how they teach them, and the way they assess student achievement remain virtually the same as in the 20th century. This leaves schools out of sync with the world for which they are supposed to be preparing students.

Furthermore, the changes that will occur in the world by 2040 or even 2030 will dwarf the changes we have had to deal with so far. We describe many of these changes in detail in *Learning Without Classrooms: Visionary Designs for Secondary Schools*, but rest assured, they will challenge educators, leaders, and school architects to adapt quickly if they are to effectively prepare students for a much different world than previous generations experienced. This requires schools to implement new instructional approaches that properly equip students with the new skills necessary for their future success. Adopting these approaches means rethinking the entire concept of classroom learning.

Brilliant minds across all of education have explored the changes educators must make in their teaching methodology to align with 21st century learners' needs (Robinson & Aronica, 2015; Thornburg, 2014; Wagner, 2012; Zhao, 2009); however, few question or explore alternatives to the 21st century schools' central paradigm—the traditional classroom consisting of four walls with a grouping of twenty-five to thirty students sitting at desks, receiving stand-and-deliver-style instruction from one teacher covering one subject in one hour. Any new instructional approaches school systems introduce largely build on this traditional classroom model because teachers can implement them with very little new training. Since there has been little movement away from the traditional classroom arrangement, there has been little need to question how districts design schools. Consequently, districts continue to construct school buildings that look much like the schools 20th century learners grew up with.

For the sake of future learners, we must explore how secondary school facilities can differ if we implement in a significant way the sound, decades-long, and research-based instructional ideas of educational experts (Andrade & Valtcheva, 2009; Bloom, Engelhart, Furst, Hill, & Krathwohl, 1956; Gardner, 2011; Vygotsky, 1978). Consider how we could design schools that facilitate individualized, learner-centered instruction that allows students to progress at their own pace. What would schools look like if we re-examine how schools use time and consider alternatives to the traditional one-hour periods? Is there a better way to configure the physical space in secondary schools to support problem-based instruction that mimics the challenges students will face when they leave the school system? What impact could truly authentic assessment have on the way we use space in schools? Could we better design schools to support the important, meaningful, long-term relationships students need with their educators?

These are all questions we answer in this book, but to really understand the significance of our ideas, we need to introduce a concept that underpins everything you will read in the coming chapters—the elements of schooling. From there we break down this book's approach to these elements and how we've organized it to propose a vision for schooling that doesn't depend on classrooms.

The Elements of Schooling

To ensure that the new schools we create are effective, every stakeholder in education needs to rethink all the factors involved in schooling. However, student learning must always be the focus of everything we do in schools. To that end, we identify six crucial and interconnected elements that factor into the learning equation (see figure I.1).

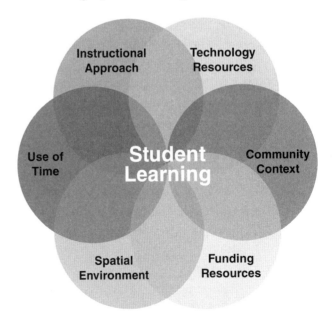

Figure I.1: The six crucial elements of schooling.

None of the components in this figure are ends in and of themselves. Instead, their effectiveness derives from how well they work together to create relevant learning environments for students. To emphasize this point, this figure specifically illustrates how each of the support areas interconnect. Note that because we reference these elements of schooling throughout the book, thoroughly understanding the purpose and role of each element, and how all elements impact each other, is *critical* to the vision we present.

The following list explains how we define the six elements of schooling.

1. **Community context:** Each school must reflect the characteristics and community needs of its location. When the community changes, schools must change to continue to be effective. We need to make different schools to serve different students in different communities. The cookie-cutter schools of the 20th century cannot work for all students in all communities.

2. **Instructional approach:** A school's instructional approach should have a direct impact on the configuration of its physical space. The problem is that schools have used the lecture approach for so long it has become entrenched as the default way to teach. This leads to default expectations, procedures, and policies in the overlapping elements in figure I.1 (page 3). However, there are many ways to teach, and we know that students learn in different ways. No instructional method works equally well for all students. We must tailor the methods we use to teach the students we serve so that we can measure learning outcomes one student at a time and not by mass statistics. Changing the instructional approach in schools will have significant ripple effects in all the other circles in the diagram.

3. **Use of time:** The amount of time that schools allot and how they organize around the time available determine much of what teaching and learning look like. We know that different students learn and work at different paces (Levine, 2011; Medina, 2014; National Education Commission on Time and Learning, 2005). If time is fixed, then learning will be the variable. Most often, students receive failing grades for not meeting learning objectives in the time allotted (a semester, for example), not because they are incapable of learning the objectives. We can make school time serve students and learning rather than make students serve time in their schools.

4. **Technology resources:** The technology the world outside the school system uses has changed dramatically in the 21st century. Not so inside schools. For example, classroom teachers often do not have access to scanners, 3-D printers, digital still and video cameras, or the photo- and video-editing software and training necessary to effectively use these tools. The technology we use inside schools must remain in sync with the technology in place in the professional world. This means the technology we use to support teaching and learning must quickly make the transition from paper based to a variety of digital resources that expand students' abilities to find any information they need at any time and from anywhere.

5. **Spatial environment:** Teaching and learning needs should shape the physical spaces in our schools rather than vice versa. Schools are not neutral containers. The configuration of a physical educational space enables and constrains the instruction that takes place within it. Consider the secondary school classroom that represents the centerpiece of school design; it is a

space with walls and a door with about seven hundred to eight hundred square feet. It serves one teacher, a class of about twenty-five students, and one subject for one period, usually about one hour in duration. This classroom configuration severely limits the opportunity for teachers and students to explore learning that is individualized and self-paced. Instead, instruction is invariably teacher-centered and lockstep because teachers want every student doing the same thing at the same time. This classroom configuration also makes interdisciplinary studies very difficult. Furthermore, facilities staff want classroom construction to be durable and lasting, which constrains flexibility to respond to changes in teaching and learning. New and renovated school spaces, like those we propose in this book, can and must support and enhance innovative ways for effective teaching and learning.

6. **Funding resources:** The funding available for schooling and facilities clearly impacts the resources available for teaching and learning. The funds coming from public sources (federal, state or provincial, and local) too often draw schools into broader discourse over taxes and politics. Many funding decisions are limited in scope without considering the wider implications of the impact schooling has on society, and many of those responsible for funding decisions may not be open to paying for schools that operate differently from what they grew up with. But consider the huge costs when we don't spend education dollars in ways that benefit teaching and learning. Students who are ill-prepared for the wider world limit a nation's ability to compete globally. Students who are unemployable because they fail or drop out generally pay fewer taxes and place larger demands on governmental entities for welfare, medical services, incarceration, and so on (Latif, Choudhary, & Hammayun, 2015; Mallet, 2016; Massachusetts Department of Elementary and Secondary Education, 2014). Conversely, successful students are a net benefit to society.

All student learning is the product of the interplay of these six elements, which are all inextricably linked—make a change to one and it affects all the others. It is our belief that many insightful and valuable education initiatives fail to achieve maximum effectiveness because they focus on just one of these elements without taking into account that the relationship each component has to the others is more important than the component itself. For example, change the funding for schools and its effect ripples through all the other elements with a positive or negative impact on overall learning. When U.S. schools cut staff in response to the 2008 recession, school districts laid off hundreds of thousands of teachers and support staff (Center for Public Education, 2010). As class sizes grew, this change impacted how schools delivered instruction. In turn, that impacted facilities as classrooms were too small to accommodate the increase in class size. That limited the programs schools could offer and reduced their ability to respond to community needs. It became a vicious circle.

For another example, what if we change the technology we use in schools? The impact of such a change also ripples through the other elements in figure I.1 (page 3). With digital technology for instruction and individual devices for students, we have the potential to dramatically alter the relationship between students and teachers. Students can have direct access to content anywhere and anytime; not just from teachers, and not just in classrooms. Subjects and courses can come to students wherever and whenever they might be versus students going to teachers for course content that teachers deliver in fixed classrooms at fixed times. The opportunity for individualized, self-paced instruction is real and practical, and we explore this opportunity in *Learning Without Classrooms*. With digital technology, we could eliminate or dramatically reduce paper text and library books, saving considerable sums and reducing the area and staff libraries require. But, the technology is not cheap, and schools must prepare to consistently update or replace it. Effective technology use dramatically impacts instruction, time, facilities, and funding.

As a final example, consider how a school might change its use of time. Since the early 20th century, we have operated on an agrarian calendar in which schools are open approximately nine months of the year. This means that while school districts have billions of dollars invested in school facilities, equipment, and so on, those capital investments sit idle about 25 percent of the year. That is enormously costly.

Altering the school year for year-round use opens the door for students to work continuously and succeed at their own pace. We would not have to fail students because they don't meet learning objectives on a fixed schedule. Instruction becomes more flexible and accommodates varied learning styles and paces, improving outcomes for students and thereby actually saving taxpayers from paying for students to repeat failed courses.

The point of all this is to convey that there are no neutral changes. Because each of these six elements has a ripple effect on the surrounding elements, improving student learning to make it effective in preparing students for life in the 21st century means we cannot focus on only one element. Instead, we must deal with them all concurrently. Failure to do this accounts for the extreme difficulty we've had for decades in truly improving and transforming education. Consider that, in most school districts, each element is an entirely separate administrative group with its own leadership, budgets, procedures, and so on. Consider that these groups are so different in their staffing and the nature of their work that they may not share a common vision for the future, may not communicate well, and may not always be fully cooperative.

We believe that it is vital that we put an end to this silo approach to education where there is little shared vision or meaningful discussion between those who represent the six elements in our diagram. In this book, we hope to engage people whose work comes from all the elements in our diagram. We want to spark conversations between all the stakeholders in education about what effective schooling should look like as we move further into the 21st century. That means examining real and substantive alternatives to traditional, classroom-centered schools.

About This Book

Learning Without Classrooms uses the elements of schooling to propose a new and highly flexible model, or concept, for schooling rooted in the advisory-school concept. This is a format that supports teachers and students in achieving individualized, self-paced, and successful technology-driven learning. To establish our vision for this concept, we organize this book to establish the scope of the challenges we face and then detail how we can design schools and curricula to meet them. This book is for grades 6–12 stakeholders across the educational world, whether you are teachers, administrators, school designers, elected or appointed officials, or parents. Although we specifically target this content toward educators working in the United States, we believe you can adapt and apply our ideas in communities throughout the world.

There are three parts to this book. Part 1 (chapters 1–4) outlines some powerful ideas about what we need to do to change our schools to better prepare our students for the world of the future. It is imperative that all educators wrestle with the issues confronting 21st century learning and the reasons *why* we need to consider dramatic changes to school design. Chapter 1 deals specifically with why traditional classrooms are ill-suited to support learning. Chapter 2 establishes key principles for modern learning, including the disruptive role technology plays in it. Chapter 3 outlines the crucial skills students need for success in the 21st century. Chapter 4 establishes multiple visions for how education must change to support students in a rapidly changing world.

Part 2 (chapters 5–7) establishes what an advisory school looks like and how a school built on this concept can successfully banish classrooms to the dustbin of education's history. Chapter 5 establishes the core vision by detailing an advisory school's instructional approach, its components, how it changes a school's use of time, its funding, and how districts can support their staff in adapting to it. Chapter 6 focuses on practical ways districts can effect these changes in its schools by establishing a vision and then executing it. This is the chapter for those most interested in answering the question: How do we establish and execute this process? Chapter 7 establishes four examples of advisory schools that could immediately function in the United States and in many other locations around the world.

The chapters in part 3 (chapters 8–15) each explore *how* your districts can apply the ideas we present in this book to an existing middle school or high school. Not every district can afford to undertake the design and construction of new school buildings, so we want to outline how to transform existing school buildings to create effective learning environments for the 21st century. Chapter 8 focuses on additional challenges educators and other stakeholders will face in establishing advisory schools in their communities and how to overcome them, while chapters 9–15 each highlight a different school and how its respective district could reinvent it as a school fit for 21st century learning.

Finally, the epilogue revisits our elements of schooling as a means to reflect on the content you absorbed from this book as well as looks at some schools in the United States that already use its tenets to positive effect.

To help people engage with the ideas we are presenting, we include a set of essential questions at the end of each chapter. It is our hope that these questions will spark lively and much-needed discussions about the nature of schools and schooling.

Although parts 2 and 3 explore physical changes to secondary schools, to address the ideas we present in part 1, you need to know that we actually wrote all of this content *for teachers* as much as we wrote it for school facilities staff, leadership, and architects. Part 1 outlines some powerful ideas about what we need to do to change our schools to better prepare our students for the world of the future, but these ideas only work in tandem with the concepts we present in the rest of the book. We believe it is imperative that all educators, regardless of professional focus, wrestle with all these issues.

Let's begin.

PART 1
UNDERSTANDING 21ST CENTURY LEARNING

Chapter 1
THE CLASSROOM HAS RUN ITS COURSE

by Ted McCain

> It's amazing how little the typical classroom has changed over the years. . . .it doesn't reflect what educators have learned about helping students and teachers do their best work.
>
> —Bill Gates

In our elements of schooling diagram (figure I.1, page 3), the *community context* element represents technological innovation's impact on the world. This element also represents the new generation of digital students entering our schools. It, combined with the *technology resources* element, is putting pressure on the other elements and creating the impetus for change. Digitally controlled machines and digital software have drastically changed the way companies manufacture and deliver products, the way marketers reach prospective clients, and the way customers place orders and communicate with companies. In addition, the students entering our classrooms have spent their entire lives using powerful digital tools that enable them to access and edit information from around the globe. These tools also empower them to publish their thoughts and visually communicate their daily life experiences in ways that are foreign to many adults. Consequently, educators feel pressure to update what they teach to keep instruction relevant for the modern world.

If we accept these ways in which technological development has dramatically changed the nature of the communities surrounding our schools, we must accept that schools must change just as dramatically to effectively prepare students for success in the world they will enter when they graduate.

We must remember that radical changes due to technological development are not a temporary anomaly that educators can wait out until everything returns to the way it was. No, the new world of constant, disruptive, and technology-driven change is here to stay. This means we can't pretend that we can fix the education system with minor improvements like adding a new course, changing a test, adding a new teacher requirement, or adopting a singular pedagogy. Such changes will not somehow make schools magically work for the 21st century. Therefore, it is time for educators to make some major structural changes to the way schools operate.

One of the greatest hindrances to updating our schools to keep them effective in this new world is schools' basic unit for spatial organization—the classroom. The basic concept for the modern classroom comes from William Wirt who, in 1908, applied mass production thinking to education (Thiede, n.d.). Wirt envisioned a factory school based on classrooms where teachers specialized in teaching a single subject. In this model, as each period ends, a bell rings, and students move to their next class as though they were on an assembly line, moving from one specialist to another. These schools sacrifice an individual student's unique interests and learning skills for the sake of greater efficiency (Cohen, 2002). The economics and efficiency of this concept were so powerful that it caught on and rapidly spread to virtually all secondary schools across the continent. Many people don't realize it, but we continue to have Wirt's 1908 assembly-line approach to education in most secondary schools.

Although the mass-production, assembly-line approach makes schools easier to organize and easier to run, it prompts certain questions: Does this approach make learning better? Does a mass-instruction approach to education maximize individual student potential? The answer to these questions is the critical point. Schools are not factories. Unlike the uniform products that come from the factory production line, the products schools produce are human beings who range widely in interests and abilities. We believe education's goal must be to shape a wide range of students from many backgrounds and perspectives into citizens who can function effectively in a pluralistic, democratic society, as well as achieve sufficient financial success to live happily while contributing to a nation's overall economic health. To meet these goals, we must move on from a 20th century mindset of assembly lines and mass production. We need to consider new ways of schooling that do not center around the traditional classroom.

To that end, what if we designed schools for mass customization rather than mass production? What if our schools could better help each student maximize his or her strengths and minimize his or her weaknesses while also allowing him or her to progress at his or her own pace and enter the wider world better prepared to be a functioning, productive member of society? These are questions we answer throughout *Learning Without Classrooms*, but we begin in this chapter by examining the hidden mindsets that affect how we approach education and how we can break our attachment to the traditional classroom.

See the Hidden Mindset

Contemplating alternatives to conventional approaches to classroom instruction is a great challenge because schooling based on traditional classroom structures has been with us since the early 20th century. As educators, we have developed great familiarity with the mass-instruction classroom model to the point that teachers, students, administrators, and parents aren't even consciously aware of all the concept's attached assumptions, expectations, and behaviors.

We all have an amazingly similar mental picture of what a school is and how it operates. It is a facility that limits access to only certain times during the day, uses bells to govern classroom activity time, and closes for more than two consecutive months each year. When the school is open, rules require students to physically meet inside a relatively small room where they often limit access to the online world that is the backbone of the world economy and the essential means of global communication. Instead, schools confront students with the long-established idea that a teacher, and supplemental textbook and photocopied materials, can provide all the information they need to fully function as citizens, employees, or entrepreneurs ready to successfully deal with the complexities of modern life.

The foundational assumption of this artificial world is the classroom. It is a concept that captures the essence of what school is and has been for a long time. Educational institutions even use the word *classroom* as a descriptor for an overwhelming number of educational concepts and terms. Classroom instruction, classroom management, classroom seating, classroom learning, classroom behavior, classroom organization, classroom resources, classroom technology, classroom staffing, classroom schedule, classroom size—the list goes on and on. The word *classroom* is so loaded with meaning for virtually anyone who has gone to school since 1920 that as soon as you use *classroom* as an adjective to describe anything, everyone knows exactly what you are talking about. This is the hidden mindset that unconsciously accompanies any school organized around the traditional classroom.

We observe an incredible number of assumptions inherent in schools built around classrooms. Many of these assumptions associated with the traditional classroom skew heavily toward preparing students for the late industrial age. The following are just a few examples of the baggage that comes along with the traditional classroom.

- The classroom is a homogenous, teacher-owned, and static space that is often visually and physically enclosed. Teachers rarely float between classrooms. The bell and class schedule generally limit student access to the space and teacher, and students do not have a personal workspace of their own.

- Classroom teachers use technology as a tool to enhance teacher-centered, stand-and-deliver instruction. Students' technology use is not integral to instruction, if the school allows it at all.

- Teachers emphasize memorizing static details and procedures for performing discrete tasks rather than on developing in students critical 21st century skills like independent problem solving, investigating, creating, and collaborating. Fostering meaningful relationships between students and teachers is not a priority.

- Classroom evaluation generally focuses on summative evaluation rather than formative evaluation.

- Uniformity and conformity are implied classroom goals. Schools group students by age and move them lockstep through their grades. Teachers instruct mass groups of students on a linear educational pathway (usually set by the district, state or province, or department or ministry of education), and schools view as a problem any student who disrupts or does not keep up with the pathway. This leads educators to view student failure for some percentage of students as an acceptable outcome. (It's not!)

- With the focus on group classroom instruction and fixed time, students who fail must repeat the very same process that did not work the first time. Thus, they lose months or even a year of their lives, and taxpayers must pay for the same education twice.

- With group classroom instruction and fixed time, reporting to parents tends to occur only at specified times and specified ways (report cards). Individual parent-teacher-student communications are infrequent.

- Many classrooms have outdated furnishings that are not appropriate for learning activities and technology use.

- School systems operate in silos. Districts do not expect teachers to know anything about school design, nor facility staff anything about instruction. Yet, having all stakeholders understand new instructional perspectives is critical for designing effective, forward-looking school facilities.

With these points in mind, consider for a moment—if you were starting from scratch—how you would define a methodology to meet students' needs for the 21st century and the spaces to house those students. Very likely, this vision bears little resemblance to the traditional classroom concept. Indeed, schools based on traditional classroom designs have been the norm for so long that educators, parents, administrators, departments of education staff, and politicians rarely consider alternate organizations of physical space. When districts build or renovate a school, they almost never ask, "Should we have classrooms?" Instead, most districts ask, "How many classrooms do we need?" To change that, we need to look beyond the classroom.

Move Beyond Classroom Attachment

Our goal throughout the rest of this book is to look at how all educational stakeholders can work together to change schools to be more effective and consider what those changes should look like. To be sure that we are objectively evaluating new thinking, it is critical that we acknowledge our familiarity and comfort with schools designed around classrooms. This is important because new ideas for delivering instruction to modern digital students using new online digital tools will most certainly stretch our thinking beyond a classroom-based approach. These ideas may be uncomfortable to contemplate because they will employ concepts and methodologies that are unfamiliar to most educators. When we confront educators and other stakeholders with our ideas for how schools could operate in the future, we often see their first response is not to like them. They can't see how such radical changes to the status quo can possibly work. They see all the reasons why it will be difficult, if not impossible, to make these changes. However, we must all resist this initial reaction because, in many cases, our attachment to the entrenched classroom mindset creates an outsized counterweight.

Instead, we must come to grips with the fact that the classroom is an obstacle to making the shift to effective, forward-thinking instruction because it does not provide the necessary flexibility in the face of new online digital tools and experiences. For example, modern digital students are completely comfortable with what Ted calls *spontaneous ad hocism*. Texting on their phones, young people form several new social and work groupings in real time over the course of a day. If several students discover they are working on the same project at the same time, they can form an impromptu work group to get the project done. They are accustomed to and successful when working in this way. Classrooms are a barrier to this kind of approach.

Classrooms, and all the behaviors and expectations that accompany them, are acting like deadweights as education stakeholders try to create much more responsive school systems that are more effective in preparing students for the 21st century. We must look beyond 20th century ideas for how to organize schools and consider what learning could be without classrooms.

To do this, it is critical that we immediately engage all stakeholders in exploring these ideas. We cannot afford to leave this until tomorrow. Whether you are a teacher, a school administrator, a school board member, a superintendent, a Department of Education employee, a politician, or a parent, you must begin looking at how your schools can and should change to meet the challenges of preparing students for their futures. The pressing need for everyone to envision new schools without classrooms is summed up in this quote from Arthur Levine (2011):

> Today's schools are an anachronism. They resemble the assembly lines of the industrial era, when they were conceived. Groups of 25 to 30 children, beginning at age five, are moved through 13 years of schooling, attending 180 days each year, and taking five major subjects daily for lengths of time specified by the Carnegie Foundation in 1910. These schools are time-based—all children are expected to master the same studies at the same rate over the same period of time. They focus on teaching—how long students are exposed to instruction, not how much they have learned. They are rooted in the belief that one size fits all—all students can benefit equally from the same curriculum and methods of instruction.

With this in mind, the following chapters explore how educators can change secondary schools to make them more effective in preparing students for success when they graduate.

Essential Questions

As you reflect on this chapter, consider the following questions.

- Think about the physical facility of the middle school or high school that you attended. Was the school built with traditional classrooms designed for one teacher to teach twenty-five to thirty students? If so, how do you think that affects your ideas for what schools look like?
- How does the traditional classroom mindset affect people's planning for new schools?
- How do your school's existing learning environments inhibit student learning?
- Given that most districts organize traditional schools for mass instruction, what would schools be like if districts organized them for mass customization and serving individual student needs?
- Close your eyes and think about designing a new school that will prepare each student for life in the 21st century. How do you see the arrangement of physical space? What would you change relative to traditional classroom-based methods that would help customize learning experiences to better support students and help them succeed after they graduate?

Chapter 2
KEY PRINCIPLES FOR MODERN SCHOOLING

by Ted McCain

The problem with our schools is not that they are not what they used to be, but they are what they used to be.

—Education Commission of the States

When we think about modern education and what students will need from their learning to be prepared for their future, there are certain things that we know: We know that technological innovation drives the world, we know that we need a significant shift in focus to help students attain the skills they require for success in the modern world, and we know that effective school design is based on what effective instruction looks like. Given these things, the next important question is: What are the key attributes of effective 21st century instruction? By identifying those attributes, we come to a subsequent question: How do we reorganize schools to make them serve that kind of learning?

To answer these questions, we look at two reasons why technology makes school change necessary—(1) how it is changing our lives and (2) how it is changing how students learn—and then focus on four principles that must form the new foundation for how we provide effective instruction for students who require much different preparation than those of us raised on 20th century learning. Those four principles are:

1. Establishing a focus on individuals
2. Building flexibility into everything we do as educators
3. Rethinking how we use school time
4. Focusing on developing students' higher-level-thinking skills

We start by examining how modern technology affects our lives.

Technology Transforms Lives

It's easy for those of us raised in the 20th century to think of the myriad ways technology has changed the world. However, the long-term impacts of technological development on how we live are only just beginning to come into focus. Like the ripples from a stone tossed into a pond, the effects of technological change are growing as time goes on, and these changes will continue to have an astounding impact on our daily lives. No one will be exempt from the effect of these changes. To give you an idea of what we will see very soon, the following is a description of life in the future by Kevin Kelly (2016), a founding executive editor of *Wired* magazine:

> It's 2046. You don't own a car, or much of anything else, paying instead to subscribe to items as you need them. Virtual reality is as commonplace as cell phones. You talk to your devices with a common set of hand gestures. Practically all surfaces have become a screen, and each screen watches you back. Every aspect of your daily life is tracked by you or someone else. Advertisers pay you to watch their ads. Robots and AI (artificial intelligence) took over your old job, but also created a new one for you, doing work you could not have imagined back in 2016. (Jacket cover)

Many of us who have been around for a while think we've already seen all the upheaval technology is going to throw at us, but the changes still to come will be very different than anything we have ever experienced. Indeed, changes like the ones Kelly (2016) describes stretch our ability to comprehend them.

Incredibly, despite these enormous changes that we know are coming, many educators don't think they will significantly affect the way schools operate. In our observations, the modern school system's amazing stability fosters a belief in educators that we will just continue to teach students the way we have always taught students. Many in education believe that although we will continue to deploy and use new technology, the basic approach to instruction, the basic organization of schools, and the basic arrangement of the physical spaces in school buildings will remain essentially as they were in the 21st century. We disagree. These waves of change will become so massive that education will no longer be immune to the technology-driven changes that will sweep over the rest of the modern world.

To help you grasp the magnitude of what education will face, we identify four major aspects of technological change that will transform education: (1) technological change is accelerating, (2) hyperinformation is transforming knowledge, (3) mobile technology is transforming access to knowledge, and (4) smart technology is transforming the teacher's role. In the following sections, we examine each aspect.

Technological Change Is Accelerating

The world has always been an evolving work in progress. But a hallmark of the transition from the late 20th century to the early 21st century is a new kind of change—technology-driven exponential change. This is change that develops at an astonishing speed, much more quickly than linear change. What this means is that the power of new technology is increasing *much* more dramatically than anything we have previously experienced (Berman & Dorrier, 2016).

The implications of exponential change, and how the changes to come will affect students' lives, are staggering. For example, exponential development of artificial intelligence makes the arrival of fully intelligent personal assistants foreseeable in the next ten to fifteen years. These assistants will be capable of natural voice interaction, able to learn from experience, and proficient at accessing all the knowledge on the internet. These smart digital personalities will provide young people with personal assistants that will monitor their schedules, interact with others on their behalf, become "friends" that accompany them everywhere, and be powerful tutors that can teach them on every topic imaginable.

Ironically, the human mind's ability to cope with new developments like these actually hinders its ability to comprehend the magnitude of technological change as it is happening (The Mind Tools Content Team, n.d.; Yamamoto, 2011). This is an important point. When most people think about the future, they naturally make a linear projection of steady change because this kind of vision for progress is much more manageable for people to deal with. But because the world is experiencing exponential change (change that is accelerating), linear projections greatly underestimate the magnitude of change that we will actually see. Exponential projections, like those in the Kelly (2016) quote or those we present in chapter 4 (page 39), often seem too incredible to believe, but in times of exponential change, you must resist the temptation to look at a projected development and say, "That will never happen!" The truth is that when we look at technology through the lens of exponential change, we quickly see that developments that were once thought of as pure science fiction quickly become reality.

Hyperinformation Is Transforming Knowledge

Hyperinformation is the term Ted uses to describe the new ways technology allows us to experience information. First, the internet provides the average person access to an incredible amount of information, much more than any individual has ever had access to. Second, technology makes it easier to find the specific data we desire. However, technology is doing more than transforming the way we get information. It is also transforming the kind of information we get. Instead of just reading traditional text-based information, we can read, see, hear, and touch new digital forms of data. Games and simulations allow us to have virtual experiences like riding on a satellite, seeing inside an atom, watching chemical reactions, and walking beside prehistoric animals. *Hyperinformation* applies to all these types of information and the sheer volume of it. Access to hyperinformation allows us to move beyond the second-hand experiences of reading about events, places, products, processes, and stories to experiencing them in a way that is, for all practical intents and purposes, firsthand.

Mobile Technology Is Transforming Access to Knowledge

Schools have always been places where experts pass on their knowledge and skills to students. Libraries have long been repositories of a wide array of learning materials. Throughout history, people have physically gone to schools or libraries when they needed to learn something (Andrews, 2016). However, online mobile technology is changing the notion that learning is tied to a physical location. Mobile technology frees learning from the confines of schools and libraries because people can learn wherever they are, whenever they need new information or they need to develop a new skill. We foresee that as the power of connected, mobile technology expands, educators will find it increasingly challenging to adapt the way they teach students. It will be critical that teachers embrace the idea that learning will increasingly happen outside the school building and beyond normal school hours (Richmond, 2015).

Having easy access to knowledge from anywhere is also changing the kinds of skills that people need to succeed in life. Historically, schools have emphasized memorization. Being educated has long been associated with what you know. But when students have access to the totality of human knowledge via an internet-connected, handheld device (a volume of data that no person can memorize), they must understand how to use those data and determine what are useful and valid from what are not. These are the sorts of higher-level-thinking skills (Anderson & Krathwohl, 2001) that empower students to do productive things with the information they find, and we write more on these skills in chapter 3 (page 29).

Smart Technology Is Transforming the Teacher's Role

Smart technology already surrounds us wherever we go. However, it's important to understand just what we mean when we refer to *smart technology*. From cars with driver-assist features, to digital assistants that listen and talk (think Google Home), to the robots that build things, smart machines are a part of our everyday lives. However, we are only just beginning to see the emergence of truly intelligent machines. The cognitive ability of digital assistants like Amazon's Alexa and Apple's Siri is an indication of where things are headed, and where they are headed is a game changer.

Rapidly, technology platforms are becoming capable of performing many cognitive functions humans do (Gillies, 2017; IBM, n.d.; UBS, n.d.). We will soon interact with smart, digital personalities as naturally as we interact with real people. This intelligent technology will process our requests, retrieve desired information, and perform a multitude of daily tasks for us. Smart machines will also anticipate our needs and do things for us before we even think of asking.

Educators are not going to be exempt from the effects of this new smart technology. We are going to have to deal with the reality that intelligent technology will very soon be capable of performing many tasks that teachers currently do. This does not mean that teachers will lose their jobs. Instead, it means that teachers will have to embrace new roles in instruction (Ostdick, 2016). This is actually a good thing. Smart technology holds the potential to relieve teachers of the drudgery of performing lower-level-information-dissemination tasks in instruction (Anderson & Krathwohl, 2001). This frees them to focus on the much more challenging and rewarding higher-level tasks of teaching critical thinking and creativity as well as the emotionally complex tasks involved in helping students mature.

Technology Changes How Students Learn

It's not just a question of how quickly the change of pace is accelerating or how easy it is to access knowledge. The kinds of change we write about in this chapter are not neutral—they profoundly impact people. Technology integration into daily living affects people at fundamental levels, especially children (Bowman, 2017). It changes how they live their lives, the way they expect others to treat them, even the way they think and the things they value. Although technology affects everyone to some degree, it most affects those who are born into it. Students in the digital generations have no experience with the way previous generations did things. Access to hyperinformation is simply what they experience and expect, and they run with it. It even changes how students think and absorb information in fundamental ways. Two important changes educators must consider when contemplating education's future include how social networking changes life experiences and how technology affects the way students learn.

How Social Networking Changes Life Experiences

Students are always on their phones and other digital devices. They use them to talk with their friends, but they use them for much more than that. They are sharing audiovisual information like sound recordings and videos shot on their phones, YouTube videos, and music files. They are also sharing textual information in text messages, email, personal writings, poems, and research for school projects. They are using their digital devices to compete and collaborate in online games and simulations. They also use social-networking technology to connect with subject-matter experts who give them instruction on topics of interest. In short, social-networking technology is not just a medium for idle chatting and posting, but a means to eliminate the barriers of distance and language that stand between people and knowledge. Friends can be sitting a few desks away in the same classroom, or they can be anywhere else around the world. We have personally witnessed students in classrooms partnering with peers from around the globe on group learning projects.

For the digital generations, there is no practical difference between the lives they live in the physical world and the lives they live while online (Palfrey & Gasser, 2010). It's all part of the same tapestry. They live in a physical world and have normal face-to-face relationships, but they also participate in a digital online culture where they have virtual relationships that augment face-to-face interactions, as well as virtual relationships that take place completely in the online world. The digital generations are as comfortable with online relationships as they are with face-to-face relationships.

How Technology Affects the Way Students Learn

Anyone who works with students in the digital generations is aware that there is something different about the way they learn. There is sound empirical research that confirms that these young people are cognitively different from older generations. A number of books, including *Growing Up Digital* (Tapscott, 2000), *Grown Up Digital* (Tapscott, 2008), *Born Digital* (Palfrey & Gasser, 2016), *Understanding the Digital Generation* (Jukes, McCain, & Crockett, 2010), and *Rewired* (Rosen, 2010), are telling us that the fast-paced bombardment of text, color, images, and sound that young people experience in the digital online world from a very young age alters the way their brains process information. Twenty-first century students are using different parts of their brains to process information than their parents and teachers. They are visual learners. In addition, information on the internet is often broken into bite-sized chunks to make it quicker and easier to consume. Ted observes that a steady diet of these information nuggets has led to a much shorter attention span in modern digital students. Further, social networking has created an online environment where learning is often a very social experience. Add all of this up, and you see that the digital generations are actually thinking and learning differently than previous generations. It is important for parents, teachers, administrators, and politicians to recognize that modern students have a much different way of learning than adults raised in a nondigital world.

The following list of some of the major attributes and expectations we observe in digital students puts this into perspective.

- They use technology as an essential tool to connect to their culture; using mobile, internet-connected devices like cell phones is not optional for the digital generations.
- They expect immediate access to up-to-date information whenever they need it.
- They are used to immediate feedback (from video games and online experiences).
- They read text only as a last resort and usually receive information in visual, auditory, or multimedia formats.
- They expect to be connected to friends all the time, with relationships and collaborations that comprise a mix of online and face-to-face interactions.
- They turn to online sources to learn new skills or acquire new information and expect those services to tailor themselves to their individual wants and needs.
- They have a much more open concept of privacy and are more comfortable with intelligent, autonomous technology than generations raised in the 20th century.
- They multitask on several simultaneous online interactions while they go about daily tasks.

The students entering schools present the adults who are in control of the school system with a significant problem—many adults can't relate to the world of the digital generations. We have witnessed in many schools, school districts, and states and provinces that neither teachers, administrators, parents, school district staff, school board members, people at the department of education, nor state or provincial politicians raised in the 20th century have any real long-term exposure to the technologically infused life experience of the students who populate our schools. There are, of course, younger teachers entering the teaching profession that have grown up in the modern, networked, digital environment, and these new colleagues bring hope for the future as they work their way into the ranks of teachers, administrators, and school district staff. However, we will not feel their most significant impacts on schooling for some time.

The core truth is that the majority of the adults responsible for teaching young people are out of touch with their students. This is a huge issue of relevancy for education. Unless teachers make it a priority to understand the world their students experience outside school, the instructional methods and examples that teachers use are almost certain to miss the mark. We believe this is a huge impediment to effective communication and to engaging learning, but we do offer solutions in the following sections to help bridge this gap.

Focus on Individuals

We have many years of research that tell us what really works and what doesn't work in terms of maximizing learning in young minds (Battro, Fischer, & Léna, 2008; Tokuhama-Espinosa, 2010). This research invalidates many of the assumptions that constitute the assembly-line foundation for how we organize most schools. The cognitive development of human beings simply does not fit into nice, neat organizational structures. Although these assumptions might have made sense from a business perspective, from a human-instruction perspective, organizational structures like grades designated by age and classrooms filled with twenty-five to thirty students for mass instruction are counterproductive at best and boring, oppressive, and damaging to individual students at worst. Trying to apply production-efficiency strategies to schools may produce efficient organizational structures, but it doesn't create an instructional environment that can handle the wide range of unique individuals that policy mandates schools teach.

In his book *Brain Rules*, John Medina (2014) writes about the disconnect between how the brains of students develop and the way schools are organized:

> The current system is founded on a series of expectations that certain learning goals should be achieved by a certain age. Yet there is no reason to suspect that the brain pays attention to those expectations. Students at the same age show a great deal of intellectual variability. These differences can profoundly influence classroom performance. This has been tested. . . . Lockstep models based simply on age are guaranteed to create a counterproductive mismatch to brain biology. (p. 67)

However, despite Medina's (2014) and other brain researchers' work to identify its flaws, a lockstep model for organizing schools is what we continue to have in education (Bransford, Brown, & Cocking, 2000; Jensen, 2005; Sousa, 2011). The question is, if we are not going to organize schools around grades and classrooms, then what should take their place? Listen again to what Medina's (2014) research has to say on this subject:

> You cannot change the fact that the human brain is individually wired. Every student's brain . . . is wired differently. That's the brain rule. You can either accede to it or ignore it. The current system of education chooses the latter, to our detriment. It needs to be torn down and newly envisioned . . . in a commitment to individualizing instruction. (p. 51)

What Medina (2014) is saying here is incredibly important. We should design schools to enable individualized instruction that meets each student's unique needs. At this point, we should note that educators have wanted to create individualized instruction for a long time, but the logistics of making that happen in the school system prevented large-scale individualized instruction.

Fortunately, technology excels at providing tools for customizing services for individuals. Consider the way 21st century businesses can target individuals with goods and services tailored to their personal needs then reflect on how educators could take advantage of those same technologies to better customize mass learning. For example, if you've ever browsed or purchased something at Amazon (www.amazon.com), you notice the company's website algorithms immediately begin to bring similar products to your attention (Amazon.com, n.d.). The more you use the site, the more information the site gathers about your preferences. Using that information, Amazon customizes your shopping experience to match your personal profile.

The way Amazon compiles and analyzes personal profiles to create a unique shopping experience for customers is part of something called *big data*. Big data refer to the use of advanced data analytics to extract value from the information it stores in a database ("Big data," n.d.). Amazon uses big-data analytics to determine individual user preferences (among other things), and it's not the only company using big data to create experiences customized to individuals. Facebook uses big-data profiles to determine how to organize each user's news feeds to reflect his or her interests. YouTube uses big-data profiles to suggest videos that will be of interest to particular people. There are many more (DeZyre, 2015). Big data are already well-established, and the ways companies use them will continue to grow and improve in the future. But consider for a moment how we can productively apply these concepts to education.

Big-data analytics can also enhance learning experiences for individual students who attend their schools. By compiling personal learning profiles, preferences, and progress for individual students, we believe school districts will be able to finally break free of William Wirt's 1908 lockstep approach to instruction. Big data will be a key to allowing students to progress at their own rate through school curriculum as well as the key to providing meaningful, automated, and personalized remedial instruction.

It is important to note that school systems will not be the only ones targeting young people with customized, personal educational programs. Already we see private companies offering instruction to students. The long-standing, entrenched approach to instruction that is prevalent in the school system doesn't encumber these companies (Herold, 2016).

Consequently, they are able to incorporate strategies for customized, personal instruction much more quickly than traditional schools. We believe this necessitates a significant shift in the attitude schools have toward students. Instead of viewing students as those the law compels to attend school, we must begin to see our students as clients who have many instructional options and whom we must engage with interesting instruction that prepares them for the world they will face outside school.

Beyond just big-data collection, an important component of reorganizing schools around individual students will be ensuring that schools provide one-on-one time between a student and a teacher. Educational experts have known for some time that a meaningful relationship with a caring adult is an important factor in students' success in school (Boynton & Boynton, 2005). The key is to create an organizational structure that facilitates this relationship and to allot sufficient time for the adult to get to know each student as a unique individual.

Build Flexibility Into Everything

In an environment of constant and accelerating change, how do you develop effective instructional methods? How do you design or modify school facilities so they will continue to be effective over their entire life span? The answer is flexibility. Educators at all levels must include flexibility as a planned component in everything they do. Since conventional school spaces are not built for flexibility, this means we must embrace a major shift in thinking about how we configure spaces for learning.

It's critical for all educators and stakeholders to keep in mind that it is their job to prepare students to succeed in environments that don't exist yet, in jobs no one has thought of yet, doing tasks no one has imagined yet, using technology no one has invented yet. How can you provide instruction that is flexible enough to equip students for the huge range of future possibilities that await them? We believe the key is to teach students processes, because a process-focused approach is the best way to future-proof our students.

The best way to understand a process-focused instructional approach is to compare it to the *content-focused approach* educators traditionally use. Content-focused approaches focus on memorization and information recall, which are concepts we discussed previously in this chapter (Technology Transforms Lives, page 18). Because it is simply not possible to memorize the enormous volume of new and changing informational content the modern world produces, what students need from educators is to learn an effective process for finding information and assessing the credibility and relevance of the information they find. From there, students can effectively use those resources to educate themselves with what they need to know in the moment. Process skills, many of which we discuss throughout chapter 3 (page 29), empower students to function in life because these skills remain the same even as the world changes.

Rethink How We Use Time

There is an old saying in education that if time is the constant, then learning is the variable. It means that if a course runs for a fixed length of time, not all students will have learned the same amount when the course is over. This has been an underlying foundation to the instructional approach in the school system for a very long time. It is an approach that virtually all of us experienced growing up, and most students still experience this approach in schools. Courses run for a fixed period—a year-long term or a four- or five-month semester. When students finish a course, teachers assess how well they learned the curriculum. Those who excel receive *A*s, those who display genuine proficiency receive *B*s, and so on down the line. Learning varies from student to student, and educators view failure as an accepted outcome for those who could not learn enough in the time allotted. Those who fail have to repeat the entire grade or course, often with the same teacher using the same instructional approach that contributed to the failure in the first place.

But what would happen if we inverted the old saying? What would schools look like if learning was the constant and time was the variable? How would we have to adjust our instruction if the focus shifted from teaching for a fixed period to continuous learning for students? It turns out that this one change to the way learning occurs changes for the better almost everything we do in schools.

Reconsider our elements of schooling diagram (figure I.1, page 3) and its six elements that support learning. When you start making changes to the use of time, you drastically change all the other elements as well. For example, if we allow teachers to make learning the constant and time the variable then we must allow for students to progress through course material at their own pace. Such a change has significant ramifications for the way teachers teach. It's much harder for teachers to stand in front of a class and talk about some aspect of a curriculum because not all students will be ready for that instruction at the same time. This means shifting instruction away from talking to whole classes and focusing more on discussions with individual students or small student groups. The teacher's role changes from being *the sage on the stage*, who talks to students to pass on his or her knowledge to them, to *the guide on the side*, who advises them on the best learning strategies and digital tools to assist students with mastering course material.

Since mastery of course material is necessary for students to progress in a school where learning is the constant, failure is no longer a part of student evaluation. Students either master part of their required learning or continue working toward mastery. Assessment of learning can shift from norm-referenced evaluation (grading *A* to *F*) to criterion-referenced assessment that uses rubrics to measure the degree to which students master course material. Using criterion-referenced assessment, the goal shifts from rating and ranking students according to their level of learning over a fixed period to all students mastering course material before they progress to new learning tasks. Although this kind of assessment may be new to many parents and teachers, it is not just an academic theory. For example, Ted has seen how schools in British Columbia, Canada, have made a significant shift in the way they evaluate students by moving away from letter grades. In these systems, reports to parents reference the evaluation criteria and are much more anecdotal in nature.

Schools will also rely more on technology for instruction because technology provides the much-needed framework for students to access course content whenever they are ready for it. This means not only delivering content when students need it but also integrating those features with analytics that record, track, and analyze student progress.

This frees teachers from much of the burden of simple information dissemination, allowing them to monitor student progress and focus instruction on creating the higher-level-thinking tasks that get students doing something useful with the knowledge they acquire. It also comes with the side benefit of making it easier for parents to see and participate in their child's progress.

Such systems can help teachers identify which students are at the same point in a course and facilitate scheduling group activities. However, students in a continuous-progress learning environment take different amounts of time to reach a particular point in a curriculum, unlike students in a traditional school, where all students receive the same amount of time for learning course material. Consequently, when a language arts teacher schedules a seminar for a group discussion on the privacy and individual rights following a student reading of *1984* (Orwell, 1949), the group may consist of two seventeen-year-olds, five sixteen-year-olds, three fourteen-year-olds, and a precocious twelve-year-old.

This kind of change in the way educators focus school time has far-reaching implications for how schools operate. For example, once students begin to progress at their own pace, some will complete certain academic coursework before reaching the typical age for graduating into postsecondary study. School districts may establish partnerships with postsecondary institutions for students to continue their studies while they are still in high school. For students who complete certain courses in career-oriented programs, school districts may establish certified apprenticeship programs so students can begin some of their postsecondary work while they are still enrolled in high school (as many have done already).

Throughout the rest of this book, we write in more detail about achieving this kind of learning and how increased technology use and getting rid of classrooms facilitate this change.

Develop Higher-Level-Thinking Skills

From our work with many educators in North America and beyond, it is clear most educators say that high on their list of instructional goals is to develop students' higher-level-thinking skills (Anderson & Krathwohl, 2001). However, the reality in most classrooms, especially in high school, is that there continues to be an emphasis on rote content memorization and regurgitation. This situation is understandable. Virtually all teachers experienced teaching with a low-level memorization focus when they were students themselves. It is completely natural for teachers to teach the way they were taught. In addition, the move toward learning standards and standardized testing produced a major focus on content and low-level procedure memorization to improve test scores (Harris, Smith, & Harris, 2011).

Consequently, many teachers feel their job is done when they convey the information in a course curriculum and then test to see how well their students can remember it. This focus on lower-level-thinking skills then becomes a ceiling for what teachers do instructionally, and they do not often go above it (Towler, 2014). Learning suffers as a result.

However, there has been a significant shift in the kinds of thinking skills people need to be successful in the 21st century world. What has become more important is what you do with the information you retrieve using technology to solve problems while working with others. Linda Darling-Hammond, professor of education at the Stanford Graduate School of Education and president and CEO of the Learning Policy Institute, underscores this point when she writes, "In 1970, the top three skills required by the Fortune 500 were the three R's: reading, writing and arithmetic" (as cited in Davis, 2013).

In 2018, the Opportunity Network (n.d.) names communication skills, teamwork, and analytical and problem-solving skills as the top three skills in demand. Given this, teachers and students alike must see learning a topic's details as providing the base for further analysis, conversation, and debate. Students must be able to rethink their assumptions in order to solve problems, form opinions, make arguments, create effective vehicles for communication, or innovate new ways of doing things. To effectively perform these tasks requires that students have higher-level information processing, problem-solving, communication, collaboration, and creativity skills. In other words, learning the specific details in a curriculum creates the floor on which high-level thought stands. We write about these skills in detail in the next chapter.

Essential Questions

As you reflect on this chapter, consider the following questions.

- How are the changes in the modern world currently reflected in your school?
- Knowing that the world is experiencing technologically driven exponential change, how can you adjust your thinking about what the future will bring?
- What steps can you take to stay current on what is happening in the world for which you are preparing your students?
- What are the implications of hyperinformation on what and how we teach students?
- Given that students are fundamentally different, how should you change how you deliver instruction?
- How can you modify instruction and learning spaces in your school to flexibly meet students' individual needs?
- What implications do the principles this chapter outlines have for effective teaching and learning in the modern world?

Chapter 3
NINE ESSENTIAL SKILLS FOR THE MODERN WORLD

by Ted McCain

Today, even when they work exactly as designed, our high schools cannot teach our kids what they need to know.

—Bill Gates

The ease of access to any and all information (hyperinformation) that we wrote about in chapter 2 creates a major shift in the kinds of skills students need to succeed in the modern world. This shift points clearly to the need for students to develop higher-level-thinking skills (Anderson & Krathwohl, 2001). Consider the task of finding information for personal, educational, or business research. In the past, such tasks involved the physical act of flipping through cards in a library's card catalogue and then walking through stacks of books containing a limited selection of sources while using the Dewey decimal system to zero in on and locate the material you wanted to access. Modern digital tools make it easy to search a global collection of sources unimaginable in the 20th century. When the challenge is less about finding information than it is about extracting the most useful and valid information from a fire hose of sources, the essential skills students need to succeed in the wider world also change.

Consider what author and creative innovator Ken Robinson (2001) says on the topic of the new skills that people need for success in the modern world:

> New technologies are transforming the nature of work. They are massively reducing the numbers of people in industries and professions that were once labor-intensive. New forms of work rely increasingly on high levels of specialist knowledge and on creativity and innovation particularly in the uses of new technologies. These require wholly different capacities from those required by the industrial economy. (p. 5)

Robinson (2001) goes on to comment on the mismatch between the skills workers need relative to the skills that schools too often focus on:

> Employers are complaining that academic programs from schools to universities simply don't teach what people now need to know and be able to do. They want people who can think intuitively, who are imaginative and innovative, who can communicate well, work in teams and are flexible, adaptable and self-confident. The traditional academic curriculum is simply not designed to produce such people. (p. 52)

Although it may seem clear and obvious from quotes like these why students in the digital generations need new skill sets to succeed in the 21st century, it is still common for us to have teachers ask us questions like: "Haven't schools always been equipping students with skills for success in life?" And, "Isn't a skill a skill? How can there be new skills?" Don't dismiss questions like these out of hand. They are very good questions that deserve answers before we go further.

Consider what happens to skills over time.

- **Some skills become obsolete:** These are skills society values at some point but that become a victim of progress. Some obsolete skills include shoeing horses, sharpening swords, running a telephone switchboard, or typesetting. These are skills some may practice for highly specialized circumstances or out of nostalgia, but other skills have superseded them in mainstream life. There's nothing wrong with these skills, but for all practical intents and purposes they are obsolete.

- **Some skills that are on their way to becoming obsolete:** These are traditional skills that are still useful to some degree but are not as important as they once were. Examples of these kinds of skills include hand accounting, using the Dewey decimal system, long division, handwriting, and even driving. Only time will tell whether these skills will fully lose their usefulness.

- **Some skills never lose their usefulness:** Traditional literacy skills, for example, remain as valuable as they ever were.

These skills include reading, writing, numeracy, social and communication skills, and so on. The reason why these skills continue to be so important is that they are the fundamental building blocks of our society, and they are an essential part of interpersonal communications.

- **Some skills become more important:** These are not new skills. They are skills that have simply received a promotion due to the shifting needs of an ever-changing world. This set of skills includes information processing, critical thinking, problem solving, understanding graphic design, video and sound production, and imaginative communication skills like storytelling and art and music creation.

- **Some new skills are unique to the 21st century:** These are the skills that weren't necessary prior to the 21st century. In fact, they may never have existed before. These skills include such things as social-networking skills, online communication skills, digital citizenship, and online collaboration.

Schools are absolutely the best places to equip students with the essential skills they need for their adult lives, but to effectively meet this goal, it is necessary to continually alter school instruction to match life changes outside of school. Because of the exponential increase in disruptive technologies, and the effects of this on the modern workplace, we see a critical need to shift our educational focus to keep skill instruction relevant for the modern world.

To that end, we have worked and researched with other educators in our industry to identify nine critical skill areas on which instruction must focus to keep schools relevant in the modern world. Ted refers to our specific skill set as the *nine Is* (McCain, in press):

1. Intrapersonal skills
2. Interpersonal skills
3. Independent problem-solving skills
4. Interdependent collaboration skills
5. Information investigation skills
6. Information presentation skills
7. Imagination creativity skills
8. Innovation creativity skills
9. Internet citizenship skills

As you read our perspective on these essential skills, it's important to understand these are not just skills the digital generations require. *Everyone* needs these skills to function and succeed in the modern world.

Intrapersonal Skills

Intrapersonal skills constitute the mental habits that enable people to work through real-world situations and respond to challenges using awareness and well-thought-out strategy within their own mind. They are habits that students can learn, develop, and enhance at school. It's easy to skip these skills because we often don't explicitly focus on them in the classroom, but these are the most important skills that students get from their school experience because they empower students for long-term satisfaction and success in their personal and professional lives.

We break intrapersonal skills into two categories: personal character skills and personal productivity skills. *Personal character skills* include self-confidence, patience, honesty, open-mindedness, self-awareness, and emotional intelligence. *Personal productivity skills* include knowing how to learn, taking initiative, overcoming boredom and self-motivating, persevering when things are difficult, managing time, evaluating one's own work, and setting long-term goals.

Each of these intrapersonal skills makes for good personal character and productivity. Although most schools go to great lengths to ensure student productivity, some schools go to great lengths to ensure they don't teach character because many view teaching these skills as a parent's responsibility. In our view, all schools should teach character because developing these intrapersonal skills is a natural byproduct of giving students work to do to learn the material in the curriculum and then holding them accountable for doing that work. Indirectly, teachers have always been helping students acquire these skills ever since formal instruction began.

In an age when employers are contracting more and more work out to individual entrepreneurs, these metacognitive and introspection skills are essential not only for personal growth but for finding and maintaining steady employment (Torpey & Hogan, 2016). The key point here is that it is critical that we state these intrapersonal skills explicitly and make acquiring them a targeted goal in instruction.

Interpersonal Skills

Face-to-face communication skills remain the most important communication skills for people to develop for success in the professional world. Interestingly, technology is making them more important than ever. As we write in chapter 2 (see Technology Transforms Lives, page 18), the rapid growth in the power of smart machines and autonomous robots threatens to replace jobs that humans traditionally do. Many of the higher-paying jobs that will survive the coming expansion of automation will require strong interpersonal skills (Mahdawi, 2017).

Interpersonal skills are outward-focused life skills that we use every day to communicate, interact, and comprehend with other people and groups. Developing these skills is essential to effectively function in a family, in relationships, and in the workplace. Interpersonal skills include conducting a conversation, listening, understanding nonverbal communication, persuading or defending in a debate, selling, asking questions, showing respect, accepting and giving constructive criticism, and asserting oneself. Interpersonal communication skills are a significant aspect of many jobs in the modern workplace, and many companies are specifically looking for these skills when they interview potential employees (Graduate Management Admission Council, 2014). The importance of acquiring these skills means we can't just expect students to develop them on their own.

Independent Problem-Solving Skills

As automation and artificial intelligence (AI) increase in sophistication in modern workplaces, employers decreasingly hire for positions that demand physical skills and low-level-thinking skills (McIntosh, 2002). High-paying jobs in the 21st century increasingly require higher-level-thinking skills, including independent problem solving. This means workers must be able to develop solutions without overreliance on external guidance.

In the 20th century, employers predominantly required high-level, independent problem-solving skills only from their management personnel, but this is changing rapidly in the modern workplace. As digital tools become more powerful and ubiquitous, management is giving frontline workers more and more decision-making authority to solve the problems that occur daily in a broad range of jobs. This means employers need fewer workers, but those they do require must be more productive and able to work independently without waiting for someone in management to learn about an issue and develop a solution. Teaching students effective thinking strategies for solving problems equips them with powerful tools for the modern workplace.

What many teachers don't realize is that there is a structured process anyone can use to solve problems, just like there is a structured process to follow when you sit down to write a paper. Ted learned about structured thinking and problem solving in his systems-analysis studies and in the computer science curriculum at Simon Fraser University. In fact, there are extensive research and resources available to you on structured problem solving (Cameron, 2015; Rasiel & Friga, 2002; VanGundy, 1988). What Ted has done is reduce the problem-solving process down to its four essential steps, the *four Ds* (McCain, 2005).

1. Define the problem.
2. Design the solution.
3. Do the work.
4. Debrief the process.

By following these four steps, anyone can develop an effective solution to any problem. It is critical that teachers familiarize themselves with this process to teach it to their students.

Interdependent Collaboration Skills

Being just as productive working within groups as when working individually has always been an important skill, and the importance of having strong collaboration skills is only increasing. Interdependent collaboration skills include such things as being able to organize functional teams with members who complement one another, criticize ideas without criticizing individuals, negotiate and brainstorm within a team, solve problems in a group setting, elicit and listen to feedback, and take responsibility for tasks.

To consider collaboration's increasing role in modern workplaces, note that many companies use collaborative workgroups with members from offices located in different time zones across a country or around the world (Flynn, 2014; Seiter, 2015). When workers on the U.S. East Coast go home at the end of their working day, workers operating on the West Coast pick up and carry that work forward. Work then begins the next morning when the workers on the East Coast start their working day, several hours before the West Coast staff start their working day. By doing work in this way, a given project progresses more rapidly and efficiently. International companies use the same strategy, but they create workgroups with members in branch offices around the globe, ensuring that project progress continues twenty-four hours a day.

Consider what it's like to work in this kind of work group. In addition to traditional teamwork skills, working effectively in this type of virtual group also requires a fundamentally different set of collaboration skills than those people use in traditional face-to-face environments because collaboration can now be synchronous or asynchronous. Synchronous collaboration is real-time. Collaborative partners or groups simultaneously work and communicate using online digital tools. However, collaborating with virtual partners who are not physically in the same place and not in the same time zone often means workers work asynchronously by doing their collaborative work at different times. Learning the skills to function effectively in these kinds of virtual work groups has already become an essential skill for the modern world, and its role is only going to increase.

Fostering this kind of collaboration goes way beyond having students work with a partner. We must encourage teachers to think beyond the classroom and develop projects that involve partners and groups across the school, across the city, across the state or province, across the country, and across the world.

Information Investigation Skills

An ever-increasing amount of information—hyperinformation—arrives daily due to the number of people in the world producing new material combined with the global reach of information technology. This avalanche of data is already far more than anyone can process. Consequently, all this material provides little, if any, real value. In his book *Information Anxiety*, Richard Saul Wurman (1989) states, "We are like a thirsty man who has been condemned to use a thimble to drink from a fire hydrant. The sheer volume of available information and the manner in which it is often delivered render most of it useless to us" (p. 36). Consider that Wurman wrote those words in *1989* and how access to information has exploded since then. When you consider the ever-growing power of digital tools' advanced-search capabilities to access this incredible breadth and depth of material, it is clear that high-level-information-investigation skills are becoming much more important in workplaces than rote-memorization skills.

Students and workers alike need to be able to investigate a specific topic, find data that are pertinent to their investigation, and then determine the data's meaning. In other words, the world needs people who can figure out the relative significance of the information they find. Having the skills to determine what is significant and meaningful gives a person great power in the new information landscape. Therefore, we must move beyond the traditional focus on low-level recall when we teach young people how to find and process information. We want students to comprehend and be able to apply in new ways what they find, not just regurgitate theoretical knowledge.

This means encouraging and empowering teachers to teach beyond the test. Schools must shift toward more complex project-based coursework that requires students to investigate a topic and evaluate the information they retrieve to form fact-based opinions, decisions, and ideas.

Information Presentation Skills

Those of us born to an analog world predominantly gained information from printed text in newspapers, magazines, and books. However, the ability to economically print images and text in color and with greater clarity created a graphic-design revolution in communication that we often take for granted. But something even bigger has occurred in communication in the modern world—communicating with full-color, audiovisual movies.

Consequently, for most daily communications, written words are not enough. We are not saying that writing and the logical thought development behind it are not relevant anymore, and we are not saying that we shouldn't teach the writing process to students. But we are saying that the vehicle for presenting those thoughts for most daily communication moves well beyond just words.

To be clear, information presentation relates to *how* one presents a message, not the content's creation. Modern information-communication skills include an understanding of graphic design, typography, effective use of color, photo composition, video composition and production, and sound recording and editing. These are basic communication skills that all students need to function effectively.

This means superseding the focus on words as the primary means for communication with a larger focus that encompasses the audiovisual communication of the modern world. This is something for which we must train teachers so they can impart the necessary information presentation skills necessary to convey ideas in this world.

Imagination Creativity Skills

There are many aspects to imaginative creativity. For example, students can use imagination creativity skills to imagine new ways to communicate ideas, messages, and stories more powerfully. These are the new ideas they need for a short story, a poem, a novel, a script, or a screenplay that communicates a thought creatively. Most of us associate this kind of communication with language arts classes in school or telling our children bedtime stories, but the reality is that imaginative communication is very much necessary in the business world as well. In fact, imagination creativity skills are vital skills for thriving in the modern world. Consider the following quote from E and S Consulting (n.d.):

> We believe that few things are as powerful for a company, organization or project as a focused, compelling story well told. We've seen how a strategic story can move people beyond mere facts, beyond the nuts and bolts of their everyday tasks, to truly embrace a larger vision they want to make real.

Another aspect of imagination creativity is using imagination to generate new ideas for the design of something to convey meaning and add value to it beyond its function. For example, Apple adds value to its products through the exterior shape of its technology to make them more desirable than its competitors (Kuang, 2011). The idea is that there are lots of companies that make computers, but only one company that makes Apple computers. Tommy Hilfiger and North Face add value to their products with the style of their clothing. Ford Motor Company makes its vehicles desirable with the design of its cars and trucks.

Rest assured, imagination creativity goes beyond adding value to functional things. It can also be about creating value purely from beauty. This is why people buy a sculpture or work of art or a piece of music. The product doesn't have to serve a function. Its value can come purely from its shape, its color, its texture, or its sound.

Teaching students imagination creativity is often not a primary focus of the school system, especially as students are progressing to higher grades, and this must change. Fortunately, it's an achievable change, because teachers can teach imagination creativity just like any other skill. The key is to have teachers explore alternatives to communicating beyond the traditional focus on logical thought development with words (Puccio & Szalay, 2014).

Innovation Creativity Skills

Innovation creativity focuses on generating ideas for how to make things function better. The world runs on ideas. Businesses are constantly looking for new ideas to gain a competitive advantage. Governments are looking for ideas on how to deliver services more efficiently. Schools are looking for ideas on how to improve student engagement in learning. There is a universal need for ideas that improve something that already exists and for ideas for something that is entirely new. More than ever before in the history of the world, there is a great need for people who can generate innovative ideas (Henderson, 2017).

The key pitfall we see in how people perceive innovation skills is the misconception that the ability to innovate is genetic, and that some people have it and some don't. This is simply untrue (Naiman, 2014; Puccio & Szalay, 2014). Certainly, some individuals are better at innovating than others, but we all have the capacity to generate new ideas. For example, have you ever watched people doing a task like loading a truck or determining how to distribute textbooks in your school and thought to yourself, "Why don't they do it this way? If they do, it will save time and energy." When you do this, you are applying exactly the kind of innovation skill that employers value. Everyone is capable of this kind of thought. Teachers can foster this innovative thinking by getting students to examine how things are made or how things are done and then ask them how they might make a product better or make a procedure more efficient.

There are two aspects to innovation creativity skills. First, we use *creative thinking* to improve something that already exists; for example, improving the design of an airport terminal to allow people to flow through the building. Second, we need *innovation creativity* to come up with the idea for something entirely new; for example, to innovate an entirely original and more efficient interface design for using a new electronic device. Both of these aspects of innovation creativity require three important attributes.

1. **Convergent thinking:** This involves linear logic and deductive reasoning.
2. **Divergent thinking:** This is nonlinear thought associated with idea generation and creativity.
3. **Metacognition:** This is thinking about your thinking; that is, reflecting on your thought processes to determine what was effective in doing something or solving a problem and how you could do better the next time you encounter a similar situation (Bransford, Brown, & Cocking, 2000; Rothstein & Santana, 2011).

Schools are generally very good at emphasizing convergent thinking, which is the kind of thought that underpins mathematics and science and the analytical skills in economics, business, and social studies. However, we believe it's critical to balance that teaching with emphasis in the kinds of divergent-thinking and metacognition skills that enhance students' abilities to create and innovate.

For example, a key aspect of divergent thinking is the ability to generate ideas by freely thinking without the fear of failure. We need for teachers to create an environment in their classrooms that fosters the kind of creative thought where students can come up with new ideas without worrying about being right or fearing for their grade if they are wrong.

It is critical to remember that failure is at the very center of learning and that we learn much more from failure than we do from success (Bryant, 2015; Madsen & Desai, 2010). Many great advances in our society have come from people who have been willing to try and fail because evaluating why an effort fails and evolving ideas based on that letdown lead to the heart of successful innovation.

So, if trying new things and failing at them are such central parts of learning, then we need to create an environment in school where we focus on the effort students put forth and what they learn from those efforts. We need to provide opportunities for students to develop their metacognition skills. This means we need to have students do more self-evaluation of not only what they produce but also the thinking that leads to those products. By examining their thinking, they will identify what thought processes were successful and those that were unproductive or need improvement.

Internet Citizenship Skills

You wouldn't give the keys to your car to your son or daughter without first teaching him or her how to drive. Instead, due to the seriousness of driving a motor vehicle, you would first outline your expectations and identify the consequences for inappropriate actions. Then you would give your child guided practice so he or she could safely develop his or her driving skills. Yet every day, parents give their children smartphones and other digital internet-accessible devices without proper guidance. Why in the world would we do that without first providing comprehensive internet education?

Without adequate instruction on the potential problems associated with using online tools, students are susceptible to engaging in dangerous and damaging behaviors while online. Sometimes this can result in tragic global consequences, such as a case at Ted's school where an individual cyberbullied a student to the point of deep depression and suicide. Just before she committed suicide, she posted a YouTube video where she told her story on handwritten flash cards. Millions of people around the world viewed her video, and it resonated with those who saw it. There were memorials for her in Italy, England, India, Russia, and Brazil. It stands as proof that the globally interconnected online world has great power to communicate. (Visit www.amandatoddlegacy.org to learn about the student's story and its impact.)

This story is also a cautionary tale for people, young and old alike, because it dramatically illustrates the two, diametrically opposed sides of online technology. This technology has huge positive upsides and incredibly mammoth negative downsides for all those who use it. Projecting this into the future, it is easy to see that the growing power of online global communications technology will greatly magnify both the positive and negative aspects of online communication. It is our job as adults and educators to adequately prepare students to function efficiently and wisely in this new online world.

We must impart to our students the following three guiding principles that lie at the heart of digital citizenship.

1. Students must protect themselves in the online world.
2. Students must respect others in the online world.
3. Students must respect the online work of others.

Building on these three principles, students need to learn about a set of ever-changing social conventions related to how people should act using digital technology. These digital citizenship conventions include online etiquette, basic courtesy, privacy considerations, and commonly understood rules and practices for email, messaging, web browsing, social networking, and the inherent behavioral expectations involved when using any online tool. As students grow as citizens, they must develop a system of ethics and accountability that starts with the individual and expands to the global level.

Essential Questions

As you reflect on this chapter, consider the following questions.

- How is the work that students do in school today significantly different than the work you did when you were in school?

- Do teachers in your school or district teach the four Ds problem-solving process to their students? What successes have they experienced from doing so?

- Who is responsible for teaching information investigation skills in your school or district? How might other teachers in your school or district benefit from their knowledge?

- How does your school or district foster meaningful collaboration between students?

- Are imagination creativity skills a priority in your school or district, or are they only secondary in importance behind the convergent thinking skills often associated with mathematics, science, and social studies?

- How could your school or district place more teaching emphasis on innovation creativity skills?

- Who is responsible for teaching internet citizenship skills in your school or district? How might other teachers in your school or district benefit from their knowledge?

- How do you keep up with the changes in the world outside school in order to alter your instruction to reflect the shifting demands for skills?

Chapter 4
HOW TECHNOLOGY WILL CHANGE EDUCATION

by Ted McCain

If you don't know where you are going, then you'll probably end up somewhere else.

—Yogi Berra

The great former Major League Baseball player and manager Yogi Berra's insightful quote provides us with an ideal starting point for thinking about the future of instruction. You can't plan effectively if you do not know where you are heading. In previous chapters, we outlined some principles to guide your thinking on instruction that will be effective in preparing modern students for success in the 21st century. We also described the nine Is students will need to thrive in the 21st century world. Although these principles and skills establish a starting point for our thinking, they do not provide enough foundation to fully realize the new school concepts we need. It's critical to consider the impact that technology will have on instruction before we begin exploring what effective new schools might look like.

Trying to project how instruction will change due to technological development is challenging because when we are dealing with technology we are dealing with a rapidly moving target. Worse, this target is picking up speed exponentially (see Technological Change Is Accelerating, page 19). To increase our chances of success, we must adopt the mentality of a grandmaster chess player. Not only must such a player understand the positioning of his or her own pieces, the grandmaster needs to understand what his or her opponent might do. He or she needs to think five, ten, or even fifteen moves ahead on the board and consider every possibility. In other words, he or she must project into the future to envision events that have not yet happened—events where all the pieces arrive at a specific arrangement to create an opportunity. To effect that future outcome, the grandmaster must understand what to do with his or her pieces in the present to successfully make it become reality.

We must think the same way the chess grandmaster does because, like his or her opponent, the modern world is moving and changing every day. If we as educators only plan for what already exists, our planning will no longer be valid when we implement it because the world will be doing things differently. Instead, we must project what instruction will look like if we hope to make effective plans for learning environments that will remain viable in the future. That is exactly what we do in this chapter.

Consider the following questions: How will technology change the way we teach students? How will these change dynamics impact interactions between teachers and students? How will these change dynamics alter course content? How can we reconfigure school facilities to best teach students in the 21st century? These are vital questions for educators to grapple with given the implications technological change has for the nature of information and the skills students will require for success. They are questions we must be able to answer if we hope to keep in-school instruction relevant for the world outside school. This means wrestling with the way technology affects student minds so that we educators can maintain our students' engagement in what we teach them. It also means that we educators must recognize smart technology's growing power to take over tasks teachers do so we can adapt to new and evolving instructional roles.

Because we believe it is of the utmost importance that educators see clearly how future technological change will impact teaching and learning, we put human faces at the center of our ideas because we want to help you envision what that future will look like. In this chapter, we project what students and teachers will do as they go about their daily lives in the future. To do that, we present you with eight future-instruction scenarios to help you see how technology development will change daily interactions. We believe that developing this vision of the future is necessary to understand the breadth of changes districts will have to undertake when organizing schools.

Please note that we present some not-yet-existent technology in the scenarios. Consequently, it will be easy to dismiss the innovations we describe as far-fetched. This is where we remind you that technological innovation is exponential. These things may seem impossible (or at least improbable), but they will be a reality much sooner than many of us anticipate.

The first three scenarios depict outcomes that are already achievable. They illustrate how schools will change as we individualize instruction and ensure learning becomes the constant and time the variable. Subsequent scenarios show how technological development will further individualize and enhance learning for both students and teachers. Remember, the technology we outline in these scenarios builds on a reasoned exponential extrapolation of what already exists.

Debra Goes to an Advisory School

The following scenario presents an organizational strategy for schools that centers on teachers working with a group of students to advise it on how to plan a daily schedule that maximizes students' abilities to effectively learn. In this scenario, we use Debra's first week at school to flesh out the advisory-school and teacher-advisor concepts we present in detail in chapter 5 (page 61). Although we present a hypothetical scenario, this advisory-school concept underpins our ideal vision for schooling.

> Noting her lack of engagement at a middle school rooted in traditional, 20th century learning concepts, Debra's parents decide to enroll her in a new high school in her district. This school is based on an advisory approach that emphasizes individualized learning, open spaces, and teacher advisors. On her first day of high school, Debra rides in the car with her father, nervously tapping her fingers against the side of her knee as they pull into the school's parking lot. She says goodbye to her dad and hops out of the car. She finds her name on a list at the main entrance to the school and discovers she is in advisory 16. Debra makes her way into the large, open-advisory hall in the west side of the school. There are clusters of student workstations, each with a workstation for a teacher advisor. After wandering around the hall for a few minutes, she finds the area for advisory 16.
>
> Debra's teacher advisor greets her and asks her to find a seat in the area in front of her advisor's workstation. Soon there are twenty-two other students sitting around her in the advisory group. Her advisor then has the group do some getting-to-know-you activities. These are fun; and before long, Debra learns all her peers' names. She discovers that there are five students who are new to the school in her group, and the others have attended the school previously and range in age from fourteen to seventeen. After this, Debra's advisor tells her she can choose her own personal workstation from one of five available designs. She chooses a chair on rollers with an adjustable writing desk and a space for storage under the seat. The first day is only a half day at school for students, so once the advisor dismisses them, Debra heads out for lunch with a couple of girls she met in her group.
>
> On her second day, Debra begins her coursework. She begins by logging onto the online registration system to look for the teacher mentors for her subjects. She finds that her advisor is also her social studies teacher. She discovers that the rest of her teachers are all located around her advisory group within a hundred feet of her workstation. Debra meets with her advisor to learn how to do her coursework. She learns that a key aspect of functioning at the school is learning how to manage her time. However, because she is just starting high school, Debra has to get a time-planner template from the school's server to manage her time. She won't be making her own time plans

until she demonstrates the ability to work independently.

Debra also learns that she must briefly meet with her advisor every morning to go over her daily plan for how she intends to use her time. Once she completes that, she has the option to begin her project work in the subjects she will be working on that day or she can walk over to one of her subject teachers to get some assistance. Debra discovers that, periodically, a group meeting for one of her subjects automatically appears in her daily schedule. Individual meetings with her subject teachers also automatically appear so she can discuss her progress. In addition to these teacher-initiated meetings, Debra learns that all her teachers have time each day for students to book individual appointments to get help or guidance with their subject work.

At the end of her first week, her teacher advisor tells her group that it gets to arrange the furniture in the advisory area to its liking. Her advisor's workstation is in one corner of the advisory's area. To get the discussion going, her advisor offers three different possible configurations for the furniture. He emphasizes that nothing is etched in stone, so students can change the arrangement as they need to. The group tries a couple of ideas and settles on a circular arrangement of workstations with the advisor's station on the outside of the circle with a couch and some beanbag chairs in the center. Just one week into her high school journey, Debra is off and running.

Combining advisory-school concepts with technology empowers schools to personalize instruction for individual students like Debra. This will change the role teachers play in schooling, and as digital tools provide more direct instruction to students, teachers can move from being the sage on the stage to being the guide on the side. This gives teachers more time to work with individual students in an advisory capacity. Advisory groups like the one in this scenario will give students adult guidance as they work their way through their courses as well as provide them a small multiage group of students that will get to know each other better than what is possible in traditional schools. These advisory groups will stay together as they progress through secondary school.

Arthur Helps Plan a Career Fair

Advisory-based schools can provide considerable flexibility for how they organize students, space, and resources. The following scenario illustrates how these schools provide the flexibility necessary to facilitate a career fair.

> Arthur arrives at school one morning and heads to his advisory. Unlike the normal individual meetings between students and the teacher advisor who helps them plan their day, all the students in the advisory meet with the teacher as a group this morning. He tells the students that the school will be hosting a districtwide career fair in two weeks. Planning for the event has been underway for several months, and now teachers are giving the students in each advisory group the task of setting up the physical space for the fair. The details are as follows.
>
> - The fair will take an entire morning from 8:30 a.m. to 12:00 p.m.
> - The district expects over 650 students from across the school district to attend the event.
> - The event will begin with a one-hour keynote address from two featured speakers—a futurist who is traveling in specifically for this event and a local engineering firm's CEO.

- Following the keynote address, there will be a series of half-hour seminars and presentations from local companies, unions, and postsecondary institutions.
- School counselors and advisors from postsecondary institutions and apprenticeship programs will be available throughout the morning after the keynote address.
- Students will be responsible for reorganizing the entire open space they normally use for advisories to facilitate these activities. (Furniture in the advisory room is already designed for easy movement for just this purpose.)
- Each advisory group should choose a student to sit in on an overall planning committee.

After a brief discussion, Arthur's group selects him to represent its advisory on the overall planning committee. He heads off to one of the seminar rooms to meet with the others on the committee. The meeting begins with a short talk by one of the school counselors who has been working on this event for several months. She outlines the activities that will happen in the large, open space on the day of the career fair. She then asks the committee to formulate a plan for how to use space for the event. The teacher advisors that are present act only as facilitators for the discussion.

They monitor plans and ensure that the committee is addressing all featured activities. They decide that seminars and presentations will take place in the seminar rooms that line each side of the advisory area, but it becomes clear that the four largest presentations must take place in the open-advisory area. The committee decides to assign a group of advisories the task of setting up for the keynote and then reorganizing the space for the four presentations. The committee assigns various other tasks to the other advisory groups. The planning committee tells each group to take photos of the furniture arrangement in its area with its phones to use as reference when restoring the existing arrangement when the event is over.

Arthur's advisory has the task of setting up the stations for the counselors and postsecondary advisors. It decides to use the teacher stations for its advisors. Since the advisory area is a large, open space, there is a concern that people will hear other presentations when they are attending one of the four sessions that will take place in that space. To address this concern, Arthur's advisory decides to arrange the counselor stations in a cross shape to create a buffer between the presentation areas.

Arthur's advisory coordinates with the group doing the reorganizing after the keynote to make sure it leaves the space it needs for the counselor stations.

On the day of the career fair, the students in Arthur's advisory meet in one seminar room and wait for the keynote address to conclude. Once it is over, the students ensure enough space is left between the four presentation areas for the counselor stations. Then, they move the teacher workstations into place. The students then attend the presentations of their choice for the rest of the morning. When the event is over, Arthur and his fellow students refer to the photos on their phones to put the furniture back the way it was before the career fair.

As technology provides new ways to teach students, it also makes it possible for schools to open up areas that previously required enclosed classrooms. Use of these open areas will be flexible and allow teachers and students to engage in a wide range of activities.

Sarah Progresses to Project-Based Learning

The following scenario projects the pivotal role big-data-driven-student-information systems will play in making an individual learning approach viable in schools. The scenario also looks at a teaching approach that uses real-world problems as the strategy for facilitating both course-content delivery and long-term personal skill development.

> Sarah is a fifteen-year-old high school student. She has been working on her grade 10 social studies course for a couple of months. She finished her grade 9 course in the middle of November and immediately moved into the next level. This is possible because the school district student-information system tracks each individual student's progress in all his or her courses. The system also communicates students' progress to their teacher advisors and to their subject teachers. This enables teachers to identify students who are having difficulty as well as those who are ready to move on to new course material. Thus, the student-information system allows students to learn at their own pace. The system also tells teachers which students are ready for group instruction or collaborative projects. The students the system identifies for group work are not like the homogenous groupings in traditional classrooms. Instead, it recommends to teacher advisors students who have progressed to a certain point in a course regardless of their age.
>
> In early January, Sarah receives a message notifying her that she is to attend a collaborative project session at her school. The following day, Sarah makes her way to the seminar room in the humanities wing of the school where she meets her group. There are five fifteen-year-old students (three boys and two girls), two fourteen-year-old boys, two sixteen-year-old girls, and a thirteen-year-old boy. The one thing they have in common is that they have all reached the point in the social studies 10 course where they look at current affairs in the world.
>
> The teacher enters and introduces herself. "Good morning, I'm Mrs. Jones, and I will be your teacher for the current-affairs unit of your social studies 10 course. We will be meeting several times over the next six weeks as we work our way through this part of the course. Our focus will be on solving problems related to a current real-world event. This group is going to be acting as the aides to the secretary-general of the United Nations. Your role is to do research for the secretary and create materials to prepare the secretary for meetings and press conferences. You must also write speeches for the secretary. You are about to have your daily morning meeting with the secretary to go over the work for the day. I will be playing the part of the secretary-general."
>
> The teacher pauses for a moment, then begins the roleplay.
>
> "OK people, we have a real problem on our hands. Rebels in Eastern Ukraine have taken control of the city of Luhans'k, and it appears they are getting ready to make an assault on Donets'k. I need to know who these rebels are and if they are acting on their own or not. If an organization or a neighboring country is supporting them, I need to know who and how they are equipping them. I also need to know what it is that they want. Now, here is the really important thing I need you to do: based on the research you have done, I need this group to come to a consensus opinion on whether they have a legitimate reason for their actions. I need all this information and your consensus opinion so that I can brief the security council one week from today. Any questions?"

From this starting point, the students then have a dialogue with the role-play character and ask questions to determine the specifics of the task they must do. All students have experienced this kind of teaching before, so they already have a structured problem-solving process to follow when they encounter these kinds of real-world problems. Since all the students are familiar with this teaching approach, once they have nailed down the task specifics, they begin planning the solution as a group. The group determines the tasks it needs to do and assigns individuals to perform those tasks. It is at this point that Mrs. Jones gives her only direction to the group—she helps the students see the importance of setting intermediate deadlines for the various tasks to ensure that the group gets all the work done by the deadline in one week. The students collaborate to set an intermediate deadline for them to complete all tasks in five days. That leaves them two days to meet and come to consensus on whether they think the rebels have a legitimate reason for their actions. Using the school district's learning management system, the students meet online in a virtual workgroup. The system allows them to have live video conferences or to communicate asynchronously via text or recorded video messages. The group agrees to get together online once a day to discuss their progress on their individual tasks.

The group assigns Sarah the task of discovering the history that led to this group rebelling against the Ukrainian government. She begins searching for online information sources. Using an internet-connected device, she finds several articles and ebooks that cover the topic. Then, she finds that the British Broadcasting Corporation website features many interviews of young and old Ukrainians speaking about the history of Eastern Ukraine. After listening to a few interviews, Sarah decides she wants to make a video report that captures the important quotes from the Ukrainians. She heads off to the media lab to record her video.

After five days, the students return to the seminar room at the school for a group meeting with Mrs. Jones. The meeting begins with a discussion of the legitimacy of the rebel's cause in Eastern Ukraine. The students don't have to report to each other on their individual work because the group has been meeting online every day to monitor each member's progress. Again, Mrs. Jones provides input when the group is getting off topic or needs a prompt for their thinking. The discussion goes well, and the students reach consensus of opinion on the validity of the rebel cause. Sarah volunteers to create the briefing notes for the secretary-general. The students set up a time for the following day to present their work to Mrs. Jones.

Information systems that smartly integrate swaths of big data will empower schools to track the progress of individual students and allow them to move through coursework at their own pace. This means students will arrive at various signposts in their coursework at different times and different ages. This self-paced structure fosters the creation of learning groups that look quite different than the homogenous class groupings we see in traditional schools. In addition, by employing a problems-first approach, the work that students do in these learning groups will change as well with a focus on higher-level-thinking skills.

Brian and Virtual Learning Environments

Future learning environments will be a mix of real-world learning and learning in virtual worlds. In the following scenario we look at how a student will blend these experiences into daily school life. This is a much more forward-looking scenario than the previous ones, but we emphasize again that this will become a commonplace reality sooner than you might think.

> One morning, Brian, a student attending a school across town, is waiting for the school bus on a busy street near his home. He arrives at the school and checks in with his teacher advisor, Mr. Gordon, to discuss his plan for the day. Mr. Gordon has been Brian's teacher advisor for the last four years. He quite likes Brian, and they have developed a good relationship. This year, Mr. Gordon is also Brian's English language arts teacher.
>
> "Hey, Mr. Gordon, how ya doin'?" asks Brian.
>
> "I'm fine, Brian. So, what are your plans for today?" Mr. Gordon asks.
>
> "I want to finish my English project. Then, if I have time, I want to work on my chemical reaction assignment," says Brian.
>
> "OK, Brian, that will be fine, but you should get that done this morning so please check in with me after lunch."
>
> Brian leaves Mr. Gordon's office and heads to the student lounge to complete his English language arts project. Brian talks with a couple of his friends for a few minutes, then he finds a place to sit down.
>
> Brian pulls out his handheld multimedia device, placing it on the table in front of him and tapping the On button for his display. Then he puts on a pair of glasses. Brian doesn't need the glasses to correct his vision. He wears them because the glasses are actually a sophisticated digital display that, when combined with the built-in earpieces and microphone, creates an interactive, 3-D audiovisual display that he can turn on and off as he needs to. This multimedia headset communicates wirelessly with the handheld multimedia device Brian put on the table. He turns on his glasses and sees his 3-D workspace superimposed over the student lounge.
>
> There is a desk with drawers he can open and shelves with books, magazines, journals, and newspapers he can pull out into the space between himself and the desk. The items he pulls off the shelf float in the air as he views or manipulates them. When Brian opens a book or newspaper it provides him with a multimedia resource he can view in many ways. He can reorganize the content to give himself quick access to relevant content according to a topic. He can watch a video on a topic, then read the text version of that information or have the system read the text to him while he looks for other material. Brian can select any information he wants to use with his fingers and bring it down onto his virtual desk. Once there, he can edit the information and reassemble it into a new document. The source of information is embedded in these data, allowing Brian to construct a dynamic bibliography on the fly that grows and changes automatically as he assembles and edits his work. He can assemble all types of media together.
>
> Brian begins pointing at items on his shelves and selecting them by snapping his fingers. Brian determines the specific items he wants on the shelves and their arrangement according to his own personal style for accessing and editing information. He particularly likes the new search engine, called *Grab It*, because it provides faster and more complete 3-D information and simulations than other search engines. He uses Grab It to begin opening books, magazines, and journals looking for information on *To Kill a Mockingbird*. He grabs videos and reviews that he likes and arranges them for his project. Brian puts together a short multimedia presentation that explains what he thinks motivated Mayella to accuse Tom Robinson and bring

him to trial. Brian records his thoughts as a commentary that will run over the top of the multimedia presentation.

After working on the project for a few minutes, Brian realizes he needs some help with understanding how southern society in the United States treated African Americans at the time the story was taking place. Brian reaches over to the side of his virtual desk and snaps his fingers on the tech button. A screen appears in front of him, floating in front of the shelves on his desk.

"Log in to the school district tutorial system," Brian says. Once he is onto the system he says, "Find *active senior English tutors*."

Brian scans the list of teachers currently available to help students with questions about their English work. He sees that a teacher from a school across town is online and is not busy with another student. "Call Mrs. Lavestrum," Brian says.

A middle-aged woman appears on Brian's screen. "Hello, this is Mrs. Lavestrum. How can I help you?"

"Oh, hi. This is Brian from Warner Heights Secondary, and I am wondering if you could help me with my project on "*To Kill a Mockingbird*?"

"What is your question, Brian?"

"I don't think I completely understand how southern states treated African Americans at the time this story is taking place. Can you help me with this?"

"Yes, I can," says Mrs. Lavestrum. "Let's discuss race relations in the southern United States during the time the novel takes place."

Mrs. Lavestrum talks with Brian for about fifteen minutes. She is quite pleased that Brian is delving more deeply into the novel's background. At the end of the conversation, she gives Brian some additional online sources to look at. Brian accesses these sources and gets some more information for his project. When he finishes his work, Brian sends it to Mr. Gordon's virtual desk.

Brian decides he better go to the virtual chemistry lab to work on his molecule assignment for his chemistry class. Without getting up, Brian returns to the school district system and selects the option for the chemistry lab. Once he is in the virtual chemistry lab, Brian navigates to the chemical reaction section. His assignment is to pour vinegar on baking soda and determine whether the reaction produces molecules that are bonded with an ionic or a covalent molecular bond. He selects the two compounds to mix together and begins pouring the vinegar on the baking soda. At first, Brian watches the reaction in the bowl, then he shrinks himself down to microscopic size so he can literally walk around the atoms in the substances and watch as they join to form new molecules. Brian slows the reaction and watches to see whether the atoms in a new molecule share electrons or whether one atom gives electrons away to another. He stops the reaction at a critical point and captures an image that shows what the electrons are doing. Brian places that photo in a new file and dictates his findings into a sound file to accompany the image. When Brian finishes his chemistry assignment, he signs out of the multimedia center and heads to lunch with his friends.

Online technology will provide powerful new ways for students to learn by allowing students to access the knowledge and wisdom of experts in various fields. Digital simulation tools will also enable students to have exciting and informative learning experiences that may seem the stuff of science fiction, but the exponential growth in the power of technology will make these tools commonplace much sooner than many people think.

Virtual environments aren't the only emerging technology that will revolutionize how we educate students. It won't be long before the growing power of artificial intelligence provides students with incredibly smart personal digital assistants. These assistants will perform many tasks we currently have students do themselves. Freeing students from the tedium or rudimentary tasks, as we describe in this section, allows them to focus on higher-level thinking.

> ### Bobby Partners With His Smart Personal Assistant
>
> It's 10:55 a.m., and Bobby is sleeping late. VX-5 has been monitoring the time and realizes that Bobby is about to miss his PE class. VX-5 is the name Bobby assigned to his personal digital assistant because using that name makes Bobby feel like he is in an old sci-fi movie. In reality, VX-5 is nothing like an old movie at all. It's the latest intelligent personal assistant software that appears in the form of a digital 3-D human face that talks with Bobby on any computer display that Bobby is using. This morning VX-5 has to sound the alarm three times to wake Bobby up, but finally he gets out of bed just in time for his physical education class.
>
> Bobby puts on his multimedia glasses and snaps his fingers to turn the glasses on. He immediately sees a 3-D display superimposed over the room he is standing in. VX-5's face appears on one side of his vision, and it reminds Bobby that he needs his exercise suit for the class. Bobby puts on a body suit that has high-tech sensors embedded throughout the suit's material. He looks at the display his glasses generated, points to the virtual icon for the school district, and touches it to access the district's online system. Then he selects to join his physical education class where he meets several friends online who are also taking it. They gather in a 3-D, virtual exercise room and listen to their teacher outline the plan for doing calisthenics in the day's class. Bobby controls his virtual digital image by simply moving his body while his teacher moves around the virtual room and helps each of the students improve the way they are doing the exercises.
>
> After class, Bobby has a shower and makes himself some lunch. As he sits down to eat, Bobby asks VX-5 about the information he requested in preparation for the presentation he is making for his social studies class the next day. Bobby is raising the issue of what to do with the seventy-five-year-old town hall. The hall is located on prime downtown property that a developer wants to use for a high-rise office and apartment tower. Bobby is proposing that the city should not approve the redevelopment permit and instead the city should keep the hall as a heritage building and renovate it so the community can continue to use it for events.
>
> "Do you have that background material on the town hall that I asked for?" Bobby asks VX-5.
>
> "Yes," says VX-5. "Are you ready to look at it?"
>
> "Can you just give me the highlights?" replies Bobby.
>
> "Of course. I have the date of construction for the town hall, a number of historical photos, the name and supporting information for all the major events held at the hall since it was built, and the restoration plans the city developed."
>
> "OK, but what I really want to know is whether people feel good about having the building in the city."
>
> "Let me see if I can find anything about that."
>
> VX-5 pauses for less than a second and then continues. "Local newspapers have eighty-six articles that contain opinions about the

town hall building. Of those, seventy-five express favorable thoughts and feelings toward the hall."

"Good. Can you put them in order from most positive to least positive? I'll have a look at them in a minute."

Bobby finishes eating and then walks to the living room, picks up his multimedia glasses, and puts them on. VX-5 appears on his display and shows him a 3-D room with a large bookshelf.

"I've put the articles in the order you requested, but I thought you might like if I grouped them by topic," says VX-5. "I put each topic on a shelf and listed the category on the front of the shelf. I ranked the articles with the most important on the top."

Bobby looks at the articles on the shelf labeled *Events*.

"I like these," says Bobby. "Please read me the important parts of the first four articles while I choose some images."

VX-5 reads him the important parts of the articles from the newspapers while Bobby looks for pictures for his presentation. As the conversation continues, Bobby and VX-5 get quotes from the articles to support the points in Bobby's presentation. As he works on making his case, Bobby realizes it would be helpful to have a live interview for his presentation. He asks VX-5 to contact the people who wrote the top ten articles who are still alive to see if anyone would agree to an interview. A reporter with a local newspaper agrees to talk about an article she wrote about the hall last year. VX-5 records the conversation for use in the presentation.

When Bobby is done preparing, he watches a basketball game he recorded the previous evening on his family's 150" wall-mounted TV. While he is watching, VX-5 appears on the TV screen and tells Bobby that his teacher advisor is calling. Bobby takes the call and has VX-5 show the video of the call in the corner of the TV screen. Bobby continues to watch the game while he talks with his advisor. She wants to go over Bobby's learning plans for the next day. She also reminds Bobby that his combined mathematics and science project is due today.

When he finishes talking with his teacher-advisor, Bobby asks VX-5 to run his mathematics-and-science simulation. Bobby has the difficult task of launching a reusable space vehicle from a launch pad in Houston, Texas, and docking it with a new type of satellite that is orbiting the Earth. This new satellite is designed to have a space vehicle capture it and bring it back to Earth for upgrades. Bobby must use physics to calculate the timing of his launch and the trajectory from Houston to catch up with the satellite and dock with it. The accuracy of his calculations is especially important because his reusable space vehicle has a limited amount of fuel on board, and he must have enough left in the tanks for the return trip to Earth.

Bobby sets up for his latest docking attempt by entering in his new physics calculations into the virtual space vehicle's console. He also specifies his launch time. As he completes his preflight preparations, Bobby is starting to get a little anxious because he has tried to dock with the satellite several times. Although he has reached the satellite more than once, he has yet to have a successful trip because he keeps using too much fuel. This time Bobby has discovered and corrected an error in his calculation for the launch time, and he is hoping that this will produce a much better result.

Bobby starts the trip simulation. He still has his body suit on from the physical education class, so he is ready for the virtual experience of being in a space vehicle. The simulation gives Bobby a full-body experience of lifting off from the launch pad and accelerating into space. Once in orbit, he pilots his vehicle toward the satellite and successfully docks with it. Bobby turns his attention to the fuel remaining in the fuel tanks and discovers that he has plenty left for returning to earth. He lets out a sigh of relief and tells VX-5 to send the successful simulation results to his mathematics and science teacher.

One of the most dynamic areas of development in digital technology is artificial intelligence. AI is exploding into almost every part of our lives. As Kevin Kelly (2016) writes in his book, *The Inevitable*, "In fact the business plans of the next 10,000 startups are easy to forecast: Take X and add AI. Find something that can be made better by adding online smartness to it" (p. 33).

The growth in the power of AI will finally make it possible to create the smart personal assistant that Apple envisioned in a short video they produced in 1987 titled, "Knowledge Navigator" (https://bit.ly/2s3j9VX). This is the kind of assistant that Bobby is using in this scenario. These powerful smart assistants will dramatically change our lives. They will also greatly change the way students learn.

Mr. Harrison Uses a Smart Assistant to Teach Differently

The types of new smart technology we outline in the previous scenario will also provide teachers with powerful, intelligent tools that will significantly change the nature of teaching. New personal digital assistants will be able to transfer themselves to different devices via wireless networks, meaning that the digital personality of the assistant can follow you wherever you go in order to help you with daily tasks. This scenario shows you how Jeeves, Mr. Harrison's personal digital assistant, follows and helps him with the task of teaching his students.

One morning, Mr. Harrison's personal robot, Jeeves, wakes him up. Jeeves is the fifteenth version of Honda's ASIMO robot line, a series of physical robotic machines that have humanoid figures with two legs, two arms, and fully functional hands. Completely independent and containing a powerful computer running artificial intelligence software, as well as wirelessly connected to the internet, the phone system, and the networks in Mr. Harrison's home and school, Jeeves has become an indispensable assistant in Mr. Harrison's daily life.

Jeeves has not only sounded the wakeup alarm, he has also made coffee and warmed a muffin and has them on a tray he is holding beside the bed. Mr. Harrison rolls over and sits up. As he takes the coffee and muffin from the tray, he asks Jeeves for the morning news which immediately appears on the TV display on his wall. Mr. Harrison views several stories while he eats his muffin and drinks his coffee in bed. Then, he gets up and heads for the bathroom. Jeeves selects the clothes for Mr. Harrison to wear, waiting with them in his arms at the bathroom door.

After dressing, Mr. Harrison walks down the hall toward the kitchen, and he asks Jeeves to show him his plan for the day. Jeeves sees that Mr. Harrison is entering the kitchen so he displays the day's schedule on the screen mounted beside the refrigerator.

"Can you get me the minutes of the last city council meeting?" asks Mr. Harrison.

Jeeves uses the internet to locate the city's website and retrieve the minutes of the last council meeting. He displays those on the screen in the dining room because that is where Mr. Harrison is eating the rest of his breakfast. Jeeves also answers a telephone call and takes a message without letting the phone ring because he has learned that Mr. Harrison does not like to be interrupted when he is eating a meal. (Previously, Mr. Harrison provided Jeeves with a list of people to always let through. This caller wasn't on that list.)

"I'd like to see the background information about the housing development being planned for the area around Fifth Avenue and Johnson Street. The council will be voting on that this morning so I want my students to have all the details."

Jeeves retrieves all the city files, newspaper articles, radio commentary, and TV news coverage relating to the housing development. There are over one hundred sources, too many to look at in the time available.

"Show me any items that contain opposition to the development."

Jeeves cuts the list down to twenty-six sources opposing the new development. Mr. Harrison discovers that the city must take down several heritage houses dating back to the late 1800s to make way for the development. Mr. Harrison selects eight of those information sources for use with his class. "Send this information out to each of my students and remind them to join me at city hall at 10:30 this morning."

Jeeves simultaneously contacts each of the students. He conducts twenty-six concurrent voice conversations with the students in Mr. Harrison's social studies class. In addition to sending the information on the housing projects and reminding the students of the lesson at city hall, Jeeves goes over each of the student's individual plans for the day and reminds them of unfinished work from the previous day.

Mr. Harrison puts on his coat and heads for his car. When he gets into the car, Jeeves greets him from the car's in-dash computer. Jeeves is able to do this because all the developing aspects of Jeeves's intelligence, memory, and personality continually update to cloud strorage and are available to all Mr. Harrison's internet-connected devices.

As they are driving towards town Mr. Harrison begins talking to Jeeves. "What did the mayor do before he was elected?" Mr. Harrison asks.

"He was a real estate salesman."

"Can you tell me how the mayor voted on any previous housing projects since he was elected?"

"There have been five housing projects considered by the council since the mayor was elected. All of them have been approved," replies Jeeves. "The mayor has voted in favor of all of them and has had the deciding vote on three of the projects."

"The students should know that before the meeting," states Mr. Harrison.

Jeeves immediately sends a message to each student to tell them of the mayor's previous occupation and voting history on housing projects in the city. Knowing their history of being late or not attending at all, Jeeves takes the opportunity to remind them that they need to join Mr. Harrison at city hall at 10:30 a.m. Mr. Harrison parks the car and heads into the secondary school where he works. Jeeves wirelessly transfers himself to the cell phone in Mr. Harrison's pocket.

"OK, let's get the class together," says Mr. Harrison as he puts on his multimedia glasses.

Jeeves contacts each of the students, and they appear in the periphery of Mr. Harrison's display as they sign in. The students will not physically attend the council meeting this morning. Instead, they will attend virtually via the school district multimedia system that taps into the video feed coming from city hall.

Mr. Harrison talks with his students via his multimedia glasses as he walks down the hall to his office. He leads the students in a discussion of the issues surrounding the housing development and asks them to predict how the vote will go. As Mr. Harrison reaches his office and sits down at his desk, he asks Jeeves to send the video feed of the council meeting out to his students. As they watch, Mr. Harrison gives his students a running commentary on the proceedings. He also answers questions the students have as the meeting progresses. The council approves the new housing development with the mayor also voting in favor.

After the vote, the city clerk gives the council notice that a developer has submitted a new shopping mall development proposal for the region's Mountain View area. This is the location of an old school that currently serves as a youth center. It is also the location of the house fire the news reported on this morning. The clerk indicates the council will discuss the development proposal at the next meeting. Mr. Harrison asks his students to find out as much as possible about this area and the new proposal. He asks the students to get back together with him at 2:00 p.m. this afternoon.

As he is walking back to the car, Mr. Harrison begins talking with Jeeves about having his students write the screenplay for a video predicting their own version of what will happen at the next council meeting. He decides to have half of the class prepare an argument for approving the shopping mall development and the other half to prepare an argument against the development. "Jeeves, create groups of four with half of each group arguing for the development and half against. Tell the students to create a ten-minute film of two students debating the issue. I want the film in before the next council meeting. You had better gather some video design tutorials for Brad and Jen because their last work was substandard."

Jeeves contacts the students and relates the specifics of the project. Then Jeeves contacts Brad and Jen to arrange a time for it to walk each student through the process of designing and filming an effective video.

Smart personal assistants will be able to take different forms, both digital and physical. These tools will greatly change our daily lives. They will also change the way teachers teach. The power of these digital assistants will enable teachers to provide interesting new learning experiences as well as to keep track of students who are progressing through their courses at different rates.

Brenda Learns Sculpture From an International Expert

Global networking will allow students to learn from teachers all around the world. This can mean virtually putting experts in rural schools, small-community schools in a shopping mall, or in any other specialized venue. In the following scenario, a student in a small rural community learns from an expert on the other side of the world. In addition, the student uses advanced 3-D art tools to create virtual art.

> Brenda lives in a small town in a rural area of her state. Brenda normally attends school at a location in a small shopping mall, located between a dry cleaner and corner market. There, she has access to a teacher advisor, but takes many of her courses virtually. Today, she is attending a lecture by a famous German sculptor as part of her high school studies in visual art. Instead of going to the school, she walks to city hall and enters the council chambers. (This is the only facility in the town equipped for hosting the lecture.) Brenda spots a couple of her friends and sits with them. Brenda has a keen interest in art and is currently working on sculpting a human head using clay. Her art teacher, who works at a high school in one of the larger cities on the other side of the state, directed her to the lecture.
>
> At 10 a.m. the sculptor appears at the front of the council chamber. After an initial flicker

or two, the sculptor appears as lifelike as a real human being. He's not, of course. He's a 3-D holographic image being transmitted from a studio in Düsseldorf. The holographic projection system has a two-way, audiovisual link that makes for completely natural interaction between the sculptor and the students in the council chambers.

"Good morning, I am Gustav Schmidt. I am a sculptor living in Germany."

There are only eighteen people attending the lecture, so the introductions only take a few minutes. Mr. Schmidt then walks over to a partially complete sculpture of a human head.

"I have been sculpting for over thirty years using clay as my primary medium. Here are a few of my best sculptures."

A screen appears over the projection of Mr. Schmidt showing a video of his works on display at the Louvre and several other museums and businesses. The people at the lecture learn that his pieces can fetch up to one million dollars. When the video ends, the screen disappears.

"I understand that you are working with clay for your projects so let's take a look at this human-head project I am doing for a mining company in Berlin. The company wants to display the piece in its main lobby. Let's discuss some clay sculpting techniques as I continue to work on this piece. I will begin by talking about how you determine the proportions of the work and how you rough in the main shape."

He starts a running commentary of his thoughts and the techniques he is using as he works on completing the sculpture. The students can virtually walk around the projection of both the sculptor and his work.

"I can't get my eyes to look real," says Brenda. "How do you make the eyelids?"

"The trick is to make them on a flat surface and then apply them to your sculpture," replies Mr. Schmidt. "Let me show you."

Brenda watches intently as Mr. Schmidt creates a very realistic looking eye on his sculpture. He then moves on and begins working on the nose. When particular topics come up in the conversation, Mr. Schmidt takes a break from his work and has discussions with the students. Mr. Schmidt's skill and creativity captivate Brenda.

Because she can do the rest of her work at home as easily as at the community school, after the lecture, Brenda heads home to work on her own sculpture. She grabs a quick lunch and then goes upstairs to her room. She puts on her multimedia headset and a special set of sensor gloves. Then, she logs in to her SimArt Center (www.simart.center) account to access a 3-D working environment. She walks over to her work area and selects the sculpting option from the list of art activities. A list of her sculpting projects appears, and she selects her human-head project. A partially complete 3-D sculpture appears in front of Brenda, and she walks around it to remind herself of the progress she has made. She reaches out with her sensor gloves and begins to work on completing the sculpture. She focuses on the cheeks, using a technique she learned from the German master earlier in the day. The gloves allow Brenda to feel the sculpture as if she was working with real clay. However, unlike real clay, she can undo work that does not go well by stepping back through her actions, even actions that she performed two or three sessions ago.

Brenda is having real success with her project as a result of the instruction she received from the session with the German sculptor. Before she knows it, her mother is calling upstairs for Brenda to come down to dinner.

When Brenda sits down at the table she announces, "I talked with a German sculptor today, and he was fantastic at showing me how to work on my human-head project."

"I can't wait to see it," her mother replies.

Brenda eats quickly while she tells her parents that her sculpture is almost finished. She goes back to her room after dinner and works on the project for another couple of hours. When she is finished, Brenda sends a copy of the completed work to her teacher. Then, she has the SimArt site send the project to her in-home, 3-D printer fabricator to create a full-sized physical copy of her work. She wants to show her work to her parents, but she knows from past experience that they get disoriented when she tries to take them out to see her artwork at the SimArt site. It takes about twenty-five minutes to create a full-sized version of Brenda's sculpture. She takes it downstairs for her parents to admire.

"Oh, Brenda, this is amazing," her father says.

"Did you really learn how to do this from a man in Germany?" Brenda's mother says rhetorically. "I think this is your best work yet. Let's send it to Grandma."

Brenda sends the plans for her sculpture, at half-size, to the 3-D printer fabricator at her grandmother's home in England.

Online technology will enable students to access learning opportunities in the community outside a school and in the modern networked world community (meaning, anywhere around the globe). In addition, the power of digital tools like these will provide students with amazing new learning experiences through complex digital simulations like the digital sculpting that Brenda is doing.

Thomas Learns in a Global Work Group

Not only will global networking give students incredible virtual access to teachers and other experts around the world, it will also allow them to collaborate with peers from around the world too. This scenario illustrates how an international group of students works together on a current affairs project for its social studies class.

Last fall, fifteen-year-old Thomas enrolled in a comparative civilizations class at his high school. He likes the idea of learning how other people in the world live, and he thought learning the relative similarities and differences between cultures would be helpful in his future career in foreign affairs. Shortly after the course begins, Thomas's teacher tells him he will be working with three other students to discuss how other parts of the world view current events. Using the site Global Student Connect (http://gsconnect.org.uk), Thomas's teacher contacts teachers in several countries around the world. She decides to put Thomas in a group that includes Monique, a sixteen-year-old girl living in Calais, France; Sergei, an eighteen-year-old boy living in Minsk, Belarus; and Mutombo, a fifteen-year-old boy living in Mwanza, Tanzania. The teacher assigns the group to meet weekly to discuss a teacher-selected current event.

Living in North America means Thomas is considerably out of sync in terms of time zone with the others in his group. To enroll in the course Thomas has had to make a commitment to get up early for group discussions. Even though the rest of his group is meeting later in the afternoon or early evening in their time zone, Thomas has to be ready at 6:00 a.m. on days when there is a group meeting.

Each of the students' schools has an online digital holographic-projection system that digitizes a person's body and sends that projection to the other schools. Students use their digital projections to meet in a virtual meeting room. They can see each other in three dimensions and speak and listen as though they were all in the same physical space. What really makes the communication natural, though, is the simultaneous translation of language done without delay as each person speaks.

Each week, the students have virtual meetings to work on their project. Their teachers take turns giving the group their assignments and facilitating group discussions. The computer system records the discussions that take place. Then, two of the students must work together to edit the raw discussion video into a ten-to-fifteen-minute presentation that captures the main points of agreement or disagreement on the topic the group discusses. The students post the edited video on a blog or video-hosting site for other students to view.

Because the technology is completely transparent to the students using it, they are soon dealing with the normal group dynamics that arise in these types of human interactions. At first, Thomas and Mutombo mostly listen to the two older students discuss the issue of the week. Monique is a confident and outgoing person who soon dominates most of the discussion. Sergei is able to hold his own in the discussions, but Thomas, being naturally shy, prefers to work with Mutombo on the production of the video blog rather than share his thoughts. Over time, Thomas begins to overcome his shyness and take a more active part in the discussions. As a result, he has been finding that his opinions are swaying the discussions and his confidence is growing.

One Monday morning, Thomas gets up early so he can make it to school for a 6 a.m. meeting with one of his teachers. Thomas stumbles into the projection room just in time and gets ready. Today, Mutombo's social studies teacher joins the students because it is her turn to present the task the students will do for the week. Mrs. Gumjali has been monitoring the group discussions for the last few weeks and wants the students to take their work to a higher level. The students have been interacting, but some much more than others. She wants to push the students into higher-level thinking as well as engage the two quieter students in the discussion.

"Good afternoon—good morning to you, Thomas. Just to remind you, I am Mrs. Gumjali, and I teach social studies at Mutombo's high school."

The words Thomas hears don't quite match the movement of Mrs. Gumjali's lips due to the automatic language translation of the system, but Thomas has already learned to ignore this when communicating with his peers and he instead focuses on the words he hears. Mrs. Gumjali places four folders on the virtual table and begins speaking.

"This week I want you to discuss the severe famine in Malawi and the problem of people trying to cross the border into Zambia to find food. I have put a folder here for each of you that contains all the video and audio I could gather on this subject. I have also included some background information on Malawi and Zambia."

Thomas picks up the virtual folder. It feels just like a real folder, and the sensor gloves he's wearing create the illusion that it has weight. Thomas looks inside and flips the pages to look at the contents. Some are videos, some are audio recordings, and some are textual documents.

Mrs. Gumjali continues, "I want each of you to take on the role of a network TV reporter. In that role, you are to create a short video that outlines what the country in which you live is doing to address this crisis. After this summary, I want you to record an editorial that answers, 'Is this enough?' This editorial is to be your opinion on the adequacy of what your country is doing. When you get together later in the week, please watch each video one at a time. Each student must then defend the opinions he or she states in his or her editorial. Your goal is to answer this question: Does anything else need to be done? And if so, what?"

"Mrs. Gumjali," Monique says, "I have heard that the Zambian border guards have started shooting people trying to enter the country. Is that correct?"

"Yes, this is true," replies Mrs. Gumjali. "It is reported in the folder I gave you."

"Can we get the video of the border cams?" asks Monique.

"No, that video is not available to us."

"Well, can we get any video that shows these shootings?" asks Monique.

"I think it would be advisable for you to look through your folder, Monique," replies Mrs. Gumjali. "You will likely find what you are looking for in there."

Mrs. Gumjali stands up, and then her figure disappears from the room.

"I think Zambia is completely justified in protecting its borders," says Monique. "They can't be expected to take in all those people."

"Yes, I think they have to protect their borders as well," adds Sergei.

"What about their duty to their fellow man?" asks Thomas. "These people are so desperate for food they are willing to leave everything. I think there must be a way of helping them. Let's get our films done and meet at our usual time on Thursday."

As they are about to sign off, Thomas turns to Mutombo. "Hey, stay behind. I want to talk to you before you go."

Mutombo and Thomas wait for the other two students to disappear from the room. Thomas says, "Mutombo, we need you to speak up in these meetings. You have really great things to say when it's just you and me talking. The rest of the group needs to hear you say those things."

"I just get scared of saying the wrong thing," replies Mutombo.

"There is no wrong thing, just say what you think," says Thomas. "And besides, we should all talk. It's time you did some more talking and let Monique do some work on the video blog."

"OK, I'll try," says Mutombo.

In addition to these weekly projects, the four students are also working on a six-month project to compare and contrast daily life in each of their countries. Using video cameras to record daily activities, they are putting together a documentary video that illustrates the similarities and differences between their cultures. They are also creating a 3-D model of a fictional town in each of their countries and embedding the real-life videos they recorded at various places around the model. For example, if a viewer walks into a model's dining room, they might see a video of a student's family eating dinner. In this way, other students traveling around the virtual town can see the videos in a more realistic context. Because the videos are embedded in a realistic 3-D model of a typical home in their respective countries, anyone using the project gets a real sense of how the four cultures are similar and how they are different.

Smart software will help to break barriers between people. The instantaneous translation we depict in this scenario is just one example. When a smart tool like this is connected to a worldwide digital network, it opens up wonderful new learning opportunities for students to communicate with others from around the world.

Essential Questions

As you reflect on this chapter, consider the following questions.

- How do you overcome the "that's impossible" response to this chapter's projections of where learning environments will be in the near future?

- How might your instructional focus change if you taught in these future scenarios relative to what you're used to teaching in a conventional classroom?

- How is the student-teacher relationship different in a virtual learning scenario as opposed to conventional classroom instruction?

- What kind of training would teachers need to be able to take the role of advisor in a school where students are engaged in virtual learning?

- How would the learning opportunities depicted in these scenarios affect students living in rural locations whose schools are not large enough to provide a full range of courses with a full range of learning tools and resources?

- Is there any shift in the kinds of skills students will need to function in these new kinds of learning environments?

- What can you do to prepare your school for learning environments like those described in this chapter?

PART 2
DESIGNING 21ST CENTURY SCHOOLS

Chapter 5
SCHOOLING FOR THE FUTURE
by Frank Kelly

We don't need to improve schools, we need to reinvent them for our times. We need people who can think like children.

—Sugata Mitra

Now that we have established a vision for what education will come to look like in the years ahead, it's time to consider how all the elements of schooling must function together to create the teaching and learning we envision. In writing this book, we reflected on studies in our previous effort, *Teaching the Digital Generation: No More Cookie-Cutter High Schools* (Kelly, McCain, & Jukes, 2009). We came to realize that a book about moving secondary schools from 20th century instructional concepts to foundations that serve 21st century students should not fully discount ideas from past generations that school administrations either botched or ignored. Never mind the magnitude of the transformation we propose in this book, we are not starting from scratch. Our ideas in this book for how education can work in the absence of physical classrooms find their roots in an old concept—open-plan schools.

In this chapter, we re-examine the concept of and logic behind open-plan schools and continue with our modern vision for schools without classrooms—the advisory school. We then use the elements of schooling we established in the book introduction to dig into every aspect of this school concept: instructional approach, technology resources, use of time, funding resources, spatial environment, and community context.

The Merit in Open-Plan Schools

Five Open Plan High Schools by Educational Facilities Laboratories (1973) sets out ideas that remain sound in the decades following its release. In some ways, its ideas are more relevant than ever. The report includes the following proposals and observations.

- Individual-progress programs should include both methods of instruction and time for teaching and learning. This is similar to the individualized, self-paced schooling about which we write in this book.

- Districts can implement the report's solutions in existing or new school facilities or in former commercial buildings. We propose and illustrate similar possibilities in part 3 (page 109).

- The relationship between teachers and students, the environment in which they work, the materials with which they work, and the way they organize time will support and guide teachers in the critically important work they must do. Transforming schools "has as much to do with personnel as with facilities" (Educational Facilities Laboratories, 1973, p. 5), which is the very issue around which the open-plan concept originally failed.

- It observes that:

    > While open-plan schooling may seem an innovation, it carries on the tradition of the one-room schoolhouse, expanded to accommodate 1,000 students. The concept also attempts to instill in students, the quality of independence that we admire in our forefathers and believe their successors were weaned away from by making teachers the directors of what, when and how to study. After educators began to overcome this cultural mismanagement of students they had to wait until the schoolhouse could provide sufficient space for open curriculum programs to flower fully. This is also a matter of the right kinds of space. Physical restraints set arbitrarily fifty years ago must be swept aside to make way for the ebb and flow of different group sizes

One should note from this that the arbitrary "physical restraints" the authors are talking about, from their perspective, originated in 1923. We are talking about a future derived from a *very* old past—and it can work.

- It describes:

   > . . . a counseling system that displaces the homeroom tradition and substitutes a daily discussion between about 20 students from all grades and an adult counselor. The same counselor works with a student throughout his life at high school. Counseling groups meet weekly or at the start of each morning, to discuss topics ranging from academic and social performance to proposals for improving the school's program or facilities. Each counselor has a broad interest in the well-being of his charges. (Educational Facilities Laboratories, 1973, p. 6)

Couple this thinking with individualized, self-paced instruction and digital technology, and schools would be a truly different place—one in which neither teachers nor students would ever float between classrooms again.

In addition to considering the aspirations laid out in the open-plan school within the context of modern students and technology, we should also include J. Lloyd Trump's thinking on open-plan schools. Even before the Educational Facilities Laboratories (1973) report, Trump (1959) calls for a very different relationship between teachers and students. He posits that classrooms are the wrong size—both too big and too small. He writes that they are too small for efficient content delivery and that giving the same lecture five or six times per day wastes teachers' time when they could deliver the same lecture just once in a lecture-hall-sized classroom. He writes that larger classrooms are poor venues for discussions, and that good discussion groups should be no larger than ten to fifteen students. As a solution to these problems, he calls for four modes of instruction.

1. **Large-group instruction:** This constitutes delivery of content to multiple classes grouped together. In 1959, Trump already imagined electronic learning devices, but could not have imagined modern technology. His vision of large-group instruction would now happen via digital online resources, and these resources help realize his ultimate goal of ensuring teachers have more time to work with individual students.

2. **Small-group instruction:** This constitutes discussions with teachers and ten to fifteen students in which everyone can participate. The question remains: How do we assemble these smaller groups for discussions? Although modern technology can provide the means for identifying and assembling students for this dialogue, we can further support and facilitate them through improved time management and specialized configuration of instruction spaces and teacher-student work areas. These are concepts we address in this chapter.

3. **Hands-on instruction:** This constitutes studies that require specialized equipment, group work, and so on. Specialized spaces and equipment will remain essential for some science, visual arts, career and technology studies, and health and wellness programs. They complement the digital resources in many areas of study.

4. **Independent study:** This constitutes time during which students are responsible

for doing the work they need to for their individual studies. This may seem the simplest of Trump's original ideas, but we believe it is among the most difficult to realize because, in the context of traditional schooling, we find that a temporary classroom seat in between bells to work on individual studies is not the answer. We believe students, just like teachers, need a personal individual place in which to work.

In *A School for Everyone*, Trump (1977) delineates a program for fully individualized self-paced instruction with no classrooms and no stand-and-deliver lecturing. He suggests that students follow paper *learning guides* with the support of teachers and access to varied specialized resources. In this vision, when both the student and teacher feel the student meets the learning objectives, the student could take an exam and, if successful, move on to the next course. We can substitute digital online resources for paper learning guides without depending on fixed time for advancement, making Trump's idea for an open-plan school far more functional for the 21st century.

It's worth noting that Trump wrote both of these books for the National Association of Secondary School Principals decades before the same organization published *Breaking Ranks: Changing an American Institution* (NASSP, 1996) and *Breaking Ranks II: Strategies for Leading High School Reform* (NASSP, 2004), which are much less forward-thinking.

In "Advent of Google Means We Must Rethink Our Approach to Education," Sugata Mitra (2013), a professor of educational technology at Newcastle University and winner of the 2013 TED Prize, writes that "It is dangerous to build a present using vague memories of the good old days." He contends there should be much less focus on facts that students can instantaneously glean from the internet as opposed to solving real-world problems that involve multiple disciplines and collaboration with others.

He proposes that we should allow students to use the internet and collaborate during examinations, and that doing so challenges learners to solve problems the way adult professionals solve them in real life. Absent stand-and-deliver lectures, he argues that we could have multiple types of teachers, both in person and digitally—from anywhere. He writes, "We don't need to improve schools. We need to reinvent them for our times. . . . We need people who can think like children" (Mitra, 2013).

Furthering this argument, we propose to create schools from the rich base of educational concepts and facilities we've inherited from the past as well as from new possibilities that digital technology affords us and from new perspectives of what students and nations need to survive and thrive. In the remainder of this chapter, we outline what schools without classrooms look like at a high level, the concepts that reflect our elements of schooling diagram (see figure I.1, page 3), how students transition from traditional elementary schooling formats to secondary schools in the advisory format, and how you prepare your staff to work within an advisory format.

Schooling Without Classrooms

Because traditional classrooms are the basic organizing element of industrial age schooling, they largely govern instructional methods, use of digital technology, student grouping, separation of disciplines, school facility configuration, and time management. We propose a very different way to approach schooling—an advisory-based concept that is applicable to both new and existing schools, including working within environments where substantial spatial modifications aren't possible.

Before digging into details, the following is an overview of our concepts as a means to understand the step-by-step descriptions that follow.

- Teachers have dual roles:
    a. As advisors for a small, multiage group of students over the full course of their time at the school
    b. As teachers in their area of expertise who support, guide, mentor, and monitor, but do little or no lecturing

  Students and teachers work together to effect learning—both are responsible for the results; however, students are responsible for managing their own studies and time with the guidance of their advisors and teachers.

- Teacher advisors, students, and their parents join together to create and maintain an individual learning plan for each student that maps out the courses he or she must complete, the learning processes (software, resources, and methods) he or she will follow, and the pace of the work he or she will adhere to—all within the guidelines of district, state or province, or other standards. In general, learning focuses on processes and skills versus specific content.

- Students advance when they meet their personalized learning objectives—this may require more or less time than allotted for them using conventional semesters. Until students realize their personal objectives, there are no *F*s. Students receive course credits only upon realizing their objectives. Transcripts note courses completed, not time expended.

- Both students and teacher advisors have workstations in the school's spaces (advisories). No one floats, and there are no generic classrooms. There are, however, spaces for programs that require specialized equipment and environments or group collaborative work; for example, project labs (makerspaces), medical labs, digital graphics spaces, culinary arts spaces, performing arts spaces, physical education spaces, and so on.

- Every student and teacher have a personal digital device and internet access. Students and teachers can access instructional content digitally, anytime and anywhere.

  - There are few or no printed learning materials. There are no paper-based libraries, but rather schools will have digital libraries with access to more content than any school library with a print collection.

  - Functioning as research teachers rather than archivists, librarians teach and support students in effectively using the internet to find information. Rather than maintain paper-based books with limited check-out times, librarians help students learn how to search for the content they need and better identify content that is valid and valuable.

- A school's enrollment does not impact what is available to students with online access to learning material. Students in large urban and small rural schools and students in affluent or economically disadvantaged schools all have equal access to learning resources online.

- There are no attendance zones. School districts create varied schools to serve varied communities. Parents and students select the school they believe best suits their needs and interests; however, for logistical reasons, a school *may* require some parents to provide transportation to and from the school.

- School districts open, modify, and close schools in response to the communities they serve. Schools fit students and not vice versa. Waiting lists and lotteries for admissions create more problems than they solve and are not acceptable for something as important as educating students (Zubrzycki, 2013).

- Schooling is a continuous, year-round service and not a time-constrained seasonal event. Learning is self-paced, and students carry varied course loads depending on their interests, capabilities, and family circumstances. As facility utilization increases, the cost of facilities per student decreases.

- Districts and regions fund schools based on courses that students successfully take and complete and not (as some do) on seats warmed, irrespective of the results. Districts and regions measure a secondary school's effectiveness in terms of the cost per graduate and not the cost of a seat per year.

- There is no age level at which schools refuse to serve a student seeking a high school diploma. A high school diploma is critical to improving one's sense of citizenship and diminishing the school-to-prison pipeline (Elias, 2013), and our schools would support any student in realizing this aim.

- Schools collect data for each student throughout their K–12 studies and any postsecondary studies. Such applications are limitless (although they must respect the need for privacy), but big-data analytics would allow schools to continually modify their curricula to address such issues as how long it takes students of different ability levels to complete courses in specific topic areas, answer specific questions regarding what areas created struggle, determine which interventions achieved improved results, address when flaws in curricula create roadblocks for students, and so on. Schools also record the student's success in postsecondary work to assess the long-term merits of their own teaching and learning.

- Students maintain digital portfolios of their work and learning as a record of their studies and accomplishments. Portfolios are far more descriptive than transcripts of a student's interests, efforts, capabilities, and accomplishments. For example, in 2015, eighty colleges united to develop a portfolio-based content platform to allow applying students to submit detailed portfolios of their high school work as part of the application process (Jaschik, 2015).

We have established throughout this book that schools must change to keep up with a changing world. We contend that if all educators and stakeholders don't deal with these concepts then new learning institutions will rise up to replace them. The big question at this date is less, Will schools change? than it is, Who will create or operate the schools our students need for the future?

Advisories as an Instructional Approach

In our vision, an advisory consists of a teacher advisor and a group of students. The teacher advisor does not teach this specific student group but does have an area of teaching expertise and works with other students in small groups or one on one throughout the day. With digitally delivered content and advanced learning management systems at students' disposal, there are no large-group lectures, and students will interact with teacher advisors on an as-needed basis. Teacher advisors may have some of the same students in their core advisory group and as part of a course students are taking, but it is not required for a student to have courses with their teacher advisor.

In an advisory capacity, teachers plan with students and individually advise, counsel, support, critique, mentor, and monitor each of them during their time at the school. These student groups should comprise a vertical cross-section of the grades the school serves (grades 6–8 or grades 9–12, for example) with some students graduating and others beginning each year. The objective is to ensure continuity between the students and advisor and among the students themselves. We intend for the advisor and students to collaborate and support each other on all manner of academic facets as they work together over time. We believe that traditional concerns about classroom management and discipline will diminish in a school that serves individuals rather than groups.

One of the advisories' most important functions is to develop and maintain an individual learning plan for every student. Teacher advisors, students, and their parents join to create an individual learning plan for each student that maps out the courses the student will complete, the learning process (including software, resources, methods, and workspaces), and the work's pace. Participation in creating and maintaining the plan is obligatory for teacher advisors, students, and parents as these plans permit them to track learning progress and make adjustments as appropriate to support and enhance the students' learning. Although all students should work toward defined curriculum requirements, students' plans for getting there will vary considerably. Collectively, individual learning plans should provide the school with data on both teaching and learning to track and project the numbers of advisor teachers and the spaces and capacities they require for advisories and specialized programs (sciences, arts, career and technology education, and physical education). The plans and related data allow schools to anticipate and plan for the optimum efficiency in how they use their spaces and funds.

In the following sections, we examine student assessment, school assessment, facility population, advisory options, advisory identities, and advisory components.

Student Assessment

In our vision, student assessment occurs at two different levels. First, advisors join with students and parents at intervals appropriate to the student's learning plan to review his or her overall progress and to update the plan as appropriate. Second, within each course, teacher advisors constantly track students' progress via instructional software, and students and teacher advisors individually meet as appropriate to support the learning process.

At each course's conclusion, students assemble an information package of their work that they include in their digital portfolio. They then share this portfolio with their teacher advisor and parents. The school should also display exemplary work around the school using monitors or printed graphics. Phillip Schlechty (1997) was right—the most important work done in schools is the work teachers get the students to do, and that work should be visible throughout the school and constantly changing. When students know what their peers are capable of, it helps inform what they can do themselves.

School Assessment

How communities and regions assess advisory-school performance draws on the same data available to teacher advisors, students, and parents plus cumulative records from students' postsecondary educational accomplishments.

If students and parents are to make informed choices in selecting the right school for them, these data must be readily available and easy to understand. If students and parents can make informed choices with regard to where they enroll, then they render the ultimate assessment—great schools will operate and thrive while, according to the laws of supply and demand, dubious schools will shrink and fail if they do not change. In this regard, why should schools be different from other institutions within the communities they serve?

Advisory Options

There are at least two variations that we envision with regard to how we recommend populating advisories (see figure 5.1 and figure 5.2). In both cases, every student has his or her own workstation in a highly flexible area, while teacher advisors are in one of two areas based on the ratio of teacher advisors to students. (Note that *CTE* in these figures refers to *consumer and technical education* spaces.)

In figure 5.1, to ensure the closest possible rapport between advisors and students, all advisors are also teachers who, in traditional schools, would otherwise operate out of typical classrooms. This primarily includes core teachers for English language arts, mathematics, science, social studies, and foreign languages. Teachers in subjects that require special spaces or equipment and group work (shops, music, or drama, for example) would not serve as advisors. In these advisories, the ratio of teacher advisors to students would be relatively high, about 1:30. (Note this ratio reflects only the size of the advisory. Any small-group instruction that takes place would feature a *much* smaller ratio.)

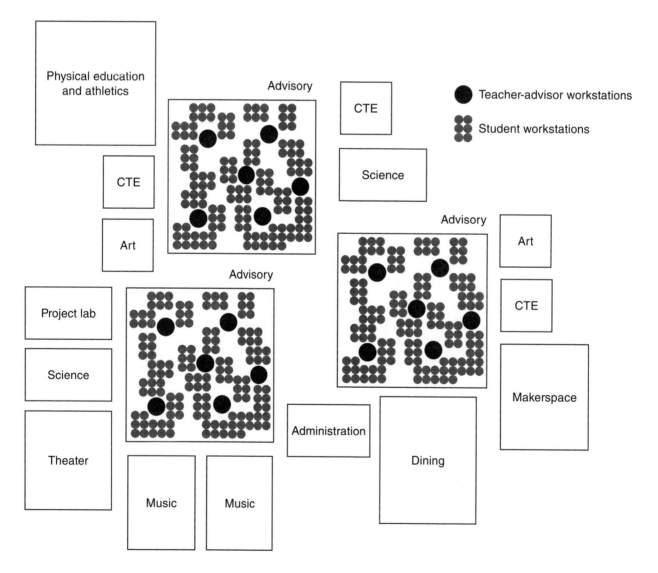

Figure 5.1: Advisory arrangement in which teacher advisors work exclusively in the open-advisory areas.

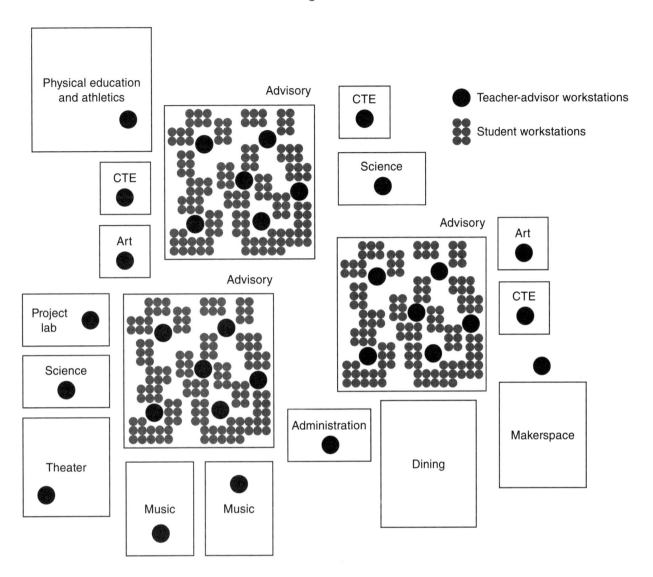

Figure 5.2: Advisory arrangement in which schools staff teacher advisors in specialized facilities in addition to open-advisory areas.

In figure 5.2, to ensure the lowest ratio between advisor teachers and students, almost every teacher in the school functions as an advisor. Those teacher advisors in core subjects (just as in the scenario for figure 5.1) would have their workstations in the advisories with those of all students. Teacher advisors in subjects that require special spaces or equipment and group work would meet with their advisory students in their specialized rooms. However, these students still work in one open-advisory area for most of the day. This concept lowers the teacher-advisor ratio to approximately 1:24, while diminishing the close spatial relationship between advisors and their students due to the separate locations. To the extent that the specialized spaces could surround and define the advisory spaces, the separation is not necessarily a problem. If the specialized spaces are at a considerable distance (certainly a possibility in a large high school), it could seriously impair the working rapport between teacher advisors and students.

Because they often require specialized workspaces, science teachers in an advisory school often blur the distinction between the two types of teacher advisors. To ensure contact between science teachers and other core subject teachers and students, workstations for science teachers should be in the open-advisory areas. We anticipate that much of what occurs in traditional science labs will occur digitally online and that science teachers and students will have access to science lab spaces and equipment on an as-needed basis (Carey, 2013).

Given that students' studies would be self-paced, they would need access to labs on widely variable schedules. To adequately monitor and maintain these spaces, schools might staff these facilities with aides rather than teachers. This is acceptable because, in this setup, there are no traditional lab or lecture science rooms. Given some of the equipment typical in science labs, the spaces may also serve as project labs (makerspaces) in which students may work to develop project materials that relate to other subjects.

Spatially, advisories would be a large cluster of workstations with furnishings, and not an enclosed space with a door. Schools should group advisories together in large, open, and highly flexible spaces. Each teacher advisor's workstation should be near the center of his or her advisory space to facilitate contact with students operating from their own workstations.

There would be no fixed elements within the advisories—the teacher advisors and students can rearrange their own spaces to reflect the work they are doing. Nor should schools identify or organize advisories according to subjects or disciplines. Rather, each teacher advisor in an advisory group should have a different area of expertise.

As students digitally pursue their studies, schools assign them to a teacher who tracks their progress and provides support as they need it. The teacher may or may not be in the same advisory. Either the teacher or students can initiate communications, schedule a meeting, and so on when they think it would help progress students' learning. Most of the day students are unscheduled, but schools should divide teachers' days into *opportunity periods* to facilitate student-teacher communications (see Use of Time, page 77).

There would be no departments spatially, but each discipline or department would have a conference room where teachers could meet and access an adjacent departmental storage room with instructional materials. The conference room would be available to others when not reserved for the department's staff.

Advisory Identities

Each advisory has two identities.

1. **Personality:** As they work together over time, each advisory develops its own personality just as each traditional classroom adopts its own personality. We expect teachers and students will add personal touches and decorate their workstations, express their personalities and enthusiasm for learning, and generally make each space unique.

2. **Expertise:** Students will come to know the area based on the teacher advisor's area of expertise—they would know to seek the teacher advisor out relative to his or her studies in his or her particular field. Both the teacher advisor and his or her area of expertise are clearly identifiable to help both students and staff navigate the school. There are no long corridors with numbers and names on the doors.

We want to be *very* clear that the character of advisories, as defined by their spaces and furnishings, should be quite diverse, and the process of creating them is different from that which districts often pursue when designing traditional schools. The intent is to create a building shell or envelope that houses, shelters, and so on, but also affords minimal constraints on the way advisories may work over time. Flexible furnishings will help flesh out and complete this shell, which will have a critical role in how the school both functions and looks.

In traditional schools with classrooms, the building and all its spaces and finishes are architect-designed and contractor-built or installed. In a separate process, the school district's purchasing office selects, purchases, and installs furnishings. As a result, there is often a substantial disconnect between the building design and the furnishings.

Given the critical role furnishings have in an advisory-based school, we propose that the architect should be responsible for the complete physical environment that teacher advisors and students experience, and the architect should design spaces and select the furnishings as one integrated process. This will enhance the coordination of the overall design and help realize the ultimate teaching and learning vision in addition to establishing the overall project budget and schedule.

In the next section, we include examples of areas with several advisories, we feature individual-component drawings that could comprise the advisories, and we include explanatory notes about each advisory's functional characteristics. The drawings we include are intentionally generic in character because numerous companies can produce these components using myriad designs and finishes. They are also time-tested, with office spaces effectively using similar furnishings since the late 1960s. The following list includes a sampling of resources from which your school can review furnishings that match what we describe in this chapter. (Visit **go.SolutionTree.com/instruction** to access live links to the websites mentioned in this book.)

- Haworth (www.haworth.com)
- Herman Miller (www.hermanmiller.com)
- Knoll (www.knoll.com)
- Bretford (www.bretford.com)
- VS (www.vs-network.com)
- Steelcase (http://store.steelcase.com)

In addition to these furnishing resources, several books explore extensive concepts for components of education environments that could serve within the advisory context we propose. These include the following.

- Scott Doorley and Scott Witthoft (2012), *Make Space: How to Set the Stage for Creative Collaboration*
- Cannon Design, VS Furniture, and Bruce Mau Design (2010), *The Third Teacher: 79 Ways You Can Use Design to Transform Teaching & Learning*
- Prakash Nair, Randall Fielding, and Jeffery Lackney (2005), *The Language of School Design: Design Patterns for 21st Century Schools*
- Victoria Bergsagel, Tim Best, Kathleen Cushman, Lorne McConachie, Wendy Sauer, and David Stephen (2007), *Architecture for Achievement: Building Patterns for Small School Learning*

Advisory Components

In this section, we examine the physical structure of an advisory. As we envision them, a group of advisories should always house several teacher advisors, each from a different discipline, to ensure that students have access to expertise in diverse areas and that there are always teacher advisors in the area to monitor the students. We use the term *workstation* to apply to individual, assigned areas for students and teacher advisors to work.

Figure 5.3 (page 72) illustrates six teacher-advisor workstations clustered in two areas. (Visit **go.SolutionTree.com/instruction** to access color versions of this and other figures in this book.) Individual student workstations surround the teacher-advisor workstations, among which are various breakout areas for discussions and collaboration. There are a few workstations for students who may be carrying less than a full class schedule. Some of the breakout areas may include projection screens, marker or tackboards to support discussions, and student work on display. There are conference rooms for those occasions where privacy is important.

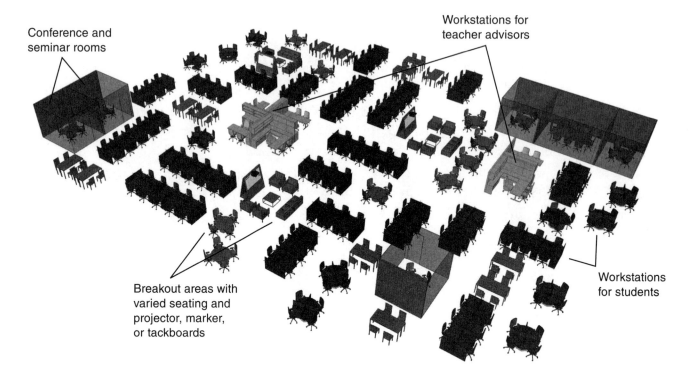

Figure 5.3: A hypothetical floor plan for an advisory area.

For direct accessibility, advisories are ideally located in major circulation routes throughout the school so they offer close access to specialized spaces (labs, CTE, and so on). If building construction dictates that walls must define advisory areas, then those walls should be substantially glass and visually open to provide real contact between the rest of the school and the advisories. Because both students and teacher advisors would spend much of each day at their workstations, each advisory should have substantial access to natural light and views to the exterior grounds. We believe that such environments are very important to both teacher and student success.

Next, we detail the structure of teacher-advisor workstations, full-time and flexible student workstations, and furnishings.

Teacher-Advisor Workstations

Our key principle for both the teacher-advisor and student workstations is that they are intermixed in the same spaces—they must be part of the same environment. The teacher-advisor workstations, as we illustrate in figure 5.4, should be landmarks in the advisory areas and they should distinguish themselves using panels approximately six feet high with graphics that identify the teacher advisor and his or her discipline or field of expertise. These workstations provide space for teacher advisors to work with, monitor, and support students online and spaces for meetings and conversations with individuals and small groups.

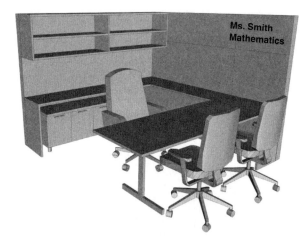

Figure 5.4: An example of a teacher-advisor workstation.

Nearby, we envision breakout areas for teacher advisors to discuss learning topics with larger groups. Schools assemble all the furnishings (including work surfaces, digital devices, phones, drawers, files, shelving, tack surfaces, and task lighting) from modular components so that the teacher advisors and students may modify their own space. Many storage drawers and shelves are lockable to secure equipment and materials. There should be easy availability to electrical power and reliable wireless access to data. The workstations are open on at least two sides so that teacher advisors may see students and ensure students can see them. Typically, advisory areas should arrange teacher-advisor workstations in groups of at least two to ensure that there will be a teacher advisor in every area throughout the school day. Encourage teachers to personalize their station and display information related to their field of expertise.

Individual Student Workstations

The school assigns each student to a workstation (see figure 5.5). This workstation should remain with that student for as long as they are a full-time student at the school. Students should not float or otherwise share workstations. Schools should ideally arrange student workstations in groups to encourage them to communicate and collaborate.

wireless data, and a comfortable chair. The work surface is enclosed on three sides with panels high enough to define the work surface and provide tack space but low enough so that students can communicate with each other and both see and be seen. Students should be able to tack or tape items on their panels related to their studies and their personal interests. The panels should also include hooks for coats because students in these environments typically do not have lockers. If a school deems that students' ability to secure valuable items is in question, they may take further steps to provide secure storage space, but any such fixtures should be movable and not interfere with advisory sight lines.

Flexible Student Workstations

As we outline in the section Use of Time (page 77), students will have widely varied schedules and carry different class loads. Students who carry less than a full-time load or are not on campus full time may not have an assigned personal workstation. While on campus, these students would use one of the flexible workstations that are also integral to the advisories (see figure 5.6).

Figure 5.5: An example of an individual student workstation.

Figure 5.6: An example of a flexible student workstation.

Similar to the teacher-advisor workstations, each student workstation should include a work surface, lockable storage drawers, access to power, access to

Because the intent is to serve and accommodate varied students and their schedules, and to efficiently use the school's spaces, part-time students should have access to lockable storage on campus that is separate from the flexible workstations.

Breakout Furnishings and Area Dimensions

Interspersed among the teacher-advisor and student workstations, there would be breakout areas with different types of furnishings for collaborative work and conferences. These include soft seating (chairs and sofas), modular conference tables, mobile tackboards, marker or projection boards, and a few flexible conference rooms that modular panels define (see figure 5.7). Teacher advisors and students would regularly move all these about in support of their work.

Figure 5.7: An example of different breakout furnishings.

Each advisory would be about the size of a typical classroom, but would be an open, highly flexible space located in the same area as other advisory groups and fleshed out with furnishings, not walls (refer to figure 5.1 and 5.2, page 68 and page 69). There would be no large-group lectures, only individual work and discussions in small groups—exactly the environment that occurs in most offices.

Existing schools could gut out classroom areas to create large, open spaces to create advisories. We recognize this is not a small renovation. It requires removing existing partitions and rearranging existing mechanical, electrical, and data systems. That said, the basic shell of the building would remain substantially intact, and most of the school building's value would be preserved such that districts could extend the useful life of the school structure. Most schools could realize this level of change over the course of a summer. We describe several examples of these changes in part 3 (page 109).

With regard to existing schools, that modify classroom areas to create advisories, the existing spaces may substantially shape the new advisories' size and configuration. Middle school advisory groups may be small, rather like pods, housing a teacher advisor from each core discipline—a total of four to six teacher advisors (mathematics, English language arts, science, social studies, reading, and foreign languages).

To provide more diverse expertise, high school advisory groups might be substantially larger, rather like the NASSP's (1996, 2004) small-learning communities that serve four hundred to six hundred students in grades 9–12. The objective is to encourage dialogue, collaboration, and projects across disciplines.

All schools will need specialized spaces for studies that require group work and for particular room configurations and equipment. These include science and project labs (makerspaces); art, music, and theater studios; facilities for consumer and technical education programs; and athletic facilities. Each school's individual character could be very different depending on how these specialized spaces relate to the advisory spaces.

A feature of this setup is that the nature of programs the school offers and instructional methods it employs can vary with the community and students it must serve—there would be no cookie-cutter schools. The school makes available software for individual courses in multiple forms to address varied interests, learning styles, and paces. The school might use project-based learning across multiple disciplines or have academies that link core and consumer and technical education studies or have mentors in the surrounding community with whom students could work. These are variations the district should develop while planning any new advisory school. Student learning, and not the programs the district offers, teaching it delivers, expenditures it makes, or facilities it provides, should be the measure of parity between schools.

Technology Resources

Although there are serious issues for schools to address in every circle of the elements of schooling (see figure I.1, page 3), the technology element has changed the world and is continuing to change the world. All that we propose in this book is feasible, necessary, and appropriate because of ubiquitous digital technology and the instant world links it provides. We propose *every* student and teacher advisor have an individual digital device for his or her use anytime, anywhere. The campus should have a robust wireless network to which everyone can connect. In the Funding Resources section of this chapter (page 82), we talk about ways to substantially offset technology costs by making changes in other aspects of schooling.

Because advisory schools eliminate stand-and-deliver, teacher-centered instruction, students digitally receive all content on their portable device whether they are at their school workstation, at home, or anywhere they have an internet connection. They can review and repeat content as many times as they need to. Likewise, teacher advisors can modify and personalize the digital materials to support individual students' learning styles. Teacher advisors also monitor and track student progress via feedback from their instructional software. They know where each student is in his or her work and, from assessments built into the software, they know how student learning is progressing. *Education Week* reports that although this is an emerging area, content options from educational content developers and stakeholders are rapidly expanding (Cavanagh, 2014). Indeed, in a joint venture, the U.S. Department of Education and U.S. Department of Defense already provide a portal, Learning Registry (www.learningregistry.org), for educators to locate digital learning resources. (Visit **go.SolutionTree.com/instruction** to access live links to the websites mentioned in this book.) The problem is not finding good materials but assembling a coherent software package that suits the special needs of each school and each student it serves. The following list includes just a handful of the many resources available to schools and teachers.

- Coursera (www.coursera.org)
- EdSurge (www.edsurge.com)
- EdX (www.edx.org)
- Instructure (www.instructure.com)
- Khan Academy (www.khanacademy.org)
- Knewton (www.knewton.com)
- Moodle (https://moodle.com)
- Schoology (www.schoology.com)
- Solution Tree (go.solutiontree.com)
- Udemy (www.udemy.com)

There is an enormous, well-funded, and rapidly growing volume of online instructional materials available for K–12 and postsecondary schooling. The content we cite in this section represents a small sampling of the sources available. Schools and teachers may generate some of these materials while universities and for-profit ventures are creating others. This creates a wealth of opportunities to provide a student body with varied materials to serve diverse interests and learning styles. Also, unlike static paper textbooks, digital materials are generally easy to update. The challenge for most districts and schools will be to assemble from this vast array of sources the set of materials appropriate for each school. We believe that consulting services, such as the Learning Registry and Education Elements (www.edelements.com) will become more readily available to help districts with this very important task.

Broad availability of online courseware is also a great benefit for students in small schools and communities. With them, any size school can offer virtually any subject. If the school's small faculty does not have the requisite expertise to support some students' work, teachers in other locations can provide online support via resources like those we listed in this section, complete with monitoring and additional support from the student's teacher advisor (see Brian and Virtual Learning Environments, page 45).

Despite the wealth of online learning opportunities, do not infer from this that anywhere, anytime access to instructional technology makes physical schools unnecessary. Schooling is about much more than content delivery. Schools provide an essential social context for students, an opportunity for contact between students and live on-site teachers, access to special equipment and resources, and access to special group programs (performing arts, athletics, and so on). In a world where all the students' parents or guardians work outside the home, schools still have an important safety and custodial role. Our advisory-school concepts suggest a process that is much more responsive to individuals and families, not a diminution of the need for schools. We believe it is possible to have many types of schools in diverse places that are very different from traditional campuses.

Advisory schools would decrease or eliminate libraries with paper collections. Online libraries and research tools give students and teachers access to many times the resources now available in the best school libraries. Some small secured stack spaces might remain for special books and periodicals at existing schools that districts convert to the advisory format, but we suggest schools should remove the rest of the printed materials. Librarians should become teachers helping students learn to use search engines effectively to locate and identify relevant and valid information. Each student's digital device would be his or her library. Schools would convert or redistribute the bulk of the traditional library space to create advisories, collaboration, discussion, small-group, and project workspaces (Gonzalez, 2014).

For further access to information students traditionally find in libraries, schools can subscribe to online libraries such as Questia (www.questia.com). Students can also connect to services like Google Books (https://books.google.com) for access to a full library of scanned and searchable books. Further, students and teachers can use specialty sites like eBooks.com (www.ebooks.com) to access more than two hundred thousand academic, copyrighted ebooks from university presses and other sources. Finally, schools can deploy learning management systems like Canvas (www.canvaslms.com) and other content-management systems like Drupal (www.drupal.org) to allow teachers to upload video, audio, and documents for sharing online.

At this point, we should note that some U.S. states require public K–12 schools to have on hand specific numbers of volumes and provide minimum floor area for libraries based on the school's projected enrollment. Although these requirements might make some sense financially, they are nonsense in terms of teaching and learning. Should the learning and research resources available to students be proportional to enrollment? Should students at a school with an enrollment of three thousand students have access to six times the information and knowledge available to those in a school with five hundred students? What information does one delete or provide to make the smaller library work for the smaller school? Although this bizarre choice is a function of paper materials, it certainly does not apply to digital information. Sources such as

Questia and Google Books are equally accessible to students in tiny rural schools and in huge urban schools. Taking advantage of this means eradicating the advantages of size and location with regard to libraries, something that can also save schools from a budgetary perspective (see Funding Resources, page 82).

Use of Time

It is indicative of the nature of schooling that in writing this chapter, we've tried to reflect on each of the six elements of schooling (figure I.1, page 3), yet each time we mention one of its elements, we find ourselves immediately embroiled with all the others. So, it should be obvious by now that everything we've mentioned about individualized student-centered instruction with the extensive use of digital technology absolutely requires comparable changes in how we think of schooling time. In this section, we include a series of diagrams that analyze traditional school days and years, along with comparable diagrams for new ways to think about school time.

Traditional School Days

Nowhere are the industrial age roots of schooling clearer than in the way schools traditionally organize time. Because secondary-level teachers must focus on single subjects and maintain a single classroom, and each student takes multiple classes every day in which he or she floats from classroom to classroom, schools usually divide days into regular periods marked by bells. Figure 5.8 describes typical days for five students.

Every hour of every day of every semester of every year, bells ring and entire student bodies move from classroom to classroom, subject to subject. Schools allot students exactly the same time for every subject for every instructional activity every day. Consider that students moving about during passing periods eats up approximately thirty minutes of every day. Then consider that students must dig out and organize their papers or books and may have to log on or off their digital devices at the end of each period and the start of the next period. All combined, that is a bunch of unproductive time. The brevity of typical periods limits opportunities for teachers to work individually with students and

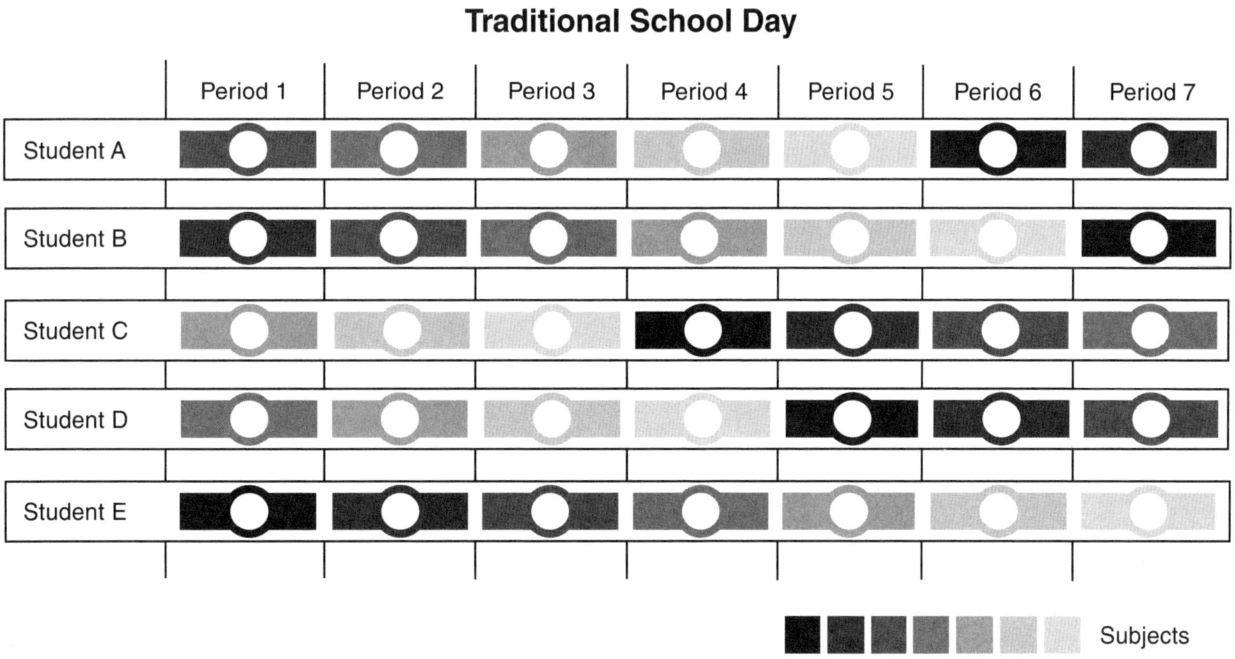

Figure 5.8: Traditional school days governed by periods and bells.

for group discussions; and, for efficiency, it requires teachers deliver content via lecture.

Although teachers loathe floating—that is, not having their own classroom—every secondary school student in a traditional school floats every day for seven years in grades 6–12. Nothing in the bell schedule responds to or reflects varied subjects, varied teaching methods, and varied learning abilities and styles. When it comes to time, apparently one size fits all with a vengeance. Not only that, the rigidity works in two directions. For some students, allotted time may be too short, and if they haven't met the learning objectives at the end of the semester or year, schools give them a failing grade and send them back the next semester to repeat exactly what did not work in the first place. The student loses a year of his or her life, and taxpayers get to pay for the same schooling twice—sometimes more. Students who excel in a subject and could easily meet the learning objectives in less than a semester must wait it out, passing the time before they can progress according to their own talents. This, again, wastes resources.

Traditional School Year

The same sort of thinking that governs school days also governs how schools organize the school year. Most school districts operate on a nine-month calendar year spanning fall to spring, with three months out of school, most of that time during the summer (see figure 5.9). In theory, this is a 19th century construct that allowed students to help their parents with farm work during the summer months (de Melker & Weber, 2014), but there were variations on this. Regardless, the idea persists despite the fact that approximately only 1 percent of the U.S. population works in agriculture (Florida, 2002). Some districts have tried operating schools all year with time organized in quarters, or thirds, but the fixed periods for schooling remain.

The key here is that school years (semester or quarters) are as rigidly organized as school days,

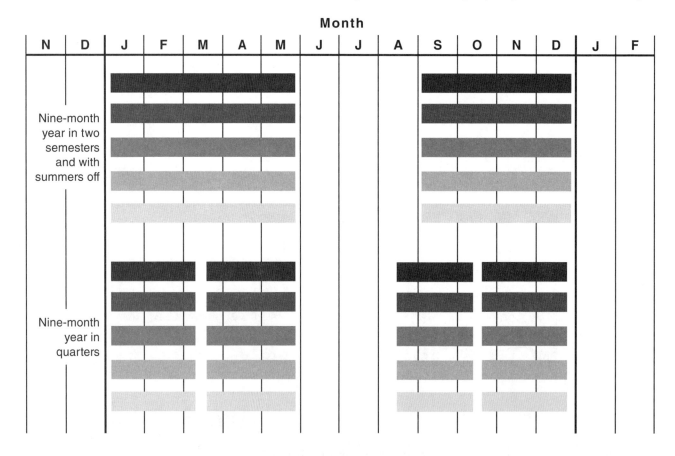

Figure 5.9: Three types of traditional school calendar years.

and they are just as unresponsive to individual students' needs. Conventional school days and school years prioritize the efficiency of the teaching process over students' learning. Time is the constant, while learning is the variable.

As if this is not enough, we've only raised questions here about the rigidity of the school year and not its length. Consider that the typical school year in the United States has 180 days, while the school years in Hong Kong and Singapore have two hundred days. Japanese students attend school for 220 days, in China it is 223 days, and in South Korea it is 225 days (Organisation for Economic Co-operation and Development, n.d.). Are those of us in the United States sufficiently ingenious in our instructional practices that 180 days in schools can make us competitive with other nations? As we shall see in the Funding Resources section (page 82), these rigid and limited times are not efficient with regard to the costs of schooling.

Advisory School Days

Although traditional schooling dictates that students move from teacher to teacher, room to room to get to subjects, technology makes it possible for teachers and content to come to students, and the difference is quite profound. The organizing link between students and teachers should be digital, not based on assigned seats in classrooms between bells. Figure 5.10 describes typical days for five students using an advisory-based model, and figure 5.11 (page 80) suggests how teachers may work with individual students or assemble groups of students for collaborative work across disciplines. Note that for our purposes, the terms *teacher* and *teacher advisor* are synonymous when talking about managing a school day.

The number of subject areas and courses in which a student might work varies each day. The circles indicate times when the student and a teacher advisor in a discipline might meet. Either the teacher advisor or student can initiate such meetings on an as-needed basis. As the figure illustrates, some students may focus on a small number of subjects on some days while others may work on every subject. Some may meet with one or two teacher advisors, while others meet with more. Students and teacher advisors shape their own working processes.

While having their own workstations, teacher advisors and students would both move about the school to tend to their individual needs—there would be no periods governed by bells and no mass

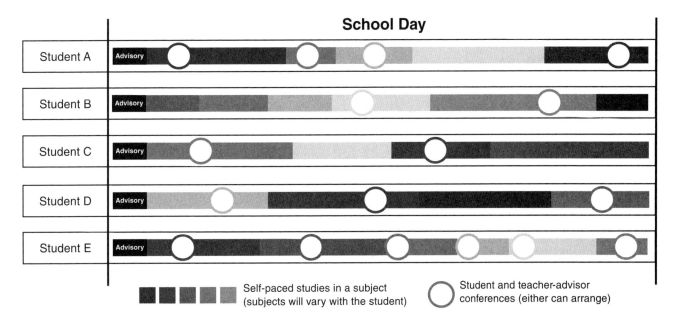

Figure 5.10: An advisory school day featuring individualized, self-paced studies.

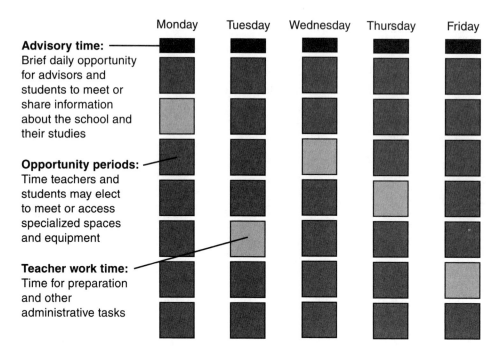

Figure 5.11: Opportunities for teacher advisors and students to meet.

movements of students. This adds back into the day the time students formerly consumed during passing periods. As a bonus, there are fewer occasions for a teacher to penalize a student for being late. Although the school day has no bells or class changes, its flexible structure helps teachers and students connect. Teachers would have a conference time each day during which to prepare instructional materials, collaborate with other teachers, and so on. The remainder of the day divides into opportunity periods during which either teachers or students may initiate meetings as they need to, to advance learning.

The sole purpose of dividing these times into opportunity periods is to help disperse students over the school day (refer to figure 5.10, page 79) and enhance their opportunity to meet with their teacher advisors. Similarly, during these opportunity periods, students have access to specialized spaces and equipment as needed for studies such as science and project labs, consumer and technical education, and the arts. However, if students and teachers need to meet at other times and their schedules permit, both are free to meet at any time. The intention is that most students do most of their work on campus at their individual workstation so that the school environment provides a supportive social context for learning. However, with the approval of their parents and teacher advisor, students may opt to do their school time from home or some other location. Figure 5.12 illustrates a highly variable school day for seven students to engage in personalized and self-paced learning.

Advisory schools remain open a minimum of five days per week from 7 a.m. to 6 p.m., and some schools may remain open parts of weekends as well. Although the school does not need full staffing during off hours, the facility should be open so students can access their workstations and the network.

Extracurricular activities should occur only outside normal school hours. To that end, schools must redefine eligibility for extracurricular activities such as athletics if learning is self-paced. To participate (and as in traditional schooling), students would have to carry some minimum number of courses during the season for the activity and sustain a level of progress to be eligible to compete.

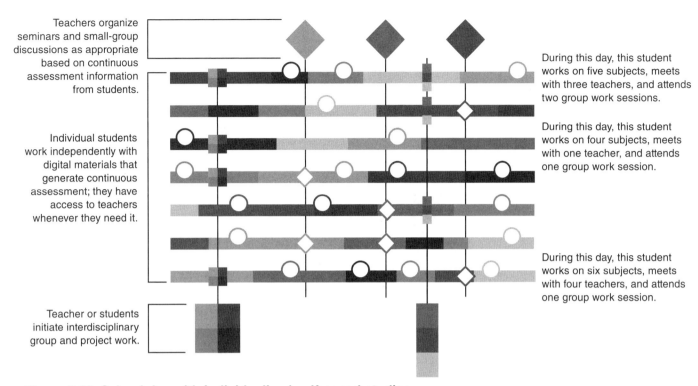

Figure 5.12: School day with individualized self-paced studies.

Advisory School Year

Just as school days require flexibility to better support students and individual learning, so too should the school year. Advisory-based schooling must be a continuous service, not a seasonal event, and schools should function twelve months a year to serve students just as hospitals are there to serve patients' medical needs as they arise. In this model, there are no semesters or quarters. The process is continuous, punctuated only by students when they complete the learning objectives of one course and begin another. Graduation is not an annual celebration, rather students receive digital diplomas certifying they completed their studies whenever that occurs.

Consider figure 5.13 (page 82), which describes the individual studies for four students over an eighteen-month period. Each shaded bar represents a different course of study, although the exact nature of the courses in this case is immaterial.

In this example, students A and B elect to carry a light academic load to suit their learning styles or to address family or health needs. At any one time during this period, these two students are taking as many as four courses or as few as one. These students would probably need more than four years to graduate high school. Student C elects to concentrate his or her studies to take off a traditional summer period but note this student could just as easily do this at any time of the year. Student D elects to take a very intense course load with five or six courses going simultaneously all year. This student would graduate in less than four years. The potential variations are as distinct as students themselves. Some students may have to attend during certain times and to stipulated levels to be eligible to participate in extracurricular programs such as athletics. Teachers may work part of the calendar year (as with the traditional agrarian calendar) or teach all year and earn proportional compensation.

Along with the improved educational outcomes we believe this model will produce, this approach to year-round schooling also has additional benefits: distributing these activities over the year and affording families the opportunity to enjoy themselves in

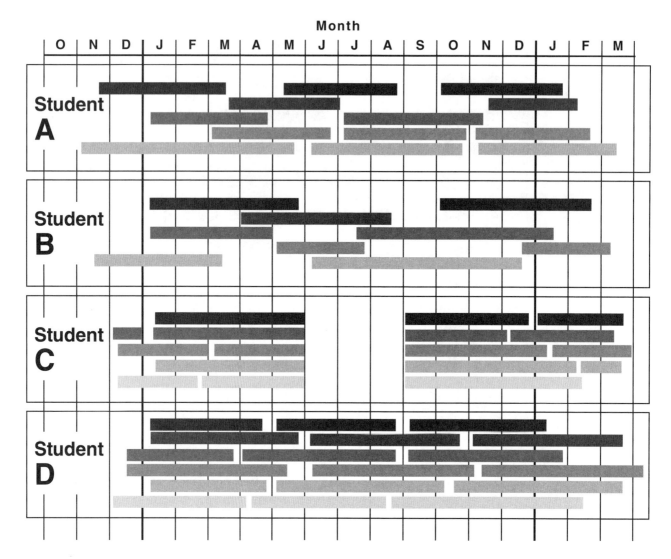

Figure 5.13: An eighteen-month snapshot of student course loads.

every season help resorts and businesses that thrive on vacationing families.

Funding Resources

Districts, states or provinces, and so on must determine funding for advisory schools much differently than funding for traditional industrial age schools. In most traditional schools, communities require students to attend the full school day, and school funding is often based on average daily attendance over a semester. The length of the school year (180 days, for example) is also prescribed for funding purposes. The school receives the same funding for students who excel and graduate and for those who fail. The methodology also assumes that every student is carrying a similar load on a similar time schedule.

Advisory school funding is based *on the classes students take and the credits they earn*, data that instructional software and learning management systems can easily track. This model accommodates students carrying varied course loads and working at different paces. The school receives most of its funds (75 percent, for example) for each course when the teacher and student begin work. It would receive the remaining funds (25 percent) when the student achieves his or her learning goals and gains credit—regardless of the time it requires. With funding tied to courses students take and credits they earn, the school receives full compensation for the successful services it provides but receives only partial payment for studies that students do not complete. It accommodates students carrying varying numbers of courses over the school year, so if a student carries less than a full load, but goes all year, the school receives funds accordingly. If a student carries a heavy load part of the year to free time for other activities during another part of the year, the school receives funds accordingly. If a student carries a heavy load and studies all year to graduate earlier, the school receives funds accordingly.

Funding is also variable for different courses. Funding requirements should generally be lower for English language arts or social studies courses, which typically do not require special facilities or equipment, but may be relatively high for some special education, science, CTE programs, visual and performing arts programs, and physical education courses that require large, specialized spaces and equipment. Funding for extracurricular programs will vary with the staff, facilities, and site improvements the programs require. Funding for each course should include an overhead factor to cover the costs of noninstructional staff and facilities. Funding data for each school related to staffing, technology and facility operations, and debt would be readily available on the school's website for parents and taxpayers. Funding for new school facilities should similarly factor types of spaces as an integral part of the facility design and funding process. All this would make schooling costs much more transparent for parents and taxpayers (Roza, 2010).

Spatial Environments

We have come to define and recognize schools as much by their facilities as what happens inside them. For most, a school is a place with classrooms, labs, shops, gymnasiums, visual and performing arts facilities, and athletic fields. The assumptions we typically make about facilities are rooted in the assumptions we make about instruction and time; but, per our elements of schooling, the changes we propose here with advisories, individualized instruction, time, and funding will dramatically change the facilities districts require. To be very clear, what we propose here *will not work* in a typical school environment with fixed classrooms and corridors, bells and semesters, and paper-based and teacher-centered instruction. To see our concepts for how changes to teaching and learning affect the design of new schools built on this model, review chapter 7 (page 101); and, for our ideas for renovating and reshaping existing school facilities, see part 3 (page 109). That said, do not think we are proposing to revive the open-plan school, which did not fully consider the ways in which all elements of schooling are interconnected and continued the use of teacher-driven lectures as if the schools still had enclosed classrooms. This is not our vision.

The school environment will be similar in both new schools and in existing schools that districts transform. Both will have very few corridors lined with lockers or fixed walls. Both will have very few spaces without natural light. Both will have large open areas with individual workstations for students and teachers. Both will have fewer corridors of any sort with no bells, and no mass movements period by period.

Schools will design almost all the teaching and learning spaces for flexibility, and how students and teachers configure spaces will evolve constantly in response to teaching and learning needs. Both will have opportunities for teachers and students to interconnect and mix in manners supportive of teaching and learning. Both will encourage students to assume responsibility for the management of their time and the realization of their objectives. The schools will be alive with displays of the work students have done. There will be no penitentiary dining spaces or lunch periods. There will be no libraries with metal detectors at their entrance.

Community Context

In the wake of desegregation in the 1950s and forward, educators have sought to provide equal schools for all students in terms of facilities, teaching, programs, funding, and so on. Somehow, we must have imagined that if we treated everyone the same way, everyone would have comparable opportunities and outcomes. We already know this kind of thinking doesn't work in hospitals when treating patients who are each there to address unique conditions, and it cannot work in schools where every student's needs are likewise unique. To the extent that students are different from one another, that approach ensures different outcomes for different students—but with our faith in parity, we believed we were doing the correct thing despite decade after decade of graduation rates and test scores that show very clearly that the approach created unequal outcomes for students—very large numbers of students.

While failing to make schools suited to the students they serve, we also failed to make schools suited to the communities they serve. More than a collection of housing, the businesses, professions, industries, shops, medical facilities, higher education, entertainment, and natural assets are what characterize communities. The article "Make K–12 Skills Relevant to Students" notes that both students and communities benefit from transforming "abstract schooling experiences into something more personal—something that can ignite student curiosity, creativity, motivation, and imagination" (Hasak, 2015). Another article, "Employers Are Integral to Career-Tech Programs," reflects on how educators can draw on expertise of businesses in their community (Adams, 2015).

To better serve a community's students, schools in varied parts of every city or town should be different in terms of the programs they offer and instructional methods they employ. This also reinforces the idea that districts should not force students to attend certain schools based on attendance zones because parents and students need to be able to pick the school that best meets their interests, needs, and future ambitions. Schools capable of flexibility and change can evolve with their communities over time, which will be necessary for them to attract students and thrive in the absence of attendance zones that guarantee enrollments and funding.

Transitions From Elementary Schools to Advisories

The transitions between elementary, middle, and high schools have long been challenging for students and teachers. While growing, maturing students and raging hormones will always be issues, we believe the differences between instruction in traditional elementary and secondary schools are not helpful.

In elementary schools, students typically learn in self-contained classrooms with one teacher for most or all the subjects, all day, every day. Each student is likely to have a personal desk in the classroom. The students and teacher are together as a group each day and get to know each other well as individuals. Starting with middle schools, students transition to the conventional schedules with which all educators are familiar, moving from teacher to teacher, classroom to classroom, and subject to subject about every fifty minutes. In most school districts, elementary schools are typically the smallest of the district's schools in terms of enrollment. The middle schools are larger, perhaps twice the elementary schools' size, and the pattern repeats at the high school level. So, elementary students not only face big changes in the way secondary schools work, but in their very size.

Because secondary advisory schools match students with teacher advisors at a personal workstation that they use most of each school day, students and teacher advisors stay together for the student's entire time at the school. The teacher advisor is responsible for knowing the student individually and for generally being mindful of the student's well-being within the school and their progress. With a mix of ages and grades, the students in each advisory also get to know each other well, with older students advising and counseling their younger colleagues. We believe this will provide a smoother and more comfortable transition as students enter secondary schooling, allowing them to progress as their personal needs dictate.

Staff Development in an Advisory

Relative to traditional industrial age secondary schools, teacher advisors in advisory schools will draw on the same expertise they develop in their discipline, but the interface with students will be quite different, which requires districts and schools to provide considerable professional development for teachers before school starts. Consider how the following details affect conventional teaching practices and how districts can best prepare teachers for them.

- There would be no classrooms and few lectures (if any). Students would individually receive their primary instruction online. Most often, it would occur at the students' workstation in their advisory but may actually occur anywhere students can log on.

- Although teachers would not lecture to large groups, they must know the software students are using—the software is the textbook for each student's studies. The software presents information using text, graphics, links to other resources, videos, and so on, and it may include questions and assignments for students that would function as ongoing assessment by which teachers can monitor each student's work.

- Teachers would still need the same expertise in their discipline and its relationship to other subjects. They would need to teach by questioning, critiquing, and guiding students in their work. Teachers and students would communicate frequently via email, instant messaging, or an equivalent communications system, and they may elect to meet when either feels it is appropriate. The need for and nature of these communications and meetings would vary quite considerably from student to student, subject to subject.

- Teachers would learn to pull students together when appropriate for small-group discussions, team projects, field trips, and so on. Teachers learn to assign projects to students to help them explore ideas and to apply them. At times, teachers would collaborate with colleagues in other disciplines, and they may collectively develop projects for their students.

- Teachers would need to learn new methods and practices to manage both their time and student time. Because students will progress at their own individual pace, teachers must be able to adapt to work with and support students regardless of where they are in a curriculum.

- Teachers would learn to help students with creating and maintaining portfolios to document their work. They must help students to develop portfolios that are more than a transcript listing courses and grades. Rather portfolios must be highly personalized and include graphics, photos, videos, text, and links to information on completed studies, projects, and so on.

Teachers must be able to help students store and access their portfolios on school servers to ensure they can't lose them. As a reflection of each student's unique nature, the portfolios should vary enormously from student to student.

- Teacher advisors would need to be curators of students' work by creating and sustaining displays throughout the school so that students may learn from and be stimulated by others in a visually engaging environment. In this regard, secondary schools should learn from elementary schools about exhibiting their own work.

Reflecting on all that we propose here, it may be helpful to recall Sugata Mitra's quote at the start of this chapter, "We don't need to improve schools, we need to reinvent them for our times. We need people who can think like children." It is time to think outside the box we've created.

Essential Questions

As you reflect on this chapter, consider the following questions.

- How do rigid time schedules and school years based on agrarian calendars inhibit learning and incur unnecessary financial and social costs for communities and taxpayers? How much impact do you feel these things have for your nation's competitiveness in the world, and how might advisory-based schools improve this picture?

- Consider the burdens high dropout rates impose on society. How can educators and education stakeholders justify allowing students to fail courses in their K–12 schooling? Should failure be an option in schooling if advisory-based schools can ensure that all students have better chances of succeeding?

- If we want to shape schooling to individual students' diverse needs and the communities in which they live, should we measure parity between schools in terms of expenditures, programs, and facilities or in terms of individual students' results? What counts most when preparing students for their futures?

- If we want to develop in students essential 21st century skills such as higher-order thinking and problem solving, what are better ways to achieve these outcomes than rigid class schedules, subject-based learning, large-group instruction, and conventional assessment practices rooted in rote memorization?

- Why are advisory-based schools in a better position to use learning technology to improve educational outcomes? Why is it critical that students and teachers have access to the same technology in schools as they would have at home?

- How does having to float from classroom to classroom inhibit learning? How would having a dedicated workspace for learning help students progress according to their own individual needs?

- If one student can meet a ten-week curriculum's learning objectives in six weeks and another takes fourteen weeks, should we fail the fourteen-week student at the end of the term or force the six-week student to delay his or her studies for the full ten weeks? What makes advisory-based schools better suited to avoiding these outcomes, and what benefit does this have for students and taxpayers in the community?

- Why is transparency in school funding critical information for all community stakeholders?

- If we don't transform our public schools, how could new schools trying new and innovative approaches displace educators? If you were a student or parent with options to choose from, what type of school would you choose? What impact would your choice have on your community?

Chapter 6
HOW TO MAKE IT HAPPEN
by Frank Kelly

Don't tell me there is something in America we cannot do. . . . We are a nation born from innovation; innovation of our ideals, innovation of agriculture, innovation in industry, innovation in science and technology. Why has the one sector in our society most in need of innovation been left in the agrarian age, and that is education? No more!

—Cory Booker

Nowhere are the elements of schooling (refer to figure I.1, page 3) more apparent than during long-range school district planning. The education stakeholders involved must ensure they represent and explore every element if the endeavor's final outcome will serve students and their futures. These stakeholders generally include the district's school board, district-level administrators (including instructional, technology, business, facilities, and transportation personnel), campus-level staff (administrators and teachers from all disciplines), parents and students, and community representatives (businesses and government entities). This is a *large* group, but when you consider the wide impact of schooling on a community, broad support is necessary.

If the planning-design process does not include all the elements and involve all stakeholders, the complete project will fall far short of its real potential. It will become a reflection of education's past tactics of implementing less-effective incremental changes, rather than a glimpse or first step into its future.

Figure 6.1 identifies the eight essential process steps for developing effective, forward-focused schools during the planning process all the way through to facility operation. This chapter's contents detail these steps in the context of building a new facility, but it also reflects a sound process for making major and minor updates to existing facilities. By reading through the entire process, it will be obvious how the steps interrelate, following from one to the next and how they relate back to the elements of schooling.

We mean for the length of the blocks in this illustration to indicate the approximate time each step might take relative to the others and the overall process, but you should clearly understand that the total time from start to finish varies with the project's scope and nature, its funding, and so on. These are variables that will change with every plan and district. For example, the total time from gathering data to full operation could easily vary from months to years. This is not a casual undertaking, and there are few things educators and stakeholders can do that are more important for having forward-focused educational strategies that aid teachers in preparing students for their futures.

Let's begin with the first step in the process.

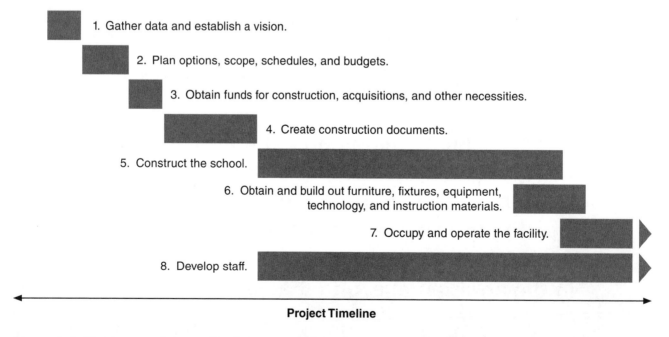

Figure 6.1: Eight essential steps to follow to effectively design and build forward-focused schools.

Gather Data and Establish a Vision

It is critical that before any planning for the future begins, districts collect substantial background data to thoroughly describe the existing conditions from which the project starts. Typically, these data include the following.

- **Demographic projections:** Is the enrollment of the school or district growing, diminishing, or changing? Is the community context changing? What are the implications for the numbers and natures of the students it serves? Some districts maintain their own data, while others use demographic consultants.

- **Enrollment capacities:** How many students will the school or schools serve, in what grades, with what programs, and with what instructional methods? Are those capacities too large or small? Are they sufficient for the enrollments the district anticipates? Is the school in the right location to serve its community? These are questions that a demographer, the district, or a planning consultant or architect can answer. For sure, districts should not measure the school's capacity based on the number of classrooms or seats, but as a function of the manner in which teaching and learning occur, the average size of instructional groups, the spaces in use, and so on. Figure 6.2 (page 92) illustrates how schools might assess existing capacity.

- **Facility conditions assessment:** What are the conditions of existing facilities? Do they require maintenance to systems or areas such as to mechanical systems, roofs, or furnishings? Do the facilities comply with life-safety and accessibility codes? Do the facilities use energy efficiently? When do individual schools require work to be done to properly function, and what will it cost? District facility personnel may do this assessment, or the district may engage an architect or other consultant.

- **Educational adequacy assessment:** How are your schools performing academically? Holistically, are the outcomes for students excellent, acceptable, or in need of improvement? Are outcomes for diverse student demographics in your district comparable or widely varied? Are the numbers, sizes, types, and equipment in your school spaces adequate and appropriate for the intended teaching and learning? Are facilities in compliance with any applicable state- (or province-) or district-defined standards? Answering these questions requires a joint undertaking from the district's instructional and facilities staff and an architect or consultant.

- **Technology assessment:** What technology systems are in place, such as networks, internet access, teacher and student devices, and instructional software? How are teachers and students using technology for teaching and learning? Do the school's and district's instructional spaces and organization of time support effective technology use? Where do students do the important work of learning? Do they float from space to space, or do they have workstations? Who operates and maintains your systems? What is the nature of your instructional materials and library? Are they predominantly paper-based or digital? Do you have general-purpose computer labs, or are teacher and student devices mobile and accessible outside schools? What do you anticipate in the next several years? The district's or school's

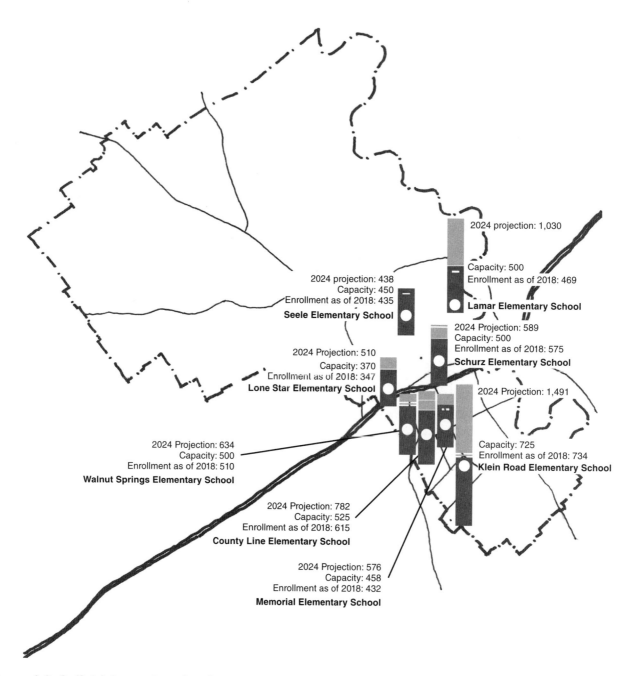

Figure 6.2: A district examines its elementary schools for current enrollment, capacity, and future projections.

instructional and technology personnel are often best-suited to answer these questions, but districts may opt to engage an outside technology consultant.

- **Financial assessment:** What is the status of the school's or district's funding as it applies to maintenance and operations, technology, and capital improvements and major purchases (properties, for example)? Does the district have the capacity to fund improvements or new construction? The district's business and finance staff may do this with the support of an outside school funding consultant.

- **Establish a vision:** This final and most critical step does not require questions to answer but is instead grounded in analyzing data from the rest of this list. It entails seriously examining how teaching and learning currently work, understanding how the educators want them to work in the future, and therefore, knowing what instructional programs are required to realize them.

Establishing a vision requires that all stakeholders involved in the planning process reflect on how long their existing schools have served their communities and that they imagine the facilities they are planning will serve just as far into the future. It challenges every tradition and assumption: Are they still appropriate? How do they serve students' futures? The participants in the visioning process should include all the stakeholders we listed at the start of this chapter. Experience tells us that diverse perspectives are essential to creating a vision for the future of a community's schools.

During the data-gathering-and-visioning process, the district may engage individuals with strong backgrounds in instruction and technology and planners and architects with substantial long-range planning experience to help structure, facilitate, and document the process. These parties should team with the school's and district's leadership to identify issues to explore to ensure that the process will be broad and thorough. The assembled group needs to meet several times for extended work to explore issues and concepts and to reach consensus. This is not a rushed process.

Documenting the vision is very important because it must be clear and provide real guidance. It must resolve issues and delineate choices and should not consist of warm and fuzzy statements with which no one could disagree. Such soft language does not help identify what stakeholders must do and what hard decisions they must make. We prefer to define visions via a series of findings and directions. In this context, *findings* are facts and policies about aspects of the district for which the board of trustees, administration, and planning committees have given *directions* that will shape the plan, the teaching and learning, and the schools the district is to create (or renovate) and operate. The district's board of trustees must formally approve the complete vision, with all its findings and directions, to guide all that is to follow in both the design and creation of school spaces and in their funding and operation thereafter.

What follows are illustrative examples of findings and directions.

Finding: The school district should tailor instruction to the learning styles, personal interests, and capabilities of individual students.

Directions:

1. Provide a teacher advisor or advocate for each secondary school student. Study how the student and teacher-advisor relationship is to work to define the optimum number of students for each teacher advisor.

2. Create for each secondary student a written personal learning plan. The teacher advisor, student, and parents should work together to create the personal learning plan.

3. The teacher advisor and his or her students should meet frequently (daily or weekly) as a group or as individuals to plan studies, monitor progress, address problems, and so on.

4. Modify school schedules (at the secondary school levels) to provide flexible time each school day to accommodate individual learning styles and multiple modes of instruction and to allow teachers and students to work together as needed to ensure student success.

5. Create varied teacher and student instructional and working spaces (in new and existing structures) to accommodate variable individualized instruction, multiple modes of instruction, and flexible schedules.

Finding: High school instruction should be student-centered and individualized, with multiple modes of instruction, flexible schedules, the development of higher-order and real-world thinking skills, and the technology use appropriate to meet tech-minded students' needs.

Directions:

1. Use multiple modes of instruction with varied sized spaces and time periods appropriate to the subject and individual student learning styles.

2. Provide the following to make subjects and teaching and learning methods more diverse, relevant, and engaging for students.

   - Expertise from the community and real world inside the schools, and sending students into the community for portions of their studies
   - Experts from the community as mentors for students
   - Project-based instruction within disciplines or across disciplines to develop higher-order-thinking skills
   - Opportunities and support for students to assume responsibility for their own learning

3. Create positive school environments that promote creative thinking and enable students to explore their own talents across content and elective areas.

4. Establish and promote additional extracurricular and cocurricular programs that meet all students' varied interests.

Finding: High school teaching and learning, and the configuration and organization of instructional spaces, are integrally related.

Directions:

1. Modify or create spaces within each high school to facilitate multidisciplinary vertical grade-level (9–12) learning communities, each with a full complement of core disciplines (including English language arts, mathematics, social studies, science, and foreign languages).

2. Provide each teacher advisor with a workstation in an open-advisory area where they may meet with and work with students and advisees as appropriate.

3. Provide workstations and small-group workspaces students may use individually and in groups.

Finding: The school district must seamlessly integrate technology into teaching and learning to achieve educational goals and objectives. The district must train staff to maximize the potential of new technologies as they become available for educational applications.

Directions:

1. Make provisions such that students may access the technology tools they need from their workstations, throughout the school, off campus, and throughout the district (particularly at home).

2. Provide each student with a personal, internet-connected digital device and ensure wireless data access. To the extent possible, promote wireless access throughout the community.

3. Utilize technology daily as the basic tool to enhance and support rigor and relevance within curricula.

4. Modify instructional methods and provide staff development to realize the potential of technology to strengthen teaching, learning, and assessment.

5. Convert computer labs to other uses, except for those serving special purposes that require software or equipment that students' personal digital devices cannot support.

6. Ensure that the technology plan reflects the district's instructional plan, and in

the future, coordinate any updates in instruction with commensurate reviews and improvements to technology systems.

7. Consistently monitor technology life cycles to ensure current and relevant technology is available for instruction.

8. Provide technology use instruction throughout elementary school to prepare students for the technology they will encounter in their secondary schools, in their homes, and in the real world around them.

9. Provide staff development such that all district employees involved with teaching and learning become effective technology users.

Plan Options, Scope, Schedules, and Budgets

If the visioning process defines where the district wants to go, the planning process defines how it will get there (see figure 6.3). Within the context of these data the district gathers and the vision it defines, the planning committee and planning architectural consultants must explore options for the district's future impact on teaching and learning, technology resources, use of time, facilities (spatial environments), and costs.

This is a fiendishly complex undertaking because these issues impact each other, and the committee

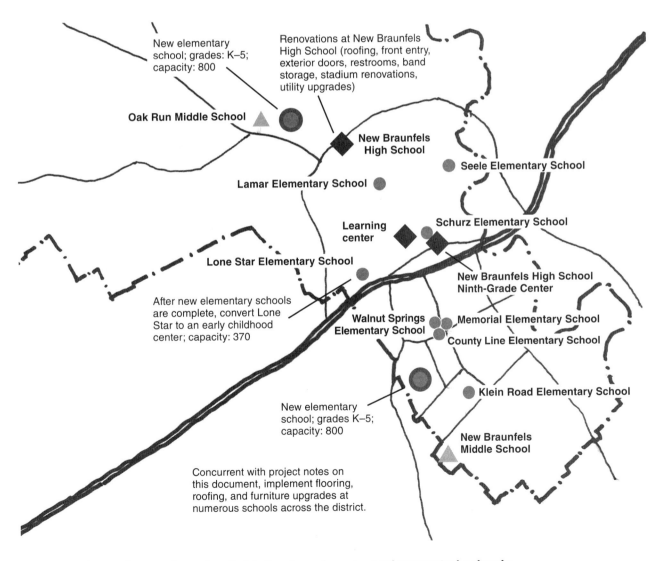

Figure 6.3: A rough overview of a district's plans for new and renovated schools.

must explore all of it within the context of funding mechanisms and community politics. It must thoroughly delineate all options including projections for time and costs to realize them. It must also analyze their consistency in conjunction with district approval. Ideally, if time and funds allow, the committee should prepare a detailed program of space requirements for each project as a solid base for projecting construction costs. As the plan develops, the district's financial advisor must review the financing implications and the impact on the district's funding capacity.

In the end, the planning committee must select the option that best realizes the vision that is within the district's funding capabilities and that will have community and taxpayer support. This option typically requires formal approval from a board of trustees or equivalent entity.

Obtain Funds for Construction, Acquisitions, and Other Necessities

With the approval of the plan and financing, the district must obtain the requisite funding. The complexities and variables involved in this process could fill a book unto themselves, and we do not explore them here. Suffice it to say, this process varies considerably from state to state and may require very different periods of time to acquire. For example, if it requires a bond election, the dates set for elections will drive when funds are available, each project's construction timeline, and when facilities will be ready for teaching and learning. These are factors that go beyond the district's control and have *huge* implications for the time schedule and school years.

Generally speaking, the time and funding required to create the new schools we propose would be quite comparable to existing schools, but with schooling as a continuous service, these schools will, over the course of a calendar year, serve more students in the same facility and thereby cost less per student or per graduate. Teachers will have opportunities to work with more flexible schedules over the year and possibly make more if they prefer to work the full year. Some operating and maintenance costs may increase as students and staff use facilities more, but the debt payments for original construction will not change.

Create Construction Documents

When the district ensures its funding, it may select the architectural or engineering team to design the first project (or projects) in the plan. Figure 6.4 is a common example of such a plan. Note that it is not necessary for you to be able to parse every detail of this image, as every architectural plan is both unique and complex. (Visit **go.SolutionTree.com/instruction** to access color versions of this and other figures in this book.) The district's instructional and facilities staff should work closely with the architectural or engineering team to develop from the established vision, scope, and budget the design and construction documents for each project.

It is very important for the district's instructional staff to be deeply involved during the first phases (schematic design and design development) to verify that the design, as defined in its program, will meet its teaching and learning objectives. This engagement in the planning process is an excellent way to begin the staff-development process we describe in the Develop Staff section (page 98). The district may then work with a number of contractors to bid or negotiate a construction agreement for each project. Typically, the process of designing and bidding the project requires several months to a year or more depending on the building's scale. This is a process that must be thorough and thoughtful—rushing it will yield costly problems during construction and afterward in the finished spaces.

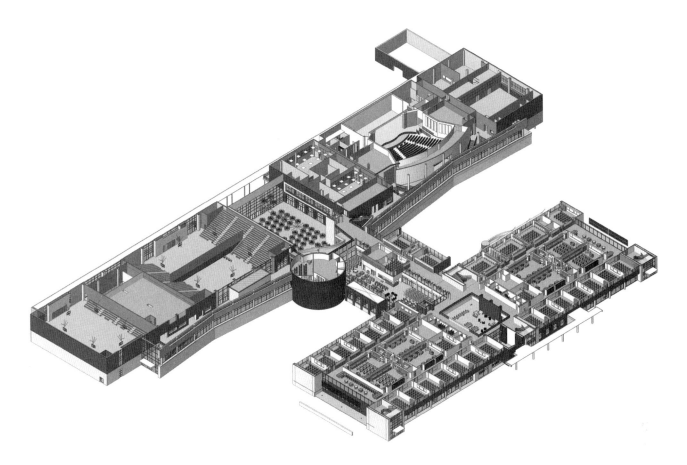

Figure 6.4: An initial architectural design for a new school.

Construct the School

The construction process for a building renovation may require only a summer between school years, whereas larger new projects may require from one to three years or more. How schools and districts opt to manage the need to use existing facilities under renovation or avoid disrupting programs is also highly variable to the particular work, but in our experience, schools routinely overcome these challenges without disruption to learning.

Recall the first steps on gathering data and establishing a vision (page 91) and recognize that planning and creating substantial new concepts and capacities for teaching and learning (of which facilities are but a part) is a major undertaking. Then, consider how long this new teaching and learning environment may serve into the future and the numbers of students it may serve. This is truly important work. The district's financial and facilities staff, along with their architect, will have primary responsibility for the construction phase, but the board of trustees should receive regular updates on the progress being made.

Obtain and Build Out Furniture, Fixtures, Equipment, Technology, and Instruction Materials

An important part of the design process is the selection of furniture, fixtures, equipment, technology systems and software, and instruction materials, all of which must be consistent with the vision and budget and must function as an integral part of the facility. Generally, either district officials or architects handle this phase; regardless, the individuals involved should select these items during the facility design and construction periods to ensure that everything is coordinated. The facility should be substantially complete two to three months before the school opens to permit the relevant parties to install all these items well before school opens.

Occupy and Operate the Facility

The full administrative, teaching, food services, and maintenance staffs should be in the building several weeks before school starts to bring the school to life and to adapt to the new facility they've helped to create. The process of learning to realize the full function and potential of the new environment may take some time, but the effort to find new ways to teach and learn should be invigorating for both teachers and students. In fact, regardless of new or renovated facilities, we think it's wonderful when schools can find ways to reinvent themselves in some way each year as a means to rethink the evolving futures for which they are preparing their students.

Develop Staff

Although establishing a vision, creating a plan, and constructing facilities are key steps for developing all sorts of new environments for teaching and learning, every vision you develop still shares one essential requirement—staff development. We should not repeat the debacle of the open-plan school and simply insert unprepared teachers into a new world. Designing and funding a new school can take up to a year or more to accomplish with another two to three years to build it. Once the instructional and spatial plans are clear, districts should begin selecting and developing the staff who will work there.

Because the facility should be complete several months in advance of the opening, there is room for districts to thoroughly introduce experienced staff and new teachers to the school's spaces, individualized-instruction concepts, technology, learning resources, scheduling, and their new dual role as advisor and teacher. If possible, use existing school facilities to model critical instructional aspects of the new or renovated facilities as well as to create learning opportunities to use new digital hardware and software. Allowing some teachers and students this experience for a new setup enables them to use what they learn to help develop the full potential of what is to come. However, unlike the construction work that stops with the school's completion, staff development should always be an ongoing process. Methods of teaching and learning need to evolve as technology resources, community contexts, funding resources, and the real world evolve.

In lieu of giant meetings that interrupt schedules, schools should have a space for professional development, where teachers are able to explore new digital technology and resources as well as explore new ways to connect with their students. This could be part of the teachers' break or work room area where it could serve multiple purposes each day. Teachers should be free to go there on an as-needed basis. When new technology becomes available—including useful websites and apps for teaching and learning—administrators must alert teachers and schedule a learning experience for them.

Ongoing staff development is important for new and seasoned teachers alike if the schooling process is to evolve, improve, and stay abreast of the exponentially evolving world outside the school.

Understand the Big Picture

Although this chapter represents only an overview of this highly variable planning, building, and staffing process, we hope it explains why working with all the elements of schooling, and making real changes, are very challenging. The process we outline in this chapter takes lots of time and involves hard work from all stakeholders, but it is also the best way to ensure that schools will serve for decades to come and simultaneously realize their full potential.

Essential Questions

As you reflect on this chapter, consider the following questions.

- How do you facilitate new thinking in all the stakeholders (based on the key principles we presented in chapter 2, page 17) to develop a shared vision for creating effective new learning environments? (Consider this in the context of the advisory concepts we detail in chapter 5, page 61.)

- Given that new teaching and learning environments may be quite different from those in existing schools, what are the role and nature of ongoing staff development in moving the shared vision into reality?

- When your school or district is considering new programs or new or modified facilities, what is the process by which you plan for these? Does it include the collection of background data and visioning described here previously?

Chapter 7
CONCEPTS FOR NEW ADVISORY-BASED SCHOOLS

by Frank Kelly

If we teach today's students as we taught yesterday's, we rob them of tomorrow.

—John Dewey

Our core argument in this book is that, because our industrial age schools are out of sync with the students and the world they serve, we are not properly serving students' essential needs, and others can and will do the job if we do not. This is equally applicable to any new schools that we build and to those that currently exist—both will be challenging.

The new schools we build going forward need to reflect the teaching and learning concepts we outlined in the preceding chapters. (We write in part 3 about transforming existing schools to meet 21st century learning needs.) The enticing part of this is that, with new schools, we have enormous flexibility in shaping school environments. The conceptual designs that follow in this chapter illustrate spatial organizational ideas to realize the aspirations we've outlined in previous chapters and are ideal guides to follow when there is an opportunity to build new schools from scratch.

To be clear, these designs are still abstract concepts that cannot account for the considerations of local school districts, communities, environmental factors, and budgets. These are variable realities that make every building site different and that should be reflected in the architecture of the schools we create. However, the designs we provide do suggest how districts might organize spaces to realize the instructional concepts we describe in this book, and they imply possibilities for adapting these ideas to local conditions and opportunities. We specifically highlight and describe four school possibilities in this chapter, but there are infinite possibilities at your disposal if you truly want to create schools to serve and respond to your own community and students. Part of the problem with traditional schools is that we've tried to apply one model everywhere. We do not want to suggest that the advisories model we outline here is or should be so constrained, but rather it is a place to begin.

In this chapter, we look at four specific variations on the advisory-school concept: (1) the comprehensive advisory high school, (2) the academy advisory high school, (3) the project-based learning advisory high school, and (4) the advisory middle school.

The Comprehensive Advisory High School

Our vision for a traditional comprehensive advisory high school intends to serve students with diverse backgrounds and interests through a broad range of academic, elective, career, performing and visual arts, and physical education and athletic programs. Depending on the community they serve and programs they offer, comprehensive advisory high schools may serve substantial enrollments—from a few hundred to several thousand students. The development of a comprehensive high school in terms of its size, breadth of program offerings, and extracurricular activities is entirely feasible with advisories, online technology, individualized instruction, and self-pacing.

Figure 7.1 illustrates the relationship between the learning halls and advisories and the other elements of a comprehensive advisory high school, links that students would have, and the movements they would make about the campus. For each student, the workstation would be his or her base. The number of learning halls and advisories varies with school size. The learning halls in the figure are open spaces that contain within them multiple advisories, each with teacher-advisor and student workstations. The smaller circles on the periphery of the learning halls indicate specialized spaces such as science labs and seminar or meeting rooms. (Visit **go.SolutionTree.com/instruction** to access color versions of this and other figures in this book.)

In lieu of departments or small learning communities, educators teach core subjects online in advisories grouped in open, flexible workspaces. This type of school integrates students of all grades into each advisory or learning space. During each day, students leave their advisory areas only for work in programs that require specialized spaces

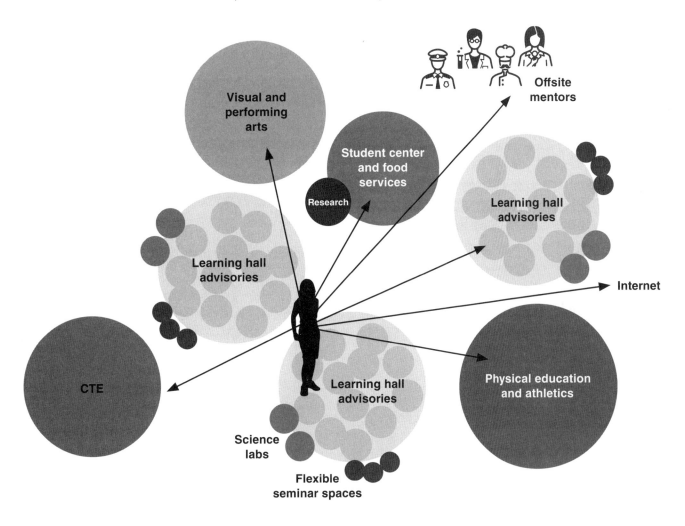

Figure 7.1: Comprehensive advisory high school.

and equipment or group work such as some CTE courses, performing arts, and physical education and athletics. This greatly reduces student circulation and passing periods during the day and saves real time for productive work.

With students primarily accessing content online, there are no classrooms, including science rooms. Students can learn most science concepts online, just as for other core subjects. Although students can do science lab work online, there are still physical labs for specialized, hands-on learning that aides monitor and service. One or more science labs should adjoin each advisory workspace. This school format operates continuously, year-round with no semesters or quarters. Each student works within his or her own individual schedule. Spaces and teacher advisors work throughout the full calendar year.

We group or departmentalize spaces for performing arts, CTE, and physical education and athletics to accommodate their special functions, equipment, and staff. Although core academic studies are continuous throughout the year, some extracurricular activities have seasonal programs, such as athletics, which impact when some students must be in school. This comprehensive school concept envisions a full complement of competitive athletic programs that link to competing school and district schedules.

The research center replaces the traditional library. It is much smaller in floor area because it houses a very small selection of books and periodicals, but it is much larger in terms of the access it provides students to information. The research center draws on online library services with vast collections (Questia [www.questia.com] and Google Books [https://books.google.com], for example). Every student in every school, small or large, has access to the same resources. Librarians are search instructors that teach students how to find things.

The research center is adjacent to the student center, which is an open space at the center of the school much like a food court in a mall. Absent bells, there are no fixed lunch periods. Students and teachers eat per their own schedules. Some food and beverage services are available throughout the day. The research center also serves as a breakout, meeting, working, and collaborating space for any sized gathering. It is highly flexible.

Relative to other schools in this chapter, this school's construction and operating costs are relatively high because of the extensive extracurricular activities it supports. A district may have a mix of high school types, and students may choose a school based on their interests. Parity of results for students is the foremost issue, not parity of programs or facilities.

The Academy Advisory High School

An academy advisory high school provides links between core subjects and real-world career programs to make schooling relevant and engaging for students. Some programs may lead to certifications in various fields, and others provide initial exposure and studies in fields for students to pursue in postsecondary studies. Students choose to attend this school and then choose the academy within the school related to their interests and career ambitions. To accommodate extensive studies in academy programs, schools may offer athletics only in the context of an academy or not at all. Although there are visual, graphic, and digital arts in every academy to help students with communication skills, the school may offer only performing arts in an academy or not at all.

Figure 7.2 illustrates how learning halls and advisories could integrate with diverse CTE or arts programs to create academies with the intent of making schooling more relevant and engaging for students. The flexibility of the advisories would help the school respond to changes in the outside world.

Each academy is a mix of core advisory, learning hall spaces, and specialized spaces related to CTE programs. Students will study some CTE subjects in specialized spaces but will use learning halls for others as appropriate. Learning halls will accommodate workstations for both core teachers and those CTE teachers whose subjects do not require special spaces or equipment.

Most of each day, students will work within their learning hall, but they may also have contact with resources in the local community—businesses, medical, retail, manufacturing, performing arts, and so on. Students work and eat within the academies most of each day and venture out to visit the student center to access the research center and exercise or attend a physical education class. If the school has no competitive athletics, physical education facilities may consist of an exercise-and-equipment room and possibly a jogging trail around the school site. This is sufficient for health and physical education purposes, but it does not require a gymnasium or athletic fields.

The Project-Based Learning Advisory High School

As we illustrate in figure 7.3 (page 106), small learning halls are ideally suited to project-based learning. Students with online resources and close communications with teachers and each other learn through projects in a stimulating, inventive environment. Students work with community resources as appropriate to their projects.

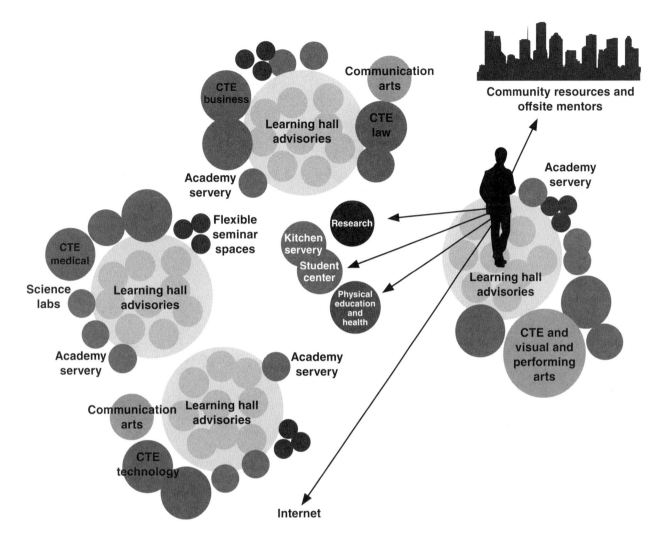

Figure 7.2: Academy advisory high school.

Each learning hall contains a multidisciplinary mix of core and CTE teacher advisors with a small group of students (100–125). The teacher advisors can collaborate to define problems that span disciplines and integrate skills and resources. The learning halls and workstations are typical of those in other models, but we add specialized spaces to complement the halls and support project work. Each hall has one or more science labs that can also house project-related activities. Each also includes an art lab with emphasis on graphic and digital arts and communications. There would also be a project lab with specialized equipment for preparing models and exhibits related to students' projects. Although the learning halls are separate spaces, the shared supporting science, art, and project labs may mix students from different halls. The learning halls will be visually open so that students moving about the school can see the work underway. Adjacent student and research centers are the hub for this school type, providing spaces for research, presentations, exhibitions (of student projects), collaboration, food consumption, and social activity. It is alive and active throughout the day.

For many student projects, the school can draw on resources in the community to provide a real-world context, information, and expertise. Students will visit with the resources off campus, and experts will come to the school to work with students. As students complete projects, they will deliver presentations that explain and describe their work to their peers, teacher advisors, and experts from the community. Students will maintain digital portfolios that document their work.

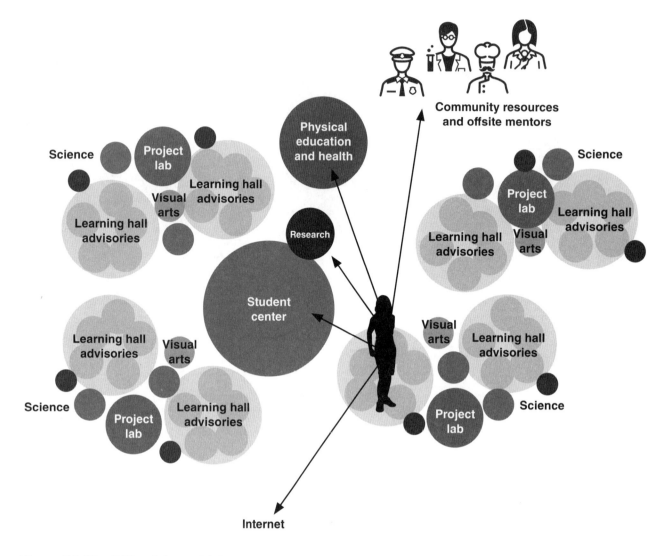

Figure 7.3: The PBL advisory high school.

The Advisory Middle School

As we depict in figure 7.4, students and teachers in this school spend the majority of their time each day in their learning halls or advisories. Each learning hall might serve a single grade level. Students would move about the school only to access shared programs such as performing arts, physical education or athletics, and the research center. There are no classrooms.

Although we propose that this school's use of online materials, advisor teachers, individualized instruction, and self-paced learning is similar to the advisory high school formats, we propose that the learning halls for middle school students be smaller in scale, similar to conventional middle school pods. Similarly, we propose to break up the student center dining area into smaller spaces near each learning hall where they can serve both as eating and breakout workspaces. The intent is to have beverage and food services close by where the students and teachers work so they are accessible throughout the school day—there would be no mass lunch periods.

Like the high school formats that we discuss in this chapter, middle schools may or may not have full programs in the performing arts and physical education or athletics. Like the high schools, each middle school program's size and character are shaped for the community it serves, and students

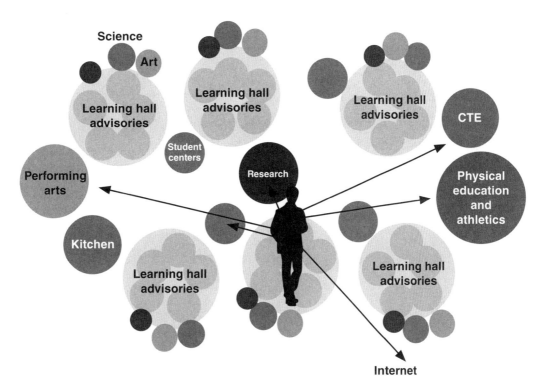

Figure 7.4: The advisory middle school.

and parents should be able to select the school they prefer to attend.

Each of the diagrams presented here is an abstraction that describes how the major parts of these advisory schools might relate to each other to create different teaching and learning environments. This sort of abstract conceptual thinking can be very helpful as a starting point in terms of envisioning the big picture before getting bogged down in important details related to the site, budget, and schedule.

Essential Questions

As you reflect on this chapter, consider the following questions.

- Reflect on the advisory-school concepts we present in this chapter. How do they reflect the concepts of the elements of schooling (refer to figure I.1, page 3)? How do these diagrams relate to your own aspirations for new or modified schools in your district?

- Does my district or state have standards that prescribe the nature and details of facilities and learning spaces the new school structures will create? Do these standards look to the future in which the facilities will serve, and are they sufficiently flexible to allow schools to tailor themselves to local or special needs?

- Would it benefit different communities in your district if you created different types of advisory schools geared to their different students? Could an advisory middle school help students transition from traditional elementary schools to advisory-based high schools? What might you need to change from our advisory middle school concept to reflect your community's unique needs?

- Does your district have attendance zones, or may students and parents select the school they believe would be best-suited to their needs or interests? What should you consider in selecting a school for your own child?

- If learning results and enrollments from campus to campus fluctuate over time, should the district and its schools modify their programs to attract and serve students?

PART 3
REIMAGINING SCHOOLS FOR THE 21ST CENTURY

Chapter 8
ADDITIONAL CONSIDERATIONS FOR TRANSITIONING TO AN ADVISORY FORMAT

by Frank Kelly and Ted McCain

> Environment shapes behavior—We have to build places of hope rather than places of despair. The public-school system here is built to contain kids, not educate them. If you build prisons, you create prisoners. Put kids in an environment where they can find dignity and purpose and they respond.
>
> —Bill Strickland

In the first part of this book, we outlined a new vision for schooling to make education relevant and effective for the 21st century. In part 2, we talked about the logistics for making this change a reality and how we can structure new schools to fit a variety of advisory-based learning formats. In this part, we must address the thorny issue of how to make the transition to this kind of schooling in existing schools. It is critical that we wrestle with this because existing schools represent an enormous investment. K–12 school districts are among the very largest property and building owners and operators in U.S. cities. Districts across the United States spent billions, and they owe billions more in debt on the existing schools they are using (Gonzales, 2012; Texas Comptroller of Public Accounts, n.d.).

Much as we need to change education to align with the world into which our students are graduating, we cannot scrap the investments we've made in our existing school buildings. Instead, we need to transform school facilities in a way that preserves the majority of every community's investment while supporting essential changes we need to make in teaching and learning to keep our learning environments relevant and effective for the 21st century.

Given that most districts will educate their students within their existing facilities for some time, the question becomes: Can districts shift instruction in these buildings beyond the long-standing traditional approaches to teaching to create more effective learning environments? Our answer is a very guarded *yes*. With a number of caveats, we believe it is possible to begin moving toward advisory-based instruction in existing secondary-school buildings.

Before we dig into the *how*, we must stress again in the absolute strongest terms that having a building with classrooms is a severe limitation for effective 21st century learning. Classrooms isolate teachers and disciplines. They force organizing students into groups or classes of twenty-five to thirty. Most important, having teachers and students in classrooms immediately brings into play all the behaviors and expectations that accompany traditional classroom instruction that we outlined in chapter 1 (page 11). We must recognize that any move to this new learning will entail some modifications to the physical building to remove classrooms.

In this chapter, we begin by looking at the minimum thresholds for effective instruction schools must achieve regardless of whether they are new or existing structures. We then examine the challenges schools face in making this transition. Finally, we specifically consider these factors in the context of existing facilities and how we can change and renovate them to work in an advisory format that eliminates classrooms.

Minimum Thresholds for Effective Instruction

Although chapter 5 (page 61) covers the key components of an advisory-based school, it is critical that educators realize that there is a minimum threshold that schools must meet if they want to make the shift to instruction that will be effective in preparing students for future success. Without meeting this threshold, schools will continue to operate largely as they have since the 20th century.

The first and most important change that must be made is that schools must individualize instruction for each student. Individualized learning allows students freedom in how, when, where, and with whom they engage with learning materials. This means schools must see students as individuals who are on their own pathway through the learning materials the school provides instead of members of age-determined groups who progress simultaneously through learning materials in a lockstep manner. Schools must stop grouping students into grades based on age. Reorganizing schools around small, multiage advisory groups is a great way to begin the shift toward focusing on individual students.

Schools must also shift to a continuous-learning approach that allows students to learn at their own pace. This is the key to individualizing instruction. One of the first things schools must do is turn off the bells and move beyond set class periods where students move from room to room on a preset timetable. Instead, they must use time more flexibly. Schools must allot time to allow students to schedule time with teacher advisors. This use of time must enable subject teachers to designate opportunities for small-group instruction using the kinds of flexible scheduling we discussed in Advisory School Days (page 79). Time use must also be flexible enough to allow students to pursue learning activities individually.

Hand in hand with the move to individualized instruction must be a shift in the role of a teacher to that of a teacher advisor. Adolescents are, for the most part, not capable of handling the adult responsibilities of self-discipline and time management vital to consistently apply themselves to their school work. Adult teacher advisors are necessary to ensure that students not only do their work consistently, but also to teach them how to make personal plans to reach goals to become independent adults themselves. The teacher advisor is an indispensable component of individualized learning. As students mature through middle school and high school, the need for the advisor diminishes because students learn how to take over more and more of the planning they need to be successful when they are learning independently.

As part of the individualizing of instruction, schools must make a long-term commitment that ensures every student has his or her own internet-connected, mobile device that can run current instructional and productivity software. Students will need to familiarize themselves with new technological tools and use these tools to enhance their learning. Purchasing new technology for students cannot be a one-shot injection of funds for a one-time purchase. Rather, it must be a continuous commitment to purchasing and upgrading technology for students and teachers like we describe in Technology Resources (page 75).

A key shift in instructional approaches in schools must be to move away from teachers teaching to students discovering. Individual and collaborative project work must replace direct instruction via lecture. Therefore, if a school retains some classrooms (see the varied spatial concepts in chapters 9–15), it should designate those rooms as bookable seminar rooms for small-group discussions. We describe the need for seminar rooms in Sarah Progresses to Project-Based Learning (page 44).

Moving to individualized learning in which students progress through course material at their own pace requires an alternative method for delivering instructional content as teachers move away from the traditional stand-and-deliver, mass-instruction method for disseminating content to a class full of students. There will be a strong tendency to make the new instructional materials paper-based. This is not optimal for modern students by any stretch of the imagination. It must be very clear that teachers using paper-based materials is a very temporary step. The best vehicle for delivering course content to students is the internet. Being online, these new resources are available twenty-four hours a day, seven days a week. This facilitates continuous learning because new course content is available to each student as soon as he or she is ready to move on. These online resources also allow students to access them when it is convenient and when it suits their personal learning styles. In addition, online digital resources are a much better match for modern students who grew up in the digital world.

The library's role is pivotal in the transition to new learning in existing schools. There is a major trend toward libraries becoming the digital hub of a secondary school due to the massive growth of online multimedia information. As learning materials transition to online, digital formats, the digital library will become an increasingly important center for student learning in the school. Let's be clear, we are describing *digital libraries* as critical resources accessible anytime from anywhere, not as a physical space in each school.

Schools must also make clear that the ultimate goal is not just to move instructional materials online, but to shift learning to be more effective in preparing students for the world that awaits them when they graduate. One way to do this is to take advantage of the interactive capabilities of online digital tools to enhance the learning experience. Another way to do this is to shift the way schools assign schoolwork to focus on developing the kinds of essential skills we outlined in chapter 3 (page 29). One pitfall to delivering instructional material online is creating learning materials that are not content-heavy, memory-recall exercises. Schools must take great care to ensure that learning tasks require more than lower-level-thinking skills. Creating these new instructional resources provides teachers with an opportunity to make a significant shift in the nature of the work that students do in school. New learning resources must emphasize project-based tasks that require students to solve problems, form fact-based opinions, and explore creative ways of communicating their thinking. Ted outlines a useful problem-solving approach to teaching in his books *Teaching for Tomorrow: Teaching Content and Problem-Solving Skills* (McCain, 2005) and *Teaching With the Future in Mind* (McCain, in press).

Schools that make the shift to meet these minimum thresholds are making the transition to 21st century learning and instruction that will better prepare their students for life in the modern world. However, we must continue to stress that these thresholds are only a temporary step in moving toward schools without classrooms.

Challenges for Creating New Learning Environments

Now that we have outlined the minimum requirements for effective instruction, we need to clarify about the challenges schools and districts face and explain why these changes will not be easy or quick. In this section, we present a few of the major difficulties that schools and districts will encounter, including challenges in developing instructional resources, monitoring student progress, and cultural and community concerns.

Instructional Resources

Schools will also encounter difficulties obtaining the instructional resources to support individualized learning. Unfortunately, because the majority of schools still employ the traditional teacher-centered, mass-instruction classroom approach to teaching, there are many resources available that support a project-based, problem-solving approach to individualized instruction; however, there are fewer resources that actually integrate those materials into entire courses for secondary school.

Therefore, teachers, school, and districts may have to initially create the overall plans for project-based courses that incorporate existing resources into a coherent progression with a focus on higher-level critical thinking and problem solving. However, there is a chicken-and-egg problem when it comes to having teachers develop these resources. Although there is a great need for developing the materials to support individualized instruction that fosters higher-level thinking and problem solving, few teachers have had any experience with this kind of instruction and will have difficulty creating effective, individualized learning materials. This is a huge obstacle to making the shift to the kind of teaching that educators need to prepare students for their futures beyond school.

Overcoming this obstacle requires a serious, significant, long-term commitment to professional development to better adopt strategies for individualized learning and higher-level thinking. This may include release time for teachers to receive training in project-based instruction away from their normal school environment as well as ongoing training sessions at schools throughout the school year.

Schools must give new teachers this training, of course, but it must extend to all teachers to make the shift to individualized learning successful. A critical part of this professional development must include instructing teachers on how to be effective student advisors, because shifting to an advisory role will also be new for many teachers. It is critical that schools and districts not follow the common short-term approach to training where the retraining effort only lasts for a limited duration. Making a shift of this magnitude, especially after the length of time the traditional classroom approach has been in effect, requires schools and districts to commit to long-term retraining efforts that will last for many, many years. Schools too often abandon good ideas before they have a chance to succeed. We cannot overstate that, in making this shift, we are asking most teachers to move on from teaching strategies many have used their entire lives.

Without constant, sustained training, teachers will naturally revert to traditional approaches to instruction to which they are accustomed. The lure of the familiar is a powerful force. We have heard the power of what is familiar, also called *nostalgic gravity* (Bergsagel, et al., 2007)—the power of what people are familiar with pulling them back to what they are used to and what they are comfortable with. Schools and districts must enter into change knowing that it will take an enormous effort to overcome the power of this nostalgic gravity.

Student Progress and Monitoring

Determining when a student is ready for more freedom to pursue instructional goals independently can be another challenge for schools moving to individualized instruction. The teacher-advisor role is central for making individualized instruction successful. The relationship teacher advisors have with individual students puts them in the best position to judge when students are ready for more freedom in their learning. However, teacher advisors need guidance for making these critical decisions. Therefore, a key component of successful individualized instruction is creating guidelines for when teachers should give students more independence in making their own learning plans.

These guidelines should identify specific behaviors for teachers to look for before giving students more independence. For example, a guideline for giving a student some independence in developing their own daily learning plan might be: *The student must demonstrate the ability to follow learning plans developed in conjunction with their teacher advisor for eight weeks before beginning to develop plans on their own.* Offering teachers that are new to advising students a comprehensive list of such guidelines would be incredibly helpful.

Another key challenge is locating and implementing the smart administrative software system that is essential for tracking student progress and gathering big-data analytics, so schools can make smart decisions about the learning activities students will do next, including what remedial steps teacher advisors can take to help students who are experiencing difficulties. In truth, no one system accomplishes our vision for what schools need from this kind of software. One reason this software does not exist is that generally schools and school districts are not asking for its development. Instead, they demand administrative software that focuses on developing timetables for school days that feature a traditional four or five periods and traditional grade recording and reporting. This must change. Software developers change their platforms to match client needs, and in this case, we need for more clients (schools) to demand the necessary functionality.

Cultural and Community Concerns

Moving to continuous learning means that you are changing a school culture and the community culture that surrounds it. You are moving from the long-standing, firmly entrenched approach to instruction with which teachers, administrators, parents, and students are familiar. We cannot overstate the magnitude of this change. Schools and districts will have to make a concerted effort to inform and explain to parents, students, businesses, and elected politicians about the need for making changes to the way they educate. Although many of these groups may grasp the need for changing how schools operate and will be very receptive to moving in the direction we advocate in this book, many members of the public may be victims of nostalgic gravity and prefer that schools continue to work the way they always have.

Consider some of the questions this degree of change raises. What if universities don't accept their child's transcript without making him or her write an entrance exam? What if test scores dip a little while teachers and students adjust to the new way of doing things? What if students are less likely to get scholarships as a result? These are just some concerns the public may have that could cause it to press for the schools to return to the way they used to operate.

Therefore, schools and districts must do much preparatory work in the community and with postsecondary institutions if they are going to make the shift to individualized instruction. They must inform parents of the reasons for making the change and make considerable effort to convince them of the long-term benefits for shifting to this new approach. Postsecondary institutions must also know about the changes so they can develop plans to better assess students' readiness for postsecondary study.

Making the shift to effective instruction for the modern world requires real courage (because you are taking the school system into a new and relatively unknown direction), a thick skin (because there will be a lot of criticism from people who prefer the familiar learning environment of traditional classroom instruction—change is scary and it creates resistance), and steadfast commitment (because making a shift of this magnitude takes time, and there will be a lot of difficulties along the way). Schools and school districts must do their utmost to prepare the community for the changes they will make and their consequences, both positive and negative, as the school makes the transition to the new learning environments that we so desperately need.

A Future for the Past

As a prelude to chapters 9–15, it's time to think about the existing buildings that will house all this change after we establish our minimum instructional thresholds and adoption challenges. In these chapters, we outline seven examples of how districts can modify existing schools to better serve the kind of schooling we describe in this book. We base each model on an existing, functioning secondary high school or middle school. Quite intentionally, the schools are very diverse. We provide considerable information about each school, but we do not identify these schools in the hope that readers will focus on basic instructional issues and search for parallels to their own schools without the school districts, cities, states, and other details and peculiarities distracting them. We gave each school we describe an abstract name and a description of its nature—all of which we summarize in the following list. The seven models describe spatial modifications districts must make to adapt these existing schools to the teaching and learning concepts we propose. Let's take a brief look at each of them.

1. **The Capital School (chapter 9, page 119):** Built in an urban state capital in 1916, it serves 1,500 students in grades 9–12.

2. **The Green School (chapter 10, page 127):** Built in a suburban community in 1953, it serves 1,055 students in grades 6–8.

3. **The Connected School (chapter 11, page 135):** Built in a rural area in 1968, it serves 334 students in grades 7–12.

4. **The Open School (chapter 12, page 141):** Built in a suburban-metropolitan area in 1973, it serves 2,013 students in grades 9–12.

5. **The District School (chapter 13, page 151):** Built as the sole high school in a suburban-metropolitan district in 1984, it serves approximately 2,700 students in grades 9–12.

6. **The Tech School (chapter 14, page 163):** Built in a suburban-urban district in 1998, it serves 766 students in grades 6–8.

7. **The Academy School (chapter 15, page 171):** Built in 1998 as a suburban office building, and renovated as a school in 2013, it serves six hundred students in grades 9–12.

As you can see, these represent a variety of school formats and community scenarios. Each presents unique challenges, all of which a creative approach can transform into assets that contribute to the school's unique presentation and culture. We are enormously grateful to old friends and clients who were very supportive and helpful as we dug through drawing files and visited and photographed their campuses. We considered lots of schools before narrowing the list to seven that are diverse in their history and character. None of those who provided information have reviewed or endorsed our proposals.

Although the information we provide in these chapters focuses on the physical transformation of these schools, the staff in each school also requires transformation as we described in this chapter. It will take considerable planning to modify each campus and several months of construction. Paralleling this, there must be a staff-development process to help teachers understand the new instructional methods, technology, continuous educational services, mastery learning, and their dual role as teachers and advisors.

Essential Questions

As you reflect on this chapter, consider the following questions.

- Is your school ready to meet the minimum threshold we outline for moving to the new learning environments we propose? If not, what can you and other stakeholders do to make it ready?

- Where will your school get the higher-level, project-based learning activities for individualized learning?

- How will you make project-based and individualized learning activities available to students?

- How will you retrain teaching staff for their dual teacher-advisor role so they can effectively educate in an individualized and continuous-learning system?

- How will you inform the wider community about the changes in the school and the possible consequences?

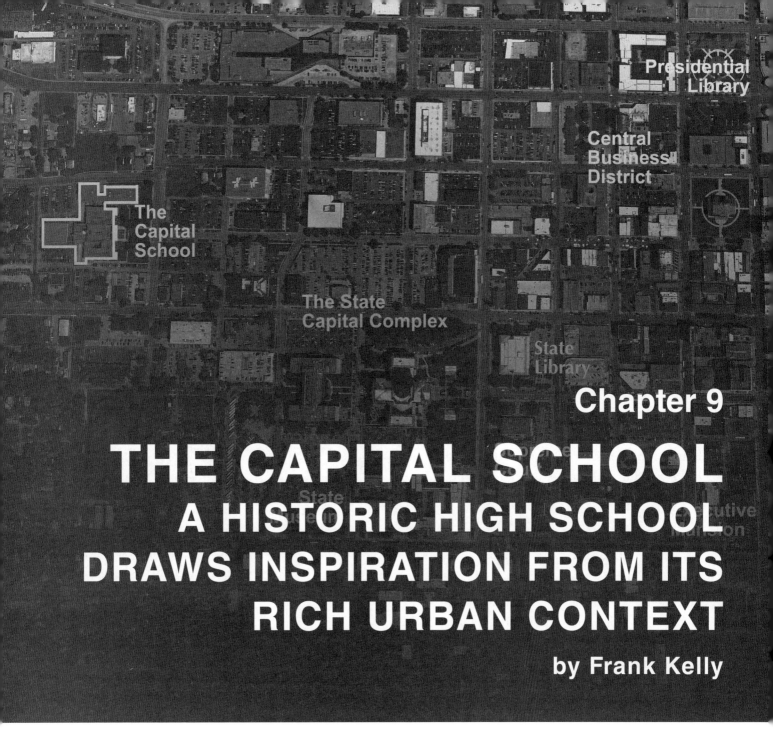

Chapter 9
THE CAPITAL SCHOOL
A HISTORIC HIGH SCHOOL DRAWS INSPIRATION FROM ITS RICH URBAN CONTEXT

by Frank Kelly

Source: Satellite imagery © 2017 Google, DigitalGlobe.

The Capital School's district serves approximately fifteen thousand preK–12 students in some thirty-five buildings, including twenty-three elementary schools (grades K–5), five middle schools (grades 6–8), and three high schools (grades 9–12). Of the students enrolled in the district during the 2010–2011 school year, just over 65 percent of the total student population received free or reduced lunch.

The most extraordinary thing about this high school is the historic urban context in which it resides. Many U.S. cities grew in the automobile-oriented 20th century and, consequently, many schools are in suburban residential areas on large sites surrounded by single-family homes and low-density commercial development. With its long history, this school is very different.

The Capital School we know in 2018 is two blocks from the front steps of its state capitol building, state office buildings, the state supreme court building, museums, the state library, the governor's executive mansion, and other important government structures. The capitol building itself is remarkable for the statues of historic figures beneath its rotunda. Immediately adjacent to the school and capitol buildings is the central business district with the city's train station, office buildings, banks, hotels, stores, and restaurants, all within easy walking distance of the school.

The Capital School is a fifth-generation facility. The first high school opened in 1857 in an existing building a few blocks away from the current facility. Another structure followed a year later, which served until 1864. In 1865, the district completed a new structure and another in 1897, but it became overcrowded and the district replaced it in 1916 with the Capital School we see in figure 9.1.

In this chapter, we examine the important details and facets that make up the Capital School and its place in its community, its current spatial environment and the modifications we believe should go into renovating it to realize our advisory-school concept, and the cost and time implications involved. Note that each of these areas invokes and

Figure 9.1: The Capital School.

reflects our elements of schooling. We conclude with some final observations for making this facility suitable for 21st century learning.

The Existing School

The district has expanded and modified the original four-story building many times to include structures with additional science spaces, a cafeteria, a performing arts venue, and physical education and athletic facilities. In 2018, the school serves approximately 1,500 students in its 243,800 square feet. The school is on a single urban block, while athletic fields are on a separate site a full block away. The combined area of these two parcels is approximately 9.5 acres. From an instructional perspective, the Capital School is a traditional comprehensive high school organized around disciplines and departments. The district has a ratio of computers to students of approximately 1:2.

The original building plan was a compact three-story mass with the first floor a half level down, which we illustrate in figures 9.2, 9.3, and 9.4. (Visit **go.SolutionTree.com/instruction** to access color versions of this and other figures in this book.) Generally, there were classrooms around the perimeter with central spaces for the cafeteria (on level 1), auditorium (on levels 2 and 3), and gymnasium (on level 2). The administration office and primary

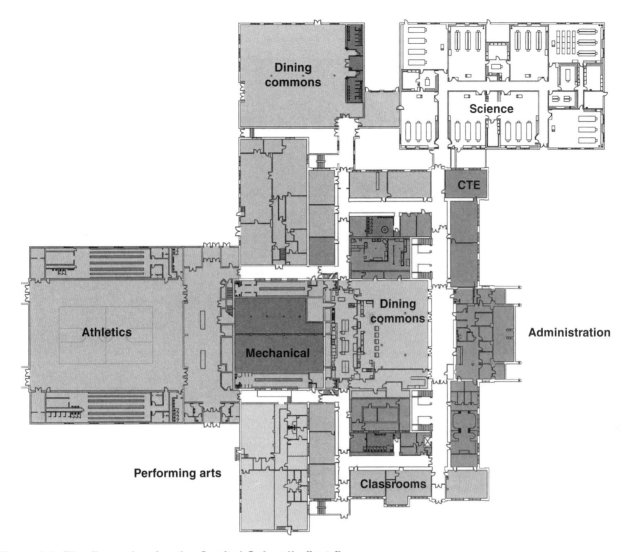

Figure 9.2: The floor plan for the Capital School's first floor.

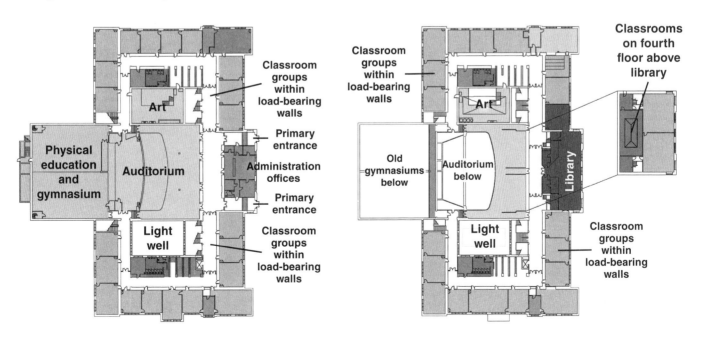

Figure 9.3: The floor plan for the Capital School's second floor.

Figure 9.4: The floor plan for the Capital School's third floor.

entrance are on level 2, and the library is above on the third floor with some classrooms above that on a small fourth level that you can see as the central tower facing the downtown area to the east. To admit light into the center of school, there were originally two light courts on levels 2 and 3, but the district subsequently in-filled it to create art spaces. The perimeter classrooms are organized in groups defined by very thick load-bearing masonry walls.

Although the school could remove or relocate most of the partitions between classrooms, the massive load-bearing corridor and exterior walls are fixed. The corridor walls are so thick that open classroom doors barely project beyond these walls' thickness.

When the Capital School first opened in 1916, it was the district's only high school and had to serve every student. In 2018, it is one of three high schools, but it is quite different from the other two, which the district constructed on larger sites in less urban locations. Although this book focuses on transforming existing schools to serve new teaching and learning, the opportunity with this location relates to both the school and its setting.

Our Proposal and Spatial Modifications

We propose to very carefully preserve the Capital School's historic character and to transform how it works instructionally by integrating the school with its context to afford its students opportunities to experience the immediate area's diverse real-world activities. The school has approximately sixty-four classrooms that it arranges in seventeen groups (each with three to five rooms), which the massive load-bearing walls define (see figure 9.5). Within these groups, nonload-bearing partitions separate the individual rooms.

As we illustrate in figure 9.6, we propose to remove these walls to create spaces that can house three to four advisories. By linking several of these, we create academies with a mix of core and career disciplines related to the state government and business activities in the immediate area. Area-based mentorships and internships would bolster the academies, and some students may spend a day or two each week off campus with their mentors.

Although load-bearing walls define each advisory area, all the original door openings to the corridors would remain. Some breakout and collaboration areas for the students and teachers would be in the corridor areas, and students would move from area to area as they need to connect with teachers and with specialized career and technology spaces (see figure 9.7, page 124).

As you can see, this school's spaces are much smaller and more numerous than those in the models that follow, but the school would function in much the same way. Within each advisory area, there would be several teacher advisors from different disciplines to ensure that there will always be someone available for the students. Students and teachers would both have workstations like those we describe in chapter 5 (Advisory Components, page 71).

Spatially, the existing school has some pluses and minuses with regard to creating advisories and flexible spaces. On the plus side, because the community built the school long before air conditioning, every classroom has natural light and ventilation (it added air conditioning in 2018), not to mention views to the capitol dome and downtown area. The transformation we propose preserves and takes advantage of all that natural light. On the plus side, the small size of the school and the open spaces we can create within the load-bearing masonry walls keep the advisory areas with the teacher advisor and student workstations relatively small, typically no more than three or four advisories in each area. That group of advisors and students will get to know each other well and provide a supportive learning context.

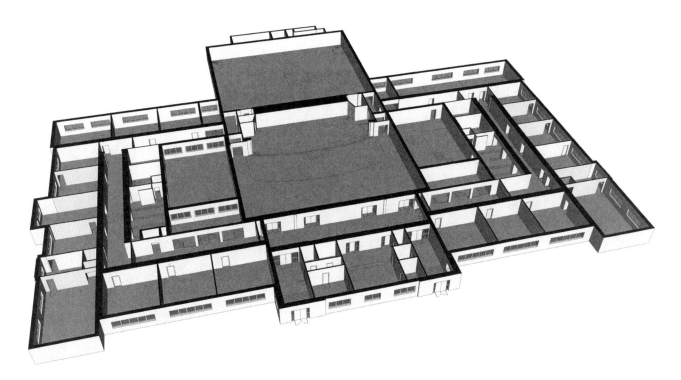

Figure 9.5: A 3-D model of a floor in the Capital School.

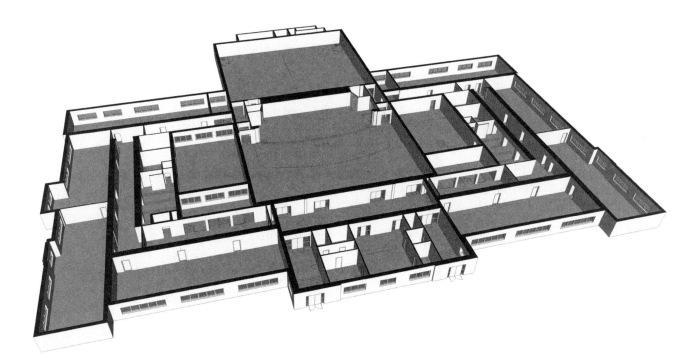

Figure 9.6: The Capital School floor plan, with nonload-bearing walls removed.

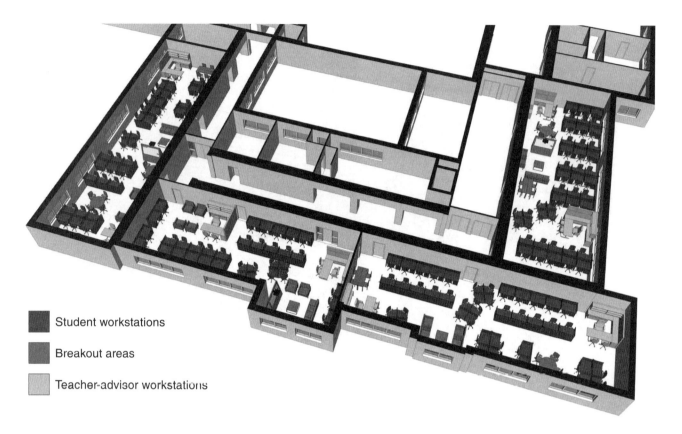

Figure 9.7: The Capital School provides room for advisory areas with nonload-bearing walls removed.

On the negative side, these small spaces will not accommodate a full mix of core teachers, nor readily allow close relationships to spaces for other studies including CTE, arts, and so on. Nor will load-bearing corridor walls allow natural light from windows to penetrate to interior corridors, which also means that those in corridors cannot see into the advisories to see student work on display, and so on. None of these are insurmountable issues. They are trade-offs for transforming an existing historic structure in an urban setting. That is a great swap!

With the focus on its urban context and academies, the school would not offer competitive athletics. Students who want to participate in athletics could enroll in either of the district's other schools or commute to those schools for after-hours athletic programs. We would preserve the existing gymnasium on the first floor for physical education and fitness programs, which might also serve the community after-school hours. The district could sell or repurpose the athletic fields to the south of the school.

We would convert the commons area on the first floor and the older, smaller gyms on the second level to specialized instructional spaces related to the academies. We would also preserve the existing music programs and continue to use the school's handsome auditorium on the second floor. The art spaces in the former light well on the north side of the school would remain, but we would complement them with a digital art and graphics studio in the former old gymnasium area on the second floor. The food services would remain on the first floor, but we would modify the serving area and dining space to function like a food court with continuous food and beverage services during the day. With students coming and going all day to connect with resources in the surrounding area, the campus would be open and students could elect to eat off campus as well.

Cost and Time Implications

All the proposed construction work would be inside the school without involving the structural system or exterior enclosure. It entails adapting the HVAC systems to the new spatial configurations and to the power and data systems related to extensive use of digital technology. These adaptations may require installing a new fire sprinkler system and new smoke detection and security systems to substantially enhance safety inside the school. The new spaces and functions would require virtually all new furnishings, but some parts will remain—administration offices, auditorium, science labs, and gymnasium—except for modifications to bring them up-to-date. As we stated previously, the district could sell or repurpose the athletic field to recover some costs. Using the school continuously all year would increase its enrollment capacity and thereby decrease the cost per student for facilities. These improvements would preserve most of the facility and site's value and give them new life for generations to come. The work would relate primarily to opening spaces, updating lighting, electrical, and mechanical systems, and installing new furnishings. Given the structure's age and the likelihood that the renovation team may need to do work in phases, it may require two summers and a school year to complete.

Observation

Confirming the concepts in our elements of schooling (figure I.1, page 3), the nature of schooling is a function of many elements interacting, and this school offers an opportunity that is sadly rare: This is a school that can benefit from its community's assets even as it serves to enhance its community. The faculty, students, and community will be mindful of ensuring their own safety and security, but this school will not be an isolated, introverted island in the city. The school's remarkable historic context gives its students direct exposure to real-life political, legal, financial, business, and commercial activities. Although the massive load-bearing walls of this very old school don't allow as extensive a spatial transformation as we describe for the other schools in the following chapters, the school's small-scale and effective use of digital technology will more than compensate.

Essential Questions

As you reflect on this chapter, consider the following questions.

- Reflect on the existing Capital School and the transformation we propose: Do we realize the elements of schooling tenets? Do you have a school of similar age or history? Could your district similarly modify it to serve 21st century teaching and learning?

- What is special about the context of your school or schools' location? Are there resources in the surrounding community that could enhance teaching and learning for your students?

- Regardless of its age, could you transform (rather than replace) your school building to support 21st century teaching and learning with online resources?

- Could access to digital research materials and online instructional materials afford your students a more individualized learning experience and increase their academic success?

Chapter 10
THE GREEN SCHOOL
A SCHOOL BUILT BEFORE AIR CONDITIONING OR COMPUTERS INSPIRES NEW TEACHING, LEARNING, AND SUSTAINABILITY

by Frank Kelly

Source: Satellite imagery © 2017 Google, DigitalGlobe.

The Green School is a grades 6–8 school very near a major interstate highway in the center of a highly developed suburban district within a very large urban area. There are businesses and offices along the freeway, including the district's administration building immediately to the east. The district serves a diverse population of thirty-three-thousand preK–12 students in twenty-five elementary schools, seven middle schools, and four high schools plus a number of specialized schools of choice. Residential areas to the north (across the freeway) and to the south serve a population that varies widely ethnically and economically.

The school enrolls 1,055 students of which 36 percent are students with economic disadvantages, 16.6 percent are students who are limited English proficient, and 39.2 percent are at-risk. The Texas Education Agency's (n.d.) rating system labels it as *recognized* in 2009 and 2010 and *acceptable* in 2011.

In this chapter, we examine the important details and facets that make up the Green School and its place in its community, its current spatial environment and the modifications we believe should go into renovating it to suit our advisory-school concept, and the cost and time implications involved. Note that each of these areas invokes and reflects our elements of schooling. We conclude with some final observations for making this facility suitable for 21st century learning.

The Existing School

Figure 10.1 and figure 10.2 reveal a picturesque, single-story building that spans 104,303 square feet and occupies an approximately twenty-one-acre site. It opened in 1953 and has had several additions for science, performing arts, food services, and physical education and athletic programs.

The building plan bespeaks its location in a hot southern city (see figure 10.3). (Visit **go.SolutionTree.com/instruction** to access color versions of this and other figures in this book.) Built before air conditioning, the school consists primarily of long double-loaded corridor classroom structures oriented to the north and south to minimize sun load and permit ample ventilation. The parallel structures define courtyards, and every classroom has a full wall of windows and natural light. Roof overhangs provide additional sun protection. Administration, food service, and performing arts link to each other on the site's west side, and enclosed corridors connect the other areas. Although the district added air conditioning to the school, the original building form remains.

It is our understanding that the courtyards' original purpose was for ventilation (the school had no air conditioning) and not for instructional activities. There is no access to the courtyards from the classrooms, and lockers that block views into the

Figure 10.1: The Green School opened in 1953 and resides on a wooded site.

Figure 10.2: The school features multiple courtyards and ample ambient lighting.

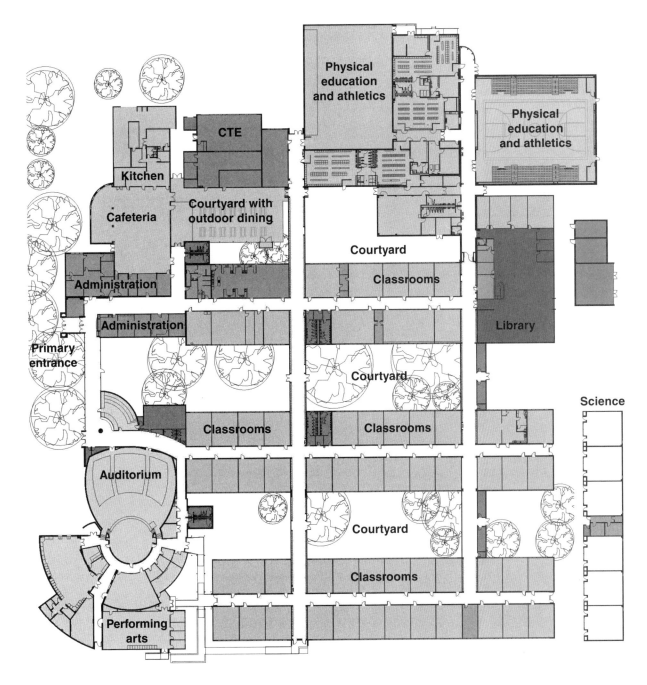

Figure 10.3: Existing floor plan for the Green School.

spaces line the corridors that link the classroom wings across the courtyards. Although the original spaces were probably quite spare with simple lawns, in 2018 they are shaded with handsome trees, making them a special asset to the school's environment. Instructionally, the school is organized around disciplines, departments, and classrooms.

Our Proposal and Spatial Modifications

We propose to remove most classrooms in the building's three wings and to create open areas with advisories (see figure 10.4, page 130). Each wing would serve a vertical mix of students in grades 6–8. The advisor teachers and students would work together for the full three years the students

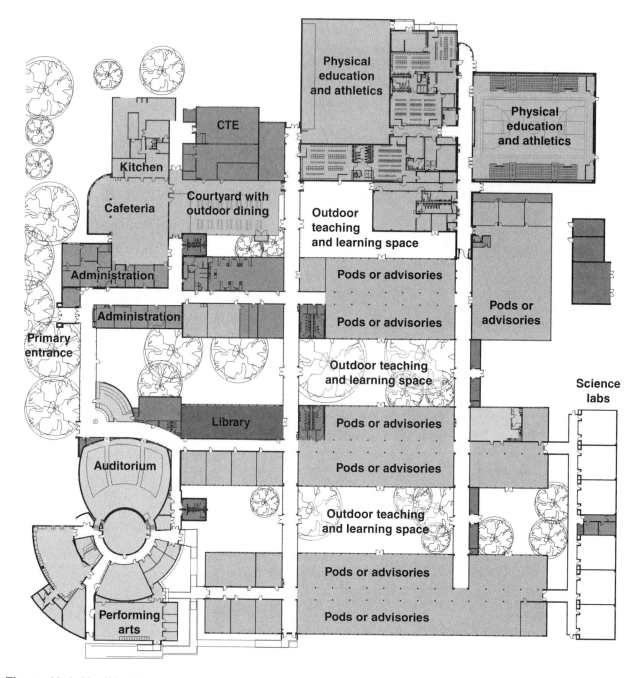

Figure 10.4: Modified floor plan for the Green School.

are in the school. Older students would mentor and counsel younger students as students progress.

With the outdoor teaching and learning spaces placed between the advisory areas, the advisory areas become very flexible. Advisor teachers and students could rearrange spaces themselves to suit the work underway (see figure 10.5).

This arrangement preserves the existing science labs, but the science teacher advisors would have workstations in each pod near the students. Students can do some experiments digitally using the technology available to them, but they would use the remaining labs whenever necessary. The school could also convert some science labs for project and graphics work where the sinks and work surfaces are most useful.

All the advisories would have natural light on the north and south sides. With new, insulated glass

Figure 10.5: The Green School's advisory pods have ample flexibility.

and light shelves, the spaces would not require artificial lighting much of the time and the school would finally realize both ventilation and energy efficiency. New doors would provide direct access from the advisories into the courtyards. We would replace the opaque walls and lockers that line the original corridors with glass to afford views into the courtyards. We propose adding gardens, walkways, and varied seating areas to each courtyard so that students can use the spaces throughout the school day. With the school building to surround them, the courtyards would represent safe and secure outdoor spaces for the students. Students would not have lockers but would have secure personal storage in their workstations in the advisory pods.

The existing library, as pictured in figure 10.6 (page 132), would become part of one of the grades 6–8 advisory groups, and we propose creating a new library near the auditorium with the bulk of its collection going online. By making those materials directly accessible to the students anytime, anywhere from their digital devices, the library can serve as an instructional space for online research and as an archive for its remaining books. The library might also serve as a project or innovation center with equipment for creating graphics, scanning, printing, and plotting.

Cost and Time Implications

The district could quickly and easily effect transformation of the interior spaces. Modifications to the exterior walls facing the courtyards might be more challenging but should yield a return in lower operating costs related to lighting and air conditioning. Restricted access to courtyards will make challenging any landscaping and paving work, but these are surmountable problems. Completing the construction work and interiors and allowing some time for staff development within the new environment would probably consume at least a traditional

Figure 10.6: The existing library with ample natural lighting.

semester and a summer, which is no small challenge for an existing school. The ultimate product of the effort should be a remarkably different new school where spaces are functionally separated but visually linked, where natural light suffuses both indoor and outdoor spaces, and where year-round instruction enlarges the school's capacity. This will not feel like a traditional cells-and-bells school for teachers or students.

Observation

More than once in these models, we have found wonderful futures for old ideas long ago abandoned, such as natural light and outdoor spaces. Maybe digital technology can change our ways of thinking to help us realize the future to which we aspire in schools from our past. Since the school opened in 1953, educators and students have found diverse ways to teach and learn, and this school's integration of indoor and outdoor spaces should support and enhance these. The courtyards are safe and secure for the students, featuring plenty of shade from large oak trees that invite both students and teachers for all sorts of outdoor projects and learning.

Essential Questions

As you reflect on this chapter, consider the following questions.

- Reflect on the existing Green School and the transformation we propose: Do we realize the tenets of the elements of schooling? Do the schools in your district offer similar opportunities to enhance existing structures and landscapes? How could you take advantage of their existing features in an advisory format?

- How might your district economically modify your school to reduce its energy consumption and exemplify environmental responsibility for your students and community?

- Are there assets (trees, views, businesses, parks) on or near your school site that could enhance or enrich teaching and learning?

- How are the spaces and subjects in your middle or high school organized: by department, in multidisciplinary grade-level pods, or something else? How might using multigrade-level groups that keep students and teachers together for all of their time at the school enhance learning?

Field house   Transportation

Administration building

Middle and high school

Elementary school

Chapter 11
THE CONNECTED SCHOOL
A SMALL RURAL SCHOOL USES SOPHISTICATED TEACHING AND TECHNOLOGY TO LINK TO THE WORLD

by Frank Kelly

Source: Satellite imagery © 2017 Google, DigitalGlobe.

The Connected School is in a district that covers 212 square miles and enrolls 685 students—351 in the elementary school serving grades preK–6 and 334 in the middle and high school serving grades 7–12. The district's two schools share a common site surrounded by rice fields and are located approximately 2.6 miles from a town with a population of approximately 647 (in 2011). Of the district's students, about 75 percent are eligible for free and reduced lunches. The common site the two schools share also includes the district's administration building and other structures for transportation, maintenance, and athletics.

In this chapter, we examine the important details and facets that comprise the Connected School and its place in its community, the modifications we propose to adapt it to our advisory-school concept, and related cost and time implications involved. Note that each of these areas invokes and reflects our elements of schooling. We conclude with some final observations for making this facility suitable for 21st century learning.

The Existing School

Six one-story buildings comprise the middle and high school, all linked to form a single structure with approximately sixty-nine thousand square feet. The district completed the school's first phase in 1968, and there have been numerous additions and renovations in the years since.

The primary entrance is a glass-enclosed corridor that links two groups of spaces (see figure 11.1). The largest single structure (to the west) houses the cafeteria and kitchen, performing arts facilities (band and choir), and physical education and athletic programs. Four structures to the east of the entry house the administration offices, library and classrooms, art facilities, family and consumer science and science labs, and agriculture spaces. All the buildings have lightweight steel frames with nonload-bearing walls so that school administrators can easily relocate or remove partitions.

Figure 11.1: The Connected School.

The district modified the Connected School in 2008, when it became part of the New Tech Network (https://newtechnetwork.org), which provides services and support to help schools reconsider how teaching and learning might work. Founded in 1996, the New Tech Network includes some 120 schools in eighteen U.S. states and Australia. New Tech Network's schools focus on project-based learning through which schooling is contextual, creative, and shared. Students work together to answer challenging questions or solve complex problems and, in the process, develop critical-thinking, creative, and communication skills. Assessment practices in the school measure both students' understanding of content and their ability to apply that knowledge to solve real-world problems.

The 2008 renovation included removing some partitions between classrooms to provide double spaces to house two teachers from different disciplines and two groups of students (see figure 11.2). (Visit **go.SolutionTree.com/instruction** to access color versions of this and other figures in this book.) Combined with block scheduling, the process gives the two teachers considerable flexibility for widely varied teaching and learning to integrate their disciplines.

The school had a 1:1 Apple laptop program before starting the New Tech Network program, and it continues that program. The school uses AB block scheduling based on a one-week cycle. The four A classes meet on two days (for two hours each), the four B classes meet on two days, and all the classes meet on Wednesday, which has eight one-hour periods. The instructional spaces have tables and chairs rather than tablet arm desks. Because most Connected School students are from families without former high school graduates, the school emphasizes students graduating. It expects every student will either go to college, a trade school, or the military following graduation.

The school uses varied modes to deliver content—digital tools, self-made videos, and lectures. There are numerous small conference rooms with green-screen walls for video-production purposes.

Our Proposal and Spatial Modifications

We propose that creating an advisory-based Connected School from the current structure requires an evolutionary process more than it does a transformative one. Figure 11.3 illustrates our ideas.

We propose replacing the double classrooms the New Tech Network program created with more

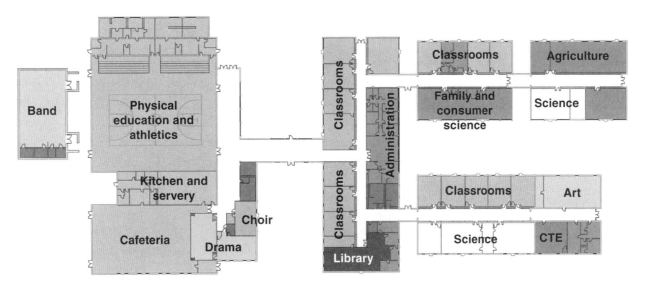

Figure 11.2: The existing floor plan for the Connected School.

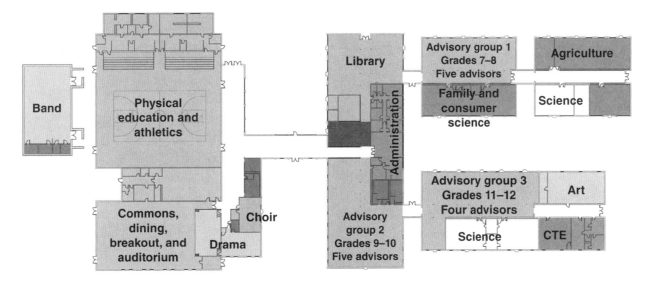

Figure 11.3: Modified floor plan for the Connected School.

open and flexible spaces to house advisories with teacher-advisor and student workstations. This expands the spirit of the double classrooms to ensure communication and collaboration across all disciplines. By adding more online digital materials, the school can further transform its teaching and learning methods to move away from lectures. Providing students and teachers with dedicated workstations gives them further flexibility to make the spaces respond to teaching and learning needs over time (see figure 11.4).

In consideration of the school's smaller student population, our design creates three separate open areas to house advisories for students in grades 7–8, 9–10, and 11–12, although the school could mix teacher advisors and students in other ways or make changes over time. Students and teachers will circulate through each advisory to reach the school's other areas, but, with the small enrollment the movement will not interrupt the students at work. It will enhance the sense of community in the school. The original school design features double-loaded corridors that characterize the four classroom structures with the only exposure to the outside and natural light coming from the corridors linking the separate buildings. The three large, open-advisory spaces we propose each come with windows and natural light. The school building will not be larger physically, but visually and functionally, this change will help it feel larger to the students and staff within.

As students move about to access the arts, CTE, administration, physical education, and other spaces, they will have opportunities to see peer-created work on display in each advisory. Although this is a small school, the open spaces and dispersed functions will help keep everyone informed about all the interesting work that occurs.

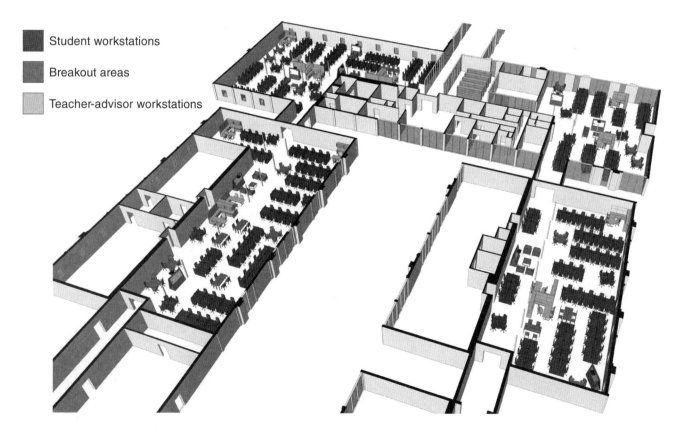

Figure 11.4: The Connected School's advisory areas are interconnected to preserve a sense of community.

Self-paced scheduling throughout the calendar year, with no need for bells, quarters, or semesters, will complement the technology and spaces. Schooling will be a continuous service. For a student body that has a highly variable agrarian context, this frees students from needing to be on the same schedule with each other. This change also increases the school's enrollment capacity, allowing the district to more effectively utilize both its staff and facilities.

Reflecting increased access to digital resources, we propose reducing the library area and relocating it to the center of the school, across the corridor from the administration offices. With digital library services available anywhere, the students in this small rural school will have access to the same resources as students in much larger urban schools. The existing science labs will remain in their current location, but the science teachers will also have workstations in the advisories, and students can accomplish much science lab work online. The art room will remain in its location, but the program will grow to include digital graphics of all sorts that students may use in their studies and presentations. Similarly, the agriculture spaces and program would remain to support the agrarian community the school services.

The teachers and students at this school are already accustomed to creating and customizing their own instructional materials, so shifting to more online instruction material (which also needs customization) should be a smooth and natural process.

Cost and Time Implications

The school could accomplish its modifications over a summer. There would be no changes to the exterior enclosure, but the school's lighting and duct work would require substantial changes relative to the new open spaces. The school also requires provisions to ensure adequate power for technology throughout the advisories. However, neither the time nor costs are comparable to those for a new structure, and with the flexibility our renovation creates, the facility should serve well into the future. Within this agrarian context, year-round continuous schooling may require more intensive community outreach and planning than it would in more urban settings; but if the district emphasizes the flexibility this format provides, it will be able to successfully coordinate and serve the special needs of students, families, and the community.

Observation

Whereas the school models we present in chapter 9 (page 119) and chapter 10 (page 127) are able to draw on their remarkable contexts and local resources, this school will use technology to the same effect, digitally drawing in more of the outside world than its students had previously experienced. That is truly powerful, and we believe this prospect is very realistic given what the school has accomplished since 2008.

Essential Questions

As you reflect on this chapter, consider the following questions.

- Reflect on the existing Connected School and the transformation we propose: Do we realize the tenets of the elements of schooling within its rural context and small enrollment? Are the possibilities here something that might serve your students better than traditional schooling concepts?

- Could online teaching and learning resources give every student, regardless of how large his or her school is or its location, access to the same educational opportunities? How would doing so increase parity between schools in diverse locations?

- Why is it particularly essential for rural schools to expand digital access to online materials and instructional resources? Why don't traditional school libraries suffice for this purpose?

- With seemingly split demands between the needs of an agrarian community and for students to gain essential 21st century skills, how will self-paced, continuous schooling allow families to serve their community's interests and still support students' learning?

Chapter 12

THE OPEN SCHOOL
A FORMERLY OPEN-PLAN HIGH SCHOOL RECONSIDERS ITS PAST

by Frank Kelly

Source: Satellite imagery © 2017 Google, DigitalGlobe.

In the 1950s, the Open School was in a suburban district on the far western edge of a growing metropolitan area. In 2018, it is an inner-city urban district experiencing redevelopment and increasing density in many areas because of its excellent location. It is also a school facing rapid change as its population diversifies. Some parts of the district comprise high-income, single-family housing, other areas have lower-income housing and apartments, and still others have substantial office, retail, and light-commercial industrial properties. In 2011–2012, the district served 32,879 students and had four comprehensive high schools.

The immediate area around the Open School includes housing and light commercial and industrial businesses. A road substantially separates the school from its context, and most structures around the site face other streets. There are no major roadways or freeways close by.

The school serves 2,013 students in grades 9–12. Of these, 633 are in the ninth grade, 538 in the tenth grade, 473 in the eleventh grade, and 369 in the twelfth grade. Economically, 88.2 percent classify as disadvantaged, 11.8 percent are noneducationally disadvantaged, 20 percent are limited English proficient, 68.4 percent classify as at-risk, and 20.8 percent are mobility students (students who relocate during the school year).

In this chapter, we examine the important details and facets that make up the Open School and its place in its community, its current spatial environment and the modifications we believe should go into renovating it to realize our advisory-school concept, and the cost and time implications involved. Note that each of these areas invokes and reflects our elements of schooling. We conclude with some final observations for making this facility suitable for 21st century learning.

The Existing School

Located on a 44.75-acre site, the Open School is a 358,200 square foot three-story building, with parking, football, track, soccer, tennis, baseball, and softball fields. Since it opened in 1973, the school has had several additions related to physical education and athletic and CTE spaces, but the most important spatial changes occurred within the classroom areas. The school's original design centered around open-plan instructional concepts, but in subsequent years, it converted the open spaces to enclosed traditional classrooms. We examine this further later in this section.

The Open School is a comprehensive high school with full core classes, CTE, visual and performing arts, and physical education and athletic programs. However, the school has no traditional CTE shop programs. The district relocated these to a separate specialized campus some years ago, and the school does not use its shop within the school.

Instructionally, the school is organized around departments or disciplines within which there are teams related to more specific areas of expertise. For example, the social studies department has teams related to geography, U.S. history, world history, and so on. Each department is in a separate area of the building, and each has its own break area and office. Social studies and science classrooms are on the third floor, English language arts and foreign languages are on the second floor, and mathematics and business classes are on the first floor. The school's bell schedule works on a one-week cycle. Monday, Tuesday, and Friday each have seven periods. Wednesday and Thursday work as a pair with block scheduling.

Spatially, the school is organized around a central dining commons area with all the core classrooms in a three-level structure on the west side, the visual and performing arts on the north side, kitchen and CTE spaces on the west side, and PE and athletic spaces on the southeast side. The primary entrance to the school is on the south side through an open courtyard (see figure 12.1) into the school commons. The bus drop entrance is on the north side through the performing arts area to the commons.

Figure 12.1: There is an open courtyard near the school's front entrance.

Within the classroom structure on the west side of the commons, there are three blocks of spaces on each of the three levels that you can see most clearly in figure 12.2. (Visit **go.SolutionTree.com/instruction** to access color versions of this and other figures in this book.) Originally the north and south blocks were either undivided or partially divided spaces for open-plan schooling and the central block contained administration, library, and special purpose spaces. Additional special purpose rooms (science labs, for example) were located adjacent to the open areas. Sometime in the mid-1980s, the school transformed the two open-plan areas on each floor into traditional, fully enclosed classrooms.

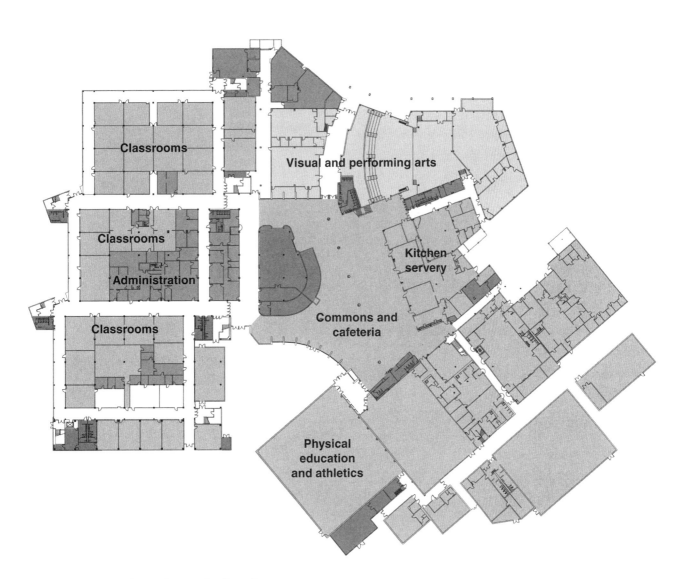

Figure 12.2: The Open School's first floor.

The second- and third-floor classroom areas repeat the pattern of the first floor each with three blocks of enclosed classroom spaces (see figures 12.3 and 12.4). There are additional administrative offices in the central block on the second floor. The library is also in this central block on levels 2 and 3. None of the classrooms on any of the floors have windows or access to natural light. The only windows in the entire classroom structure are adjacent to the two exit stairs on the west side.

Our Proposal and Spatial Modifications

The Open School is an especially relevant model for our studies because, like many schools across the United States, the district originally constructed it as an open-plan school. Although the instructional and spatial concepts we propose here share substantial similarities with the open-plan school ideas we discussed in chapter 5 (see The Merit in Open-Plan Schools, page 62), there is one giant game-changing tool we have that those who created the open plan never imagined—internet-connected digital technology. We believe we can retain and expand on all the merits of open-plan schooling while avoiding the pitfalls that sunk the original efforts. As a bonus, the Open School provides a wonderful background by which to illustrate the similarities and differences between the original concepts and our own vision.

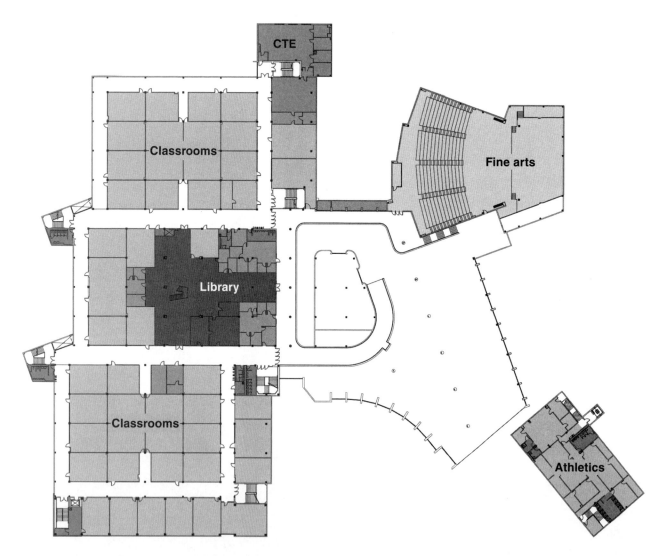

Figure 12.3: The Open School's second floor.

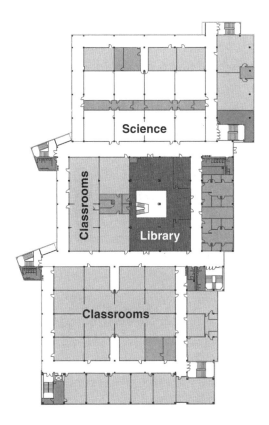

Figure 12.4: The Open School's third floor.

On each of the structure's three levels, we propose removing the classrooms in the north and south blocks to create open-advisory spaces. We would retain the central block to house various support spaces such as administrative offices (some on each floor) and the library (on the second and third floors). We illustrate this in figure 12.5.

Around the perimeter of the advisories and within parts of the central blocks, we would retain or create spaces to house programs that require special equipment or group work in fields such as science and CTE. That said, major parts of the walls between these specialized spaces and the open-advisory areas would be transparent and even operable to ensure close contact between the two. With these changes, the school becomes much more open and easier for students and staff to understand and navigate. Although the academies will be large, students and staff will perceive them as a single space and the school can aid in this by using colors and

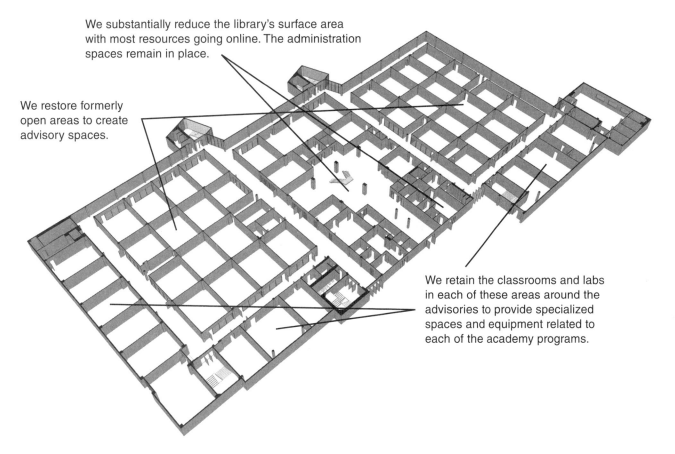

Figure 12.5: The second-floor core instruction spaces.

graphics to further distinguish them. Around each space's perimeter, we would include large, flat-screen TVs for the school to display information, academy content, presentations, and student work.

It's ironic that the original open-plan classroom areas on all three floors were not open, but windowless, with the exception of a small area of glass at each stairwell on the school's northwest side. We propose to open both the spaces and the exterior walls with windows so that students and teacher advisors will have real light and views (see figure 12.6). With the school's tilt-up exterior wall panels this will not be easy. Some workstations will be distant from these new windows, but everyone will get to enjoy the light and views as they move about the school to access other functions.

Each of the six open-advisory areas would be a small learning community, as the NASSP (1996, 2004) describes in its books *Breaking Ranks* and *Breaking Ranks II*. Each advisory should serve approximately twelve to fourteen teacher advisors and approximately 370 students in grades 9–12. Students would join a community when they first come to the school and remain with that group and their advisor through graduation.

Each of the small learning communities would have a different focus that integrates core subjects and a group of closely related CTE studies programs with the objective of making schooling more relevant, engaging, and motivating for the students. When students first enroll at the school, they would choose a community based on their interests at that time. During their time at the school, the school would allow students to move to another community as their knowledge of the world and themselves evolves. The initial communities might include the following, but it is highly likely that these will change over time as the world around the school changes.

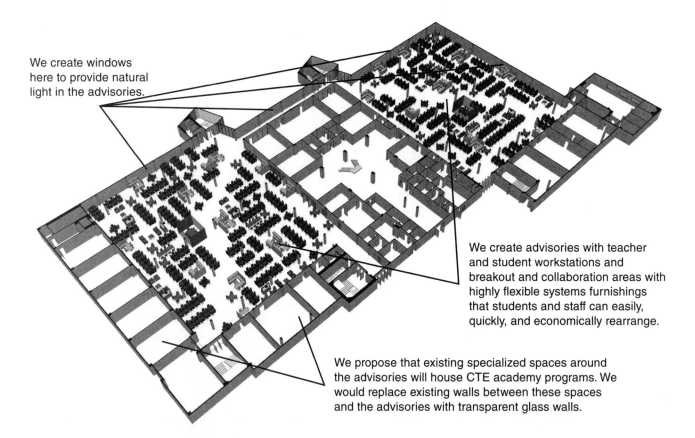

We create windows here to provide natural light in the advisories.

We create advisories with teacher and student workstations and breakout and collaboration areas with highly flexible systems furnishings that students and staff can easily, quickly, and economically rearrange.

We propose that existing specialized spaces around the advisories will house CTE academy programs. We would replace existing walls between these spaces and the advisories with transparent glass walls.

Figure 12.6: Modified second-floor advisories.

- Architecture, engineering, and construction
- Visual and performing arts, audiovisual technology, communications, and marketing
- Business, management, finance, and law
- Hospitality, tourism, and food services
- Information technology and computer science
- Health sciences

Most students will work most of the time on the campus, but we anticipate that some may have mentors with businesses in the community with whom they will occasionally work. The flexibility of the school's self-paced studies will readily accommodate these individual needs. The school's urban context contains many businesses with whom students may work.

The learning communities are large spaces, each with advisories and breakout and collaboration areas. Schools should loosely and very flexibly configure each area so that teachers and students may rearrange them over time (see figure 12.7). Dispersed among the advisor and student workstations are breakout spaces with varied seating areas for small-group discussions and collaboration.

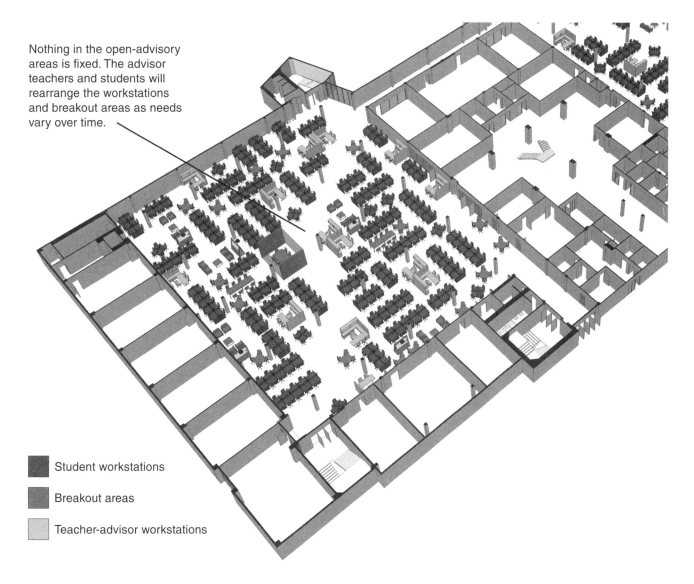

Nothing in the open-advisory areas is fixed. The advisor teachers and students will rearrange the workstations and breakout areas as needs vary over time.

- Student workstations
- Breakout areas
- Teacher-advisor workstations

Figure 12.7: Workstations in advisory areas are highly flexible due to the large, open spaces that house them.

Within the open-advisory areas and in the surrounding spaces are several small conference rooms with glass enclosures to afford some acoustically private areas.

Students will spend the majority of each school day within their learning community for all of their core, CTE, and elective subjects. Students will leave their learning communities only for food services, performing arts, and physical education and athletics, which will help make this large school feel smaller to those attending it.

Given the three-story classroom part of the school configuration, each of the six learning communities is a distinct, separate space, and there will be little or no circulation through them as teachers and students move about the campus. Every student will have his or her own individual digital device and a workstation.

We would convert the former CTE shop space on the first floor behind the kitchen to support the new learning-community programs and provide space and equipment for students doing projects as part of their course work. The library will remain in its present location in the center block on the second and third floors, but we would convert parts of the space on both levels to specialty classrooms to work with the adjacent academies.

Cost and Time Implications

Although the Open School's new advisories require substantial renovations to create, the nature of the work is not complex. Our proposal is comparable to the sorts of spatial modifications architects frequently make to office buildings. We would remove partitions that were not part of the original structure, while adding new floor finishes, lighting, and ceilings. The new floor finishes and ceilings are to provide new electrical power distribution. With plenty of advanced preparation and time to order the furniture systems, a skilled team could complete the necessary work over a summer and extra semester. There would be little or no work outside the existing classroom areas.

The ultimate cost question could relate to the cost per graduate. This new approach to instruction could significantly reduce the disparity between the sizes of the freshman class (633) and senior class (369), and in the process use the spaces more effectively, benefiting both teaching and learning and facility and operating costs.

Observation

Although returning the building to its original open-plan configuration is an interesting bit of history, it has the added benefit of making this project economical and easy to realize, positioning this school well as a powerful place for 21st century schooling. It would be wonderful if some of the individuals involved in the original school are still around to see their vision finally realized.

Essential Questions

As you reflect on this chapter, consider the following questions.

- Reflect on the existing Open School, its original aspirations, the changes the district made to it over the years, and the proposals we make for it: Do we realize the elements of schooling within its urban context and large enrollment? Does the facility's history make it an ideal place to realize our advisory-school concept?

- Dig into your district schools' history: Are there formerly open-plan schools within your district that were converted to conventional classrooms? How might their decades-old aspirations finally become reality?

- Does the area near your high school contain businesses and other resources that your district could engage to provide relevant, motivating contacts and experiences for your students?

- Given its urban context, the Open School's students and their families are clearly not engaged in agriculture. In lieu of the traditional agrarian calendar, how could schooling as a continuous service benefit and, in turn, take advantage of teaching and learning in this community? How could it accommodate the varied lives of the families it serves?

- How might a school like this Open School reconcile its flexible schedules and continuous services with the seasonal nature of extracurricular athletic activities?

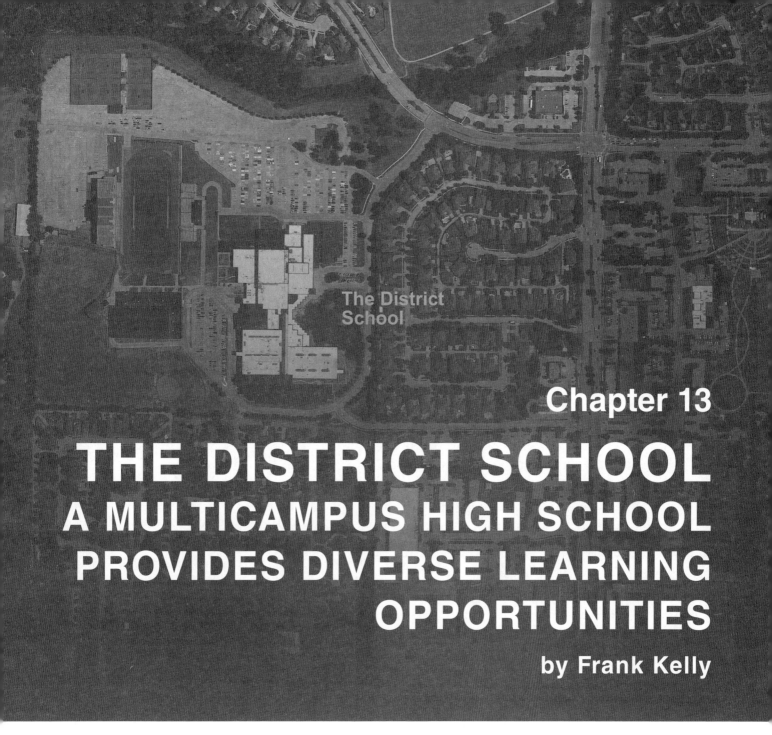

Chapter 13
THE DISTRICT SCHOOL
A MULTICAMPUS HIGH SCHOOL PROVIDES DIVERSE LEARNING OPPORTUNITIES

by Frank Kelly

Source: Satellite imagery © 2017 Google, DigitalGlobe.

Located within a very large and rapidly growing metropolitan area, the school district for the District School encompasses twenty-five square miles and has an enrollment of 10,190 students. The community has built out the district for some time, but it reacquired a large parcel of land for residential development after a local power plant closed. For many years, the district had a single, large, and comprehensive high school (the District School), but it also has a new, smaller high school (the New Tech School) that provides additional capacity and specialized instruction. The district plans to convert an existing middle school to a ninth-grade center to increase its total high school capacity. It seems improbable that further population growth will justify a second comprehensive high school, but the District School's large size makes it capable of absorbing further growth. In addition, the district has three middle schools and nine elementary schools.

The District School grounds have residential areas to its east and south. Athletic facilities and parking wrap around its west and north sides, and there are some retail stores along a major thoroughfare to the southeast. Beyond these, the community the high school serves is primarily comprised of low-density, single-family neighborhoods and with related retail services along the major thoroughfares. The community does not include high-density office, commercial, or industrial areas.

The district's population is relatively affluent, and its schools' academic records are excellent. Approximately 19 percent of students are classified as at-risk, with 1.7 percent who are classified as limited English proficient. As of 2018, there are 739 ninth-grade students, 688 tenth-grade students, 676 eleventh-students, and 595 twelfth-grade students.

In this chapter, we examine the important details and facets that make up the District School and its place in its community, its current spatial environment and the modifications we believe should go into renovating it to realize our advisory-school concept, and the cost and time implications involved. Note that each of these areas invokes and reflects our elements of schooling. We conclude with some final observations for making this facility suitable for 21st century learning.

The Existing School

The District School first opened in 1984 and has had three additions in the ensuing years. The two-level building has 437,050 square feet on a 63.54-acre site and serves 2,698 students in grades 9–12. The core instruction classroom areas are split between two floors while the remainder of the school is on the first level. Site improvements include a stadium with football and track, softball and baseball fields, and tennis courts. Adjacent to the stadium is a multipurpose building with a fifty-yard indoor football practice field, locker rooms, meeting and weight rooms, and offices.

The original 1984 plan appears to center around multidisciplinary learning communities, but apparently each area served a single discipline with the exception of science, which was distributed among the communities. An addition in 2000 created a separate area for ninth-grade students to increase the school's capacity. The school has extensive programs and spaces for the visual and performing arts, and physical education and athletics.

Every student since fall 2013 has had an iPad. The school retains two existing general-purpose computer labs and converted another to provide spaces for a growing number of blended learning courses. The school's library is already evolving to become a learning commons where desktop computers are available for students. It will also contain what the school calls a *juice bar* for iPad charging stations and a customer service desk.

Spatially, the very large footprint of the District School is organized around a two-story mall, which extends some 770 feet from the physical education, athletic, and arts spaces on one end of the school to the classrooms and ninth-grade center on the opposite end. The school's primary entrance (figure 13.1) is near the center of the mall (see figure 13.2), which itself connects with the dining area and library (see figure 13.3).

Figure 13.4 (page 154) illustrates the school's first-floor layout. One end of the building houses physical education and athletic facilities and the visual and performing arts areas, which include a theater and auditorium. (Visit **go.SolutionTree .com/instruction** to access color versions of this and other figures in this book.) At the opposite end of the mall, there are two-story classroom areas. The classrooms were originally organized into four distinct groups (with two on each level), but with the subsequent additions, including the ninth-grade center, this organization is no longer so clear. Over a typical school day, students will move about the entire school to connect with all of their teachers.

As we illustrate in figure 13.5 (page 155), second-floor spaces are only in the classroom end of the school. The layout of the groups of classrooms is much easier to see at the second level. Each of the two groups contains typical classrooms around the perimeter with additional classrooms and science labs and lecture rooms in the center. The ninth-grade center is at the far end of the building.

Figure 13.1: The District School's front entrance.

In 2008, to provide additional instructional opportunities for its high school students and increase its high school enrollment capacity, the district teamed with the New Tech Network (https://newtechnetwork.org) to create a new small high school of choice (the New Tech School), located in a former elementary school approximately a mile

Figure 13.2: The District School's mall connects its major facilities.

Figure 13.3: The District School library provides ample natural lighting.

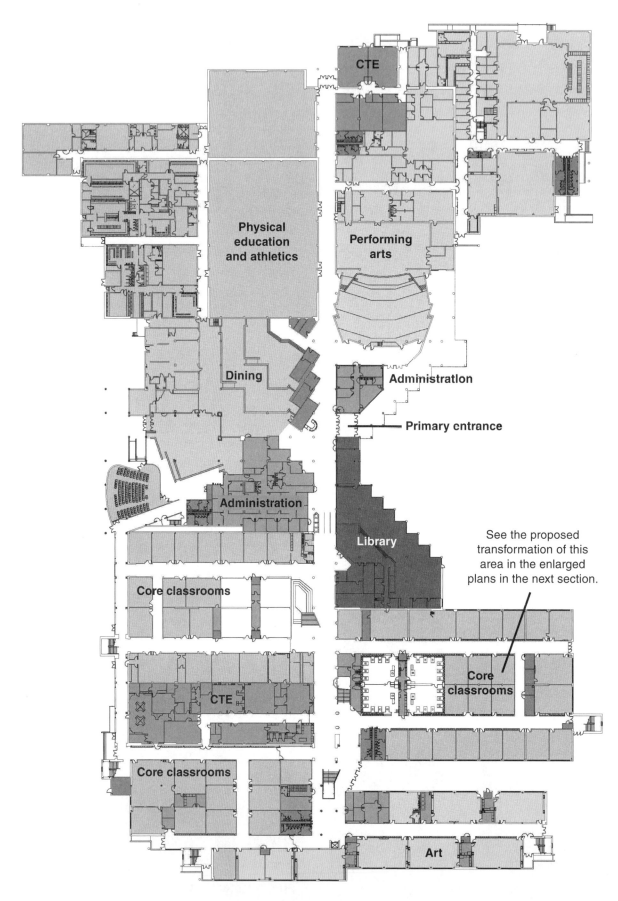

Figure 13.4: The floor plan for the District School's first floor.

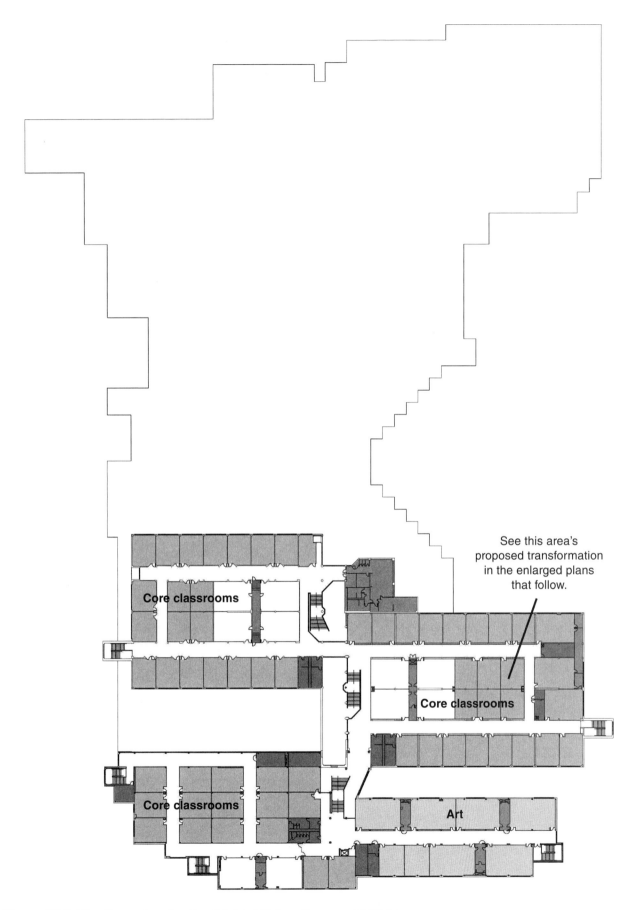

Figure 13.5: The floor plan for the District School's second floor.

from the District School (see figure 13.6). This is not an unusual arrangement, as the New Tech Network teams with more than a hundred similar districts across the United States successfully serving tens of thousands of students.

This New Tech School serves 486 students in grades 9–12 in a 62,700 square foot structure. The original elementary school closed at the end of a spring semester and reopened in the fall as a high school. The modifications cost the district $35.63 per square foot. The previous elementary school was based on conventional classrooms (see figure 13.7), while the district designed its revised layout specifically for project-based learning (see figure 13.8).

When the district renovated the school, it removed partitions between alternating classrooms to create double spaces for two teachers, each in a different discipline, and two classes of students for a double-time period. The two teachers control how to use the time and how to mix the disciplines.

Figure 13.6: The New Tech School front entrance.

The New Tech School provides all the programs students need to graduate, but it does not include extracurricular activities. Its students may participate in these programs at the District School. Both New Tech School and District School graduates receive diplomas from their respective schools.

Achieving accountability ratings of *recognized* and *exemplary* from the Texas Education Agency

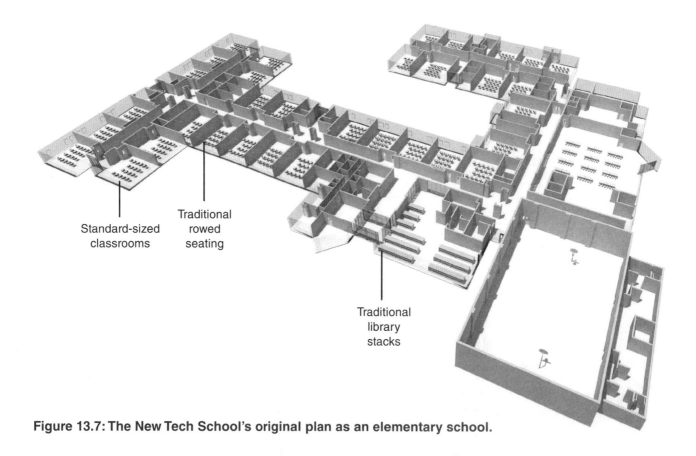

Figure 13.7: The New Tech School's original plan as an elementary school.

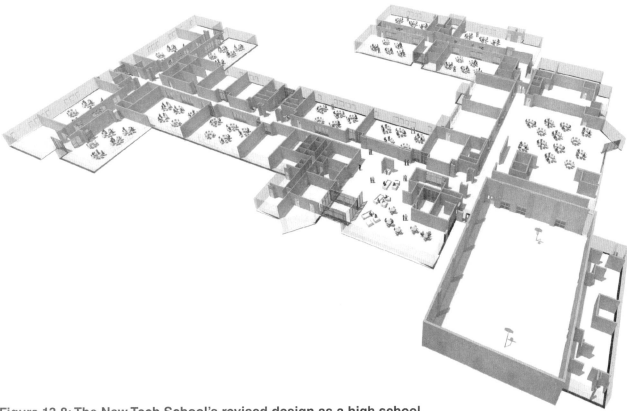

Figure 13.8: The New Tech School's revised design as a high school.

(n.d.), the District School has a very successful academic track record. Yet, after the New Tech School opened, parents and students have put forth huge efforts to enroll in the newer, smaller project-based learning school. Clearly, despite the very high quality of the District School, students and parents have real interest in alternative methods and contexts for teaching and learning.

Our Proposal and Spatial Modifications

The district has one high school and is essentially built out with limited opportunities for additional housing. It is unlikely that the district will grow enough to require a second school of comparable size, but accommodating every student on the one campus could produce a very large school. Fortunately, the district's New Tech School has been a big success, something of which we can take advantage.

We propose to create a single school that is an assembly of diverse learning communities designed to meet the community's varied needs and interests. We propose to create academies or learning communities on the district's main campus and in separate satellites (think of the New Tech School's campus), each different in terms of instruction and focus or theme. We would reconfigure each department to create academies with diverse themes.

Students and their parents would select an academy within the District School just as they choose to attend the New Tech School. The district can add additional satellite campuses in other schools or commercial structures just as they did with the New Tech School should it require additional high school capacity in the future.

Over time, the district will need to respond to changes in what students and parents choose, and that will require real spatial and instructional flexibility. Eventually, the District School may have multiple campuses that function as a single secondary school.

The modified plans for the existing facility in figure 13.9 (page 158) and figure 13.10 (page 159)

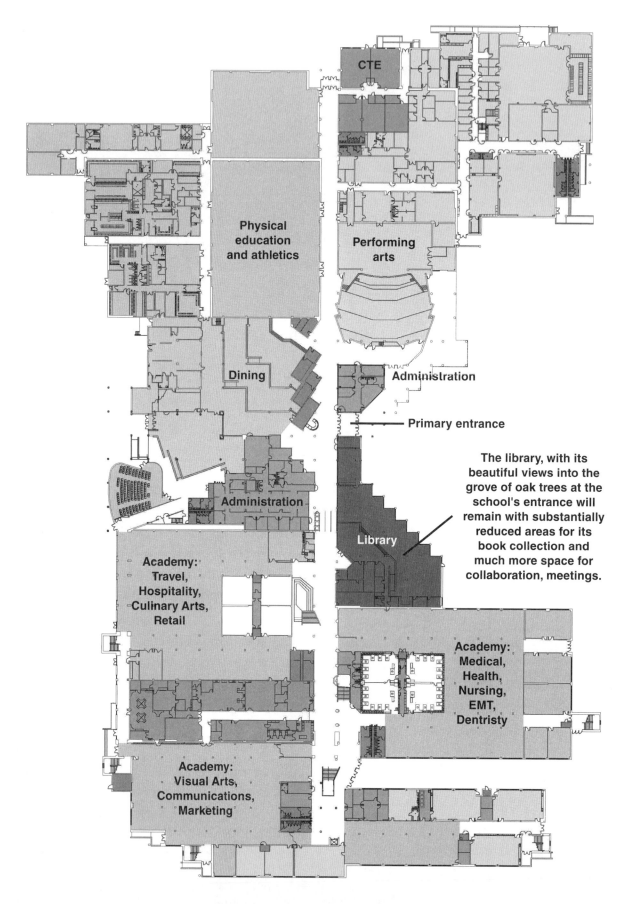

Figure 13.9: The District School's modified floor plan for the first floor.

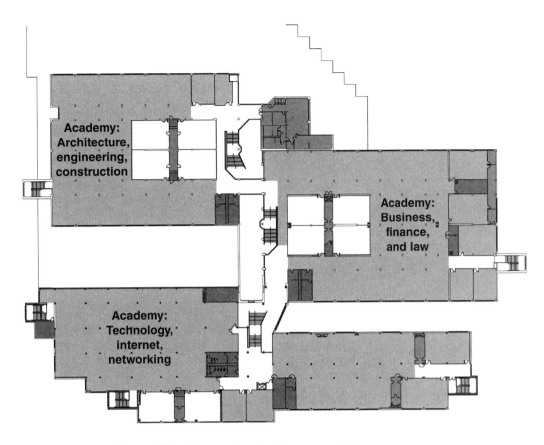

Figure 13.10: The District School's modified floor plan for the second floor.

show the creation of the new academies within areas that are already clearly defined in the plan. The existing structure subdivides these spaces into classrooms and corridors. We propose removing lockers along the corridors and partitions between most classroom spaces to open spaces. We would create highly flexible advisories for teachers and students within the open areas.

Each academy would serve students in grades 9–12 with a mix of core and CTE subjects. Whereas many of the school's existing spaces do not have windows and natural light, with the open spaces there would be light and views through most communities. Time would be flexible in all academies, but each community can organize its own time and separately schedule events. The school will operate as a continuous service throughout the year, which will significantly increase the enrollment capacity and may forestall the need for additional satellite campuses for years to come.

Initially, the academies in the modified school might house the following themes. But over time, the themes will change as the world the school serves changes. The academies must stay current both to serve and to attract students. The academies on the first floor include the following.

- Visual arts, communications, and marketing
- Travel, hospitality, culinary arts, and retail
- Medical, health, nursing, dentistry, and emergency medical technician

The following are the academies on the second floor.

- Architecture, engineering, and construction
- Technology, internet, and networking
- Business, finance, and law

Figure 13.11 (page 160) describes one of the existing first-floor departments with its corridors and classrooms.

Figure 13.12 shows the same space transformed as an academy with advisories.

The existing learning community is accessible from the school's central mall. Near the two entrances, there's a small suite of secondary administration offices plus toilets. The remainder of the community consists of double-loaded corridors with classrooms and science lab and lecture spaces.

Our modified plan preserves the offices, toilets, and science labs (with their costly utilities and casework) while replacing and opening the majority of the classrooms with advisories. We retain some existing specialized spaces to support classes related to the business, finance, and law academy.

The school will only use the science lab and lecture spaces for lab and project work. Science teachers will also function as advisors and have workstations in the open-advisory areas. The school will instead staff the science labs with aides, and students will independently conduct most of their lab work based on where they are in their individual studies. The labs will also provide workspaces with water, tables, and various graphics equipment for preparing projects and presenting exhibition material related to all the areas in which they are working.

Cost and Time Implications

Given that the work to convert the existing departments and communities consists almost entirely of removing partitions; replacing floor coverings; adjusting ceilings, lights, and power-distribution systems; and installing new furniture, fixtures, and equipment, the district could implement a substantial portion of the work over a single summer. The New Tech School's conversion of 62,700 square feet of elementary school space to high school spaces is indicative of the potential

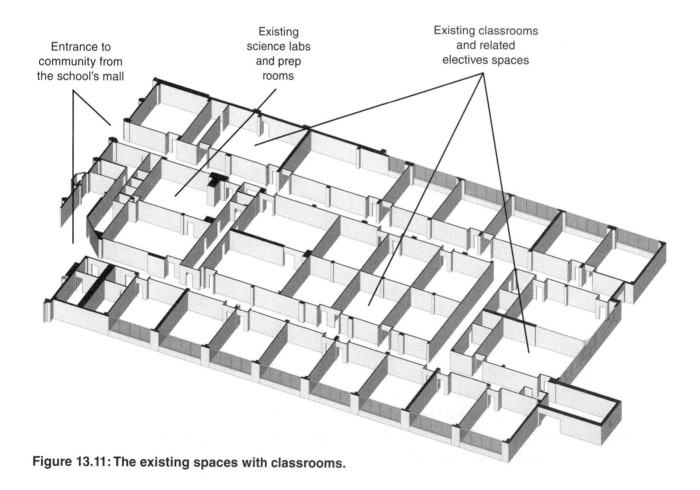

Figure 13.11: The existing spaces with classrooms.

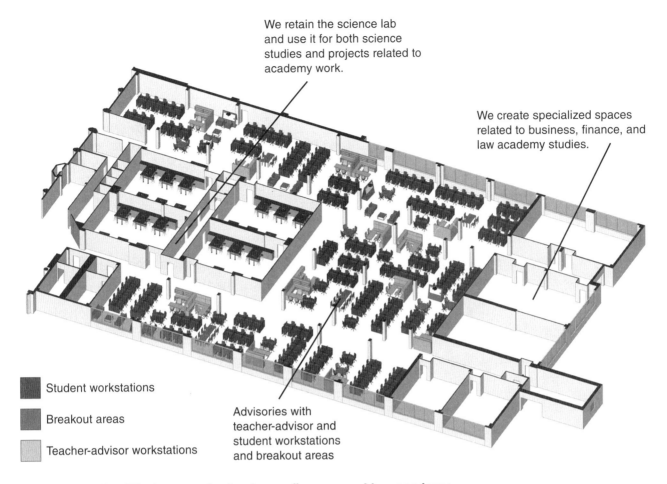

Figure 13.12: Modified spaces for business, finance, and law academy.

costs ($35.63 per square foot). Even if the work volume takes two summers, the existing school could continue to operate over the intervening school year under its current arrangement. Operating this very large campus year-round would quite significantly increase its capacity to serve teaching and learning thereby reducing the facility cost per student.

Observation

The District School and its New Tech School component are similar to the Academy School concept we discuss in chapter 15 (page 171) in terms of how quickly and economically districts can convert existing buildings to serve 21st century teaching and learning. Our District School concept, in particular, suggests ways to give students and parents multiple choices within a single campus to serve diverse community interests.

We believe that all these designs confirm that the traditional comprehensive high school need not be the only way to serve high school students. Costs and construction are not insurmountable constraints to realizing 21st century schooling.

Essential Questions

As you reflect on this chapter, consider the following questions.

- Reflect on the existing District School, with its multiple campuses and varied small learning communities: Do we realize the tenets of the elements of schooling within its framework for enabling multiple opportunities for diverse communities? How does the district's use of satellite campuses like the New Tech School make our advisory-school concept even easier to realize?

- Can a single high school function on several campuses—at several locations?

- How can a single high school support multiple learning communities when each has a different instructional focus and different learning environment?

- What are the benefits for teaching and learning when a district offers varied options from which parents and students can choose to serve diverse interests and needs?

- In what ways can a single, large high school in a district offer both educational and extracurricular options that might otherwise be unaffordable?

- How can having multiple, highly variable campuses dispersed about the district help integrate the school into the community and help the school to draw on the community's resources for the students' benefit?

Chapter 14

THE TECH SCHOOL
A MIDDLE SCHOOL THAT PACES TECHNOLOGY'S PROGRESS

by Frank Kelly

Source: Satellite imagery © 2017 Google, DigitalGlobe.

The Tech School is a middle school in a suburban district that spans approximately fifty-three square miles in a large and growing metropolitan area. The area around the school is a mix of single and multifamily housing, shopping, and suburban office structures. The district serves 26,423 students in four comprehensive high schools, seven middle schools, and twenty-four elementary schools.

The Tech School, specifically, serves 766 students in grades 6–8. Students with economic disadvantage constitute 46.9 percent of the school's enrollment, with 5.5 percent classifying as limited English proficient and 29.1 percent classifying as at-risk. Just over 2.1 percent of the school's students transferred there due to disciplinary problems at other schools, and 21.6 percent are mobility students who transferred into the district during the school year. The school's three most recent accountability rankings from the Texas Education Agency (n.d.) include ratings as *recognized* and *acceptable*.

In this chapter, we examine the important details and facets that make up the Tech School and its place in its community, its current spatial environment and the modifications we believe are appropriate to realize our advisory-school concept, and the cost and time implications involved. Note that each of these areas invokes and reflects our elements of schooling. We conclude with some final observations for making this facility suitable for 21st century learning.

The Existing School

Built in 1998 on a twenty-three-acre site, the single-story building has 142,000 square feet of space and offers the International Baccalaureate (IB) program, a university-recognized, two-year curriculum that involves extended essay work, an instructional focus on theories of knowledge, and emphasis on personal growth (see figure 14.1).

Responding to rapid growth in the mid-1990s, the district built a number of schools that were very forward-thinking. It built a new high school with small learning communities before the National Association of Secondary School Principals (1996) published *Breaking Ranks*, and it tried in numerous schools to make provisions for the technology it anticipated in the near future. The district wanted every teacher and student to have ready access to technology and not just a computer lab down the hall from the core classrooms.

For the Tech School, the district organized classrooms in multidisciplinary pods around shared labs, each with enough computers for a full class of students. Each classroom had windows into the shared space for collaboration and supervision. This provided a very high level of access and encouraged dialogue between teachers and disciplines.

Figure 14.1: The Tech School's primary entrance.

The school organized pods in three grade-level groups around a central space (see figure 14.2). (Visit **go.SolutionTree.com/instruction** to access color versions of this and other figures in this book.) These groups contain two pods each with a science lab and lecture space and four classrooms around a shared computer lab plus classrooms for related studies such as foreign languages.

The three groups of pods cluster around a central area housing the school's library, an enclosed sculptural form that contrasts with the surrounding pod areas. Art and CTE spaces are nearby in the corners of the building. A central spine aligned with the school's primary entrance links these instructional areas with the performing arts spaces (band,

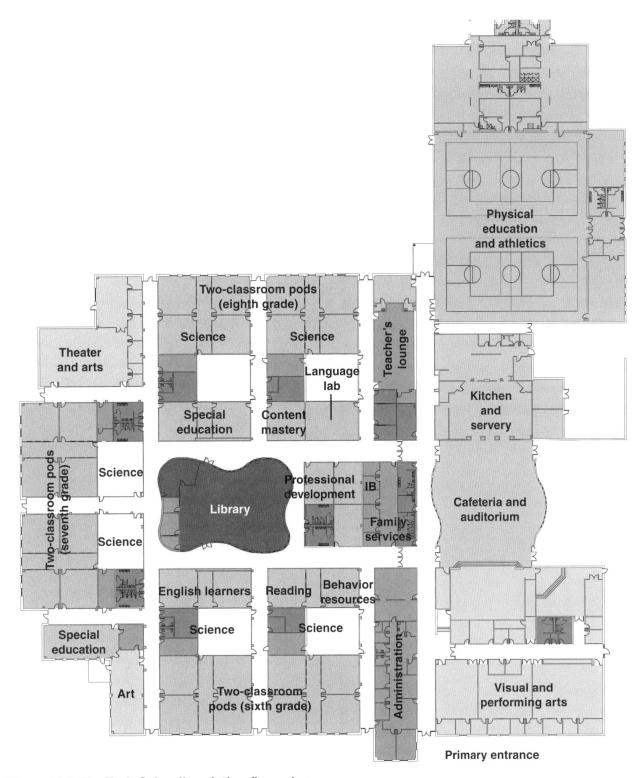

Figure 14.2: The Tech School's existing floor plan.

orchestra, choir, and theater), cafeteria, auditorium, and physical education and athletic spaces (see figure 14.3, page 166). The typical school day has seven periods.

They organized classrooms in multidisciplinary pods around shared labs, each with enough computers for a full class of students (see figure 14.4, page 166). Each classroom has windows into the shared space for collaboration and supervision. This provides a very high level of access and encourages dialogue between teachers and disciplines.

Figure 14.3: The Tech School's central spine connects all of its major spaces.

Our Proposal and Spatial Modifications

The school's challenge is that changes in technology that were unforeseeable and unimaginable at the time of the school's initial construction are already here. Ubiquitous, 1:1 technology in many forms is the reality, and the school now uses for furniture storage the shared computer labs that were forward-thinking in 1998 (see figure 14.4). The computer labs no longer knit teachers and students together but separate them and occupy valuable space as well.

Figure 14.4: One of the Tech School's computer labs.

We propose to retain the building's basic organizational plan but reconfigure the spaces within the pods to allow much greater flexibility and fully utilize 1:1 technology (see figure 14.5). Our plan removes the corridors and computer labs and incorporates that space into the teaching and learning spaces. Within these areas, only the partitions around the science labs and related supporting spaces would remain. The scale of these pods would still be quite small and appropriate for the younger students in grades 6–8. The science teachers would join the other teachers as advisors in the open spaces with student workstations.

Originally the three groups of pods were clustered around a central library to form a highly efficient layout (five to seven classrooms per pod), but only two rooms per pod had windows and the central library area had no natural light at all. By opening the pods, virtually everyone in each area will have some access to natural light and views to the lawns around the school.

Although teacher advisors will have conventional workstations, the students may have rolling desks to facilitate and encourage rearranging spaces daily to accommodate individual studies and work in variable-size groups. Students would spend about 70 percent of their typical day in their pods, going out primarily for art, CTE, physical education and athletics, and dining, which all require special equipment or spaces and group versus individual work. Whereas the original pods housed a single grade level, the larger groups will house a vertical mix of students in grades 6–8 so that they will remain with their group all three years they are on the campus. Digital devices will deliver most content with teachers monitoring students online and working directly with them individually as students need them. Work will be self-paced with no bells or periods during the school day.

The existing library lies within a free-form curving wall in the central space defined at the heart of the groups of pods. It mostly fills this central space and separates the pods. We propose to make the

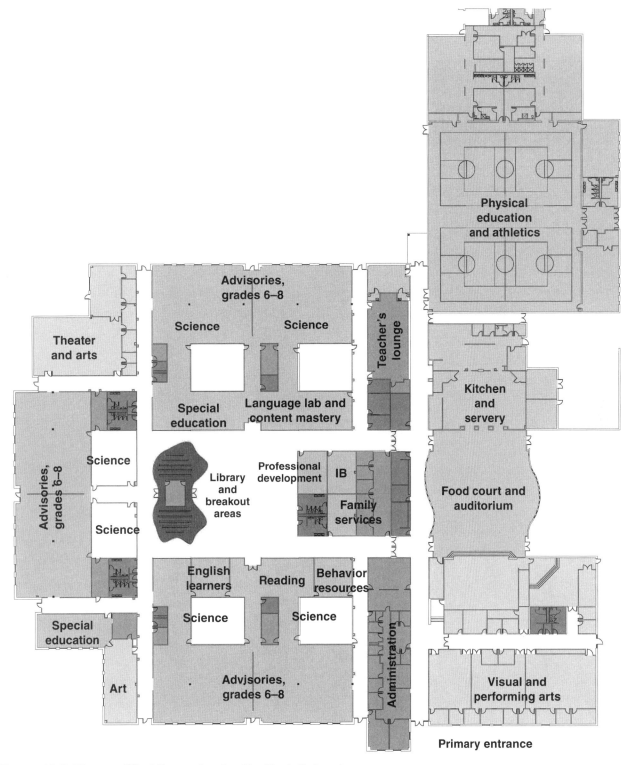

Figure 14.5: The modified floor plan for the Tech School.

enclosed part of the library significantly smaller to house only a small stacks area, a librarian office, and an instructional area to help students learn to use the library's digital resources. The remaining original library space would provide informal breakout areas for group work and collaboration.

We would add skylights punched through the roof above this space to provide natural light in the heart of the school.

With self-paced studies and no bells, the cafeteria would have no set lunch periods and would function like a food court. Students could go there when they are hungry. They could eat there or in the new breakout area near the library in the center of the pods. During other parts of the day, they may go there for beverages or snacks. The cafeteria would have highly flexible tables and chairs rather than the current folding tables with attached fixed seats.

Figure 14.6 and figure 14.7 further illustrate the school's transformation from its classroom pods to the open, advisory pods. Figure 14.6 shows a traced line around two existing groups of pods, with each pod requiring five teachers. There are other classrooms that face the central library space and serve students from all the pods.

Under the existing organization, when students change classes per the bell schedule, they walk from room to room through their computer lab or use the perimeter corridors. Although the computer labs internally link the pods, they have no identity along the corridors around them or in the central space around the library. Likewise, even though the library's curvilinear form distinguishes it from the surrounding classrooms, its wall is largely opaque, and the corridor has no natural light and little to make it interesting and active.

Figure 14.7 shows the same area with many of the partitions removed to house new pods or advisories. With the exception of the science labs and related support spaces, we remove almost all the partitions within the pods. We also remove the corridor between the original pods and replace it with a single floating wall to define but not enclose the areas of the two pods. Teacher advisors have open workstations within the pods surrounded by workspaces for the students, and students pursue their studies according to their own pace with no bell schedules. We intend for teachers and students to, over time, rearrange and regroup these as they pursue their studies.

Science teachers will have workstations within the pods and will join their students when appropriate for work within the labs. Between the labs and the related support spaces, there will be presentation

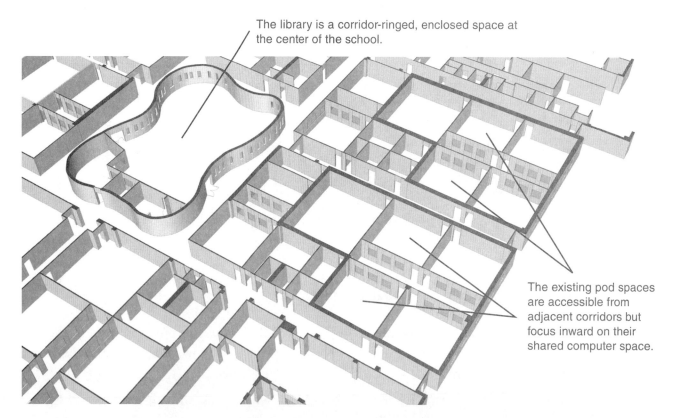

Figure 14.6: How the Tech School organizes classroom pods.

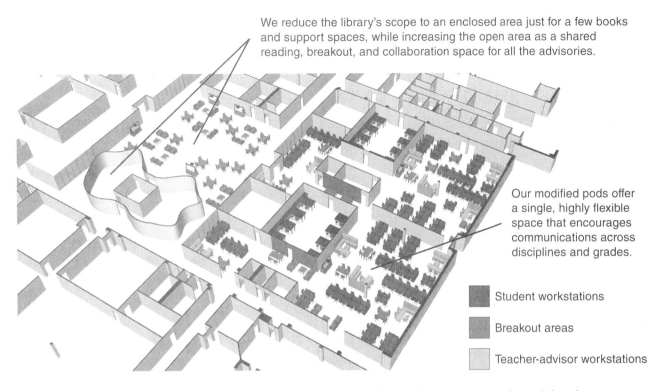

Figure 14.7: **Modified spaces to reduce the library's footprint and create space for advisories.**

exhibition spaces for all students and teachers to share. We propose using the science labs' walls as surfaces for displaying student work.

This design creates a central, open space around the much smaller stack space that is only interrupted by several small, visually open but acoustically closed conference spaces for private meetings. Around these, there will be tables and chairs similar to those the library previously provided.

Cost and Time Implications

Transforming the pods consists of removing partitions, replacing finishes, modifying the ceiling, lights, air-conditioning registers, and power distribution, and installing new furnishings. Reconfiguring the library walls and creating the new stack spaces are similar undertakings. Installing the skylights on the roof to obtain natural light requires some substantial coordination between the rooftop mechanical units, the structural systems, and the interior duct work, ceiling, and lighting. This is not a big project, however. With planning preparations during the spring, the school could accomplish the total job over a summer.

Observation

Of all the schools we selected as models in previous chapters, the Tech School is the newest and most forward-thinking. Yet, since its construction in 1998, advances in technology and related changes in instruction have made important parts of the school obsolete. The moral here is that schools need to be able to respond to change as quickly, easily, and economically as office and retail buildings. We can no longer argue that the best use of taxpayers' dollars is to build schools that are durable and long-lasting when they will need to change multiple times over any reasonable life span.

Essential Questions

As you reflect on this chapter, consider the following questions.

- Reflect on the existing Tech School, with its initial forward-looking design that still can't keep pace to sustain learning for the 21st century: Do we realize the tenets of the elements of schooling within our proposed changes to its pods and central library?

- How does the spatial configuration of your school reflect or support your current thinking about the use of digital technology for teaching and learning?

- Can your district modify your school building to easily, quickly, and economically support inevitable changes in instruction and technology?

- How long has your school been in its current spatial configuration? Has the world outside your schools changed appreciably during this period?

- With advances in technology, with new entities creating teaching and learning materials, with ongoing pressures on the costs of schooling, and with concerns about the competitiveness of our schools, is it likely that your school will need to change repeatedly in the coming years?

Chapter 15

THE ACADEMY SCHOOL
A HIGH SCHOOL THAT USES THE FLEXIBILITY OF AN OFFICE BUILDING TO SERVE TEACHING AND LEARNING

by Frank Kelly

Source: Satellite imagery © 2017 Google, DigitalGlobe.

The Academy School is in a suburban district within a large metropolitan area with many municipalities and school districts. During the 2010–2011 school year, the district served approximately 55,300 students. It has three senior high schools (grades 11–12), six high schools (grades 9–10), thirteen middle schools, and forty-four elementary schools. In terms of enrollment, 25.9 percent of students are economically disadvantaged, 12 percent are students who are limited English proficient, and 22.5 percent are students at-risk.

To the west of the Academy School's site there are large areas of single-family homes. To the east, there are low-rise retail and commercial developments and a major interstate highway. Immediately adjacent to the building are open properties for future commercial developments.

During its creation, the school received financial support via a substantial grant from a local company which allowed the school to hire ten facilitators (teachers) for a year of work and study before it opened. In addition, the program attracted other corporate groups to support the school both instructionally and financially. All instruction in the school focused on technology-supported, project-based learning with instruction in the core subjects organized around and through these projects. In the spring of 2016, the Academy School awarded its first degrees.

In this chapter, we examine the important details and facets that make up the Academy School and its place in its community, its current spatial environment and the modifications we believe should go into renovating it to realize our advisory-school concept, and the cost and time implications involved. Note that each of these areas invokes and reflects our elements of schooling, which are particularly unique for this facility given its context as a former office building. We conclude with some final observations for making this facility suitable for 21st century learning.

The Former Building and Existing School

Originally built to provide office lease space, a regional phone company purchased it to house its call center. Completed in 1998, the building and its parking occupy a 6.36-acre site with 439 parking spaces, and the building has 107,054 square feet on three floors (see figure 15.1). Having purchased the site and building during the 2009–2010 school year for $6.3 million ($59.64 per square foot), the district repurposed them to serve six hundred high school students.

Figure 15.1: The front-facing entrance for the Academy School.

It took approximately five months to renovate the building for the district's purposes, and the Academy School opened for the fall semester of 2013. In addition to core spaces for elevators, toilets, mechanical rooms, and exit stairs, the phone company had some enclosed spaces for conference rooms and other special purposes. However, most of the space on all three floors was entirely open with flexible furnishings for employee workstations (see figure 15.2). There are windows and natural light around the entire perimeter of the building on all three levels. In addition to the original building and site purchase, the renovation work to convert the building into high school spaces cost $5.3 million. This included costs for construction, new furnishings,

Figure 15.2: The Academy School has large, open spaces.

Figure 15.3: These large open spaces are ideal for advisories.

and various fees. The total cost of the project including the purchase of the building and site was $11.7 million ($109.51 per square foot).

The Academy School is a STEAM (science, technology, engineering, arts, and mathematics) school that uses project-based learning to serve students in grades 9–12, and it incorporates many facets (though not all) of the elements of schooling that we deem critical to education's future. We aim to take this solid foundation even further.

For example, the school already provides a different experience for its students via collaborative team projects, STEAM classes, and the opportunity to attend classes without structured periods. The district has dwo other academy programs, one with studies in health sciences and the other being the International Baccalaureate (IB) program. Most of the school already has the open spaces that would house the advisories we propose (see figure 15.3), and it already includes three science labs, a fabrication lab, and three presentation spaces. With 1:1 technology, students may pursue their studies in individual manners, including dual-credit classes, via a major university in the area.

As we illustrate in figure 15.4, the first floor is typical of all three floors in the existing building. (Visit **go.SolutionTree.com/instruction** to access color versions of this and other figures in this book.) There are two elevators and an exit stair in the center of the building. The primary building lobby opens to the adjacent parking area. Additional core spaces (toilets, mechanical and electrical spaces, and fire stairs) appear in the center of each of the two arms of the building. The building-support spaces house building management and janitorial areas. Although there are some enclosed office spaces in the center of the building, most space is completely open and flexible making it well-suited for the advisory spaces we propose.

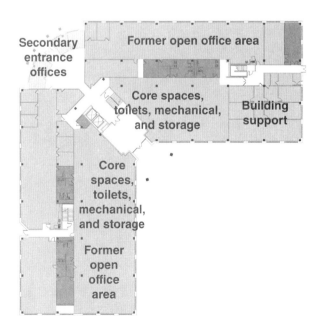

Figure 15.4: The Academy School's existing first-level floor plan.

The existing second floor features offices clustered in the center near the elevators, and there is a round conference presentation room (see figure 15.5).

The third floor is much the same as the second, only without the conference room (see figure 15.6). Offices cluster in the center near the elevators with the remainder of the floor open.

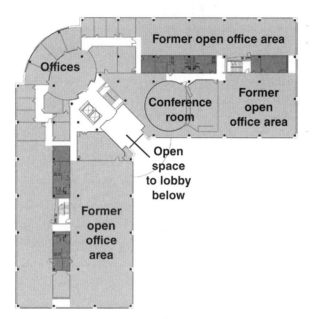

Figure 15.5: The Academy School's existing second-level floor plan.

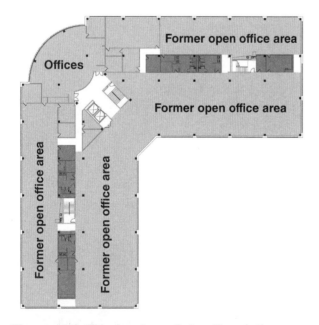

Figure 15.6: The Academy School's existing third-level floor plan.

Our Proposal and Spatial Modifications

Given the remarkably forward-thinking instruction layout the Academy School plans, our proposal springs from and elaborates on its existing thinking. We envision this facility as a school of choice within the district. Students will select among the teacher-advisor groups with each representing an academy that links core and CTE subjects with a different technology focus and corporate sponsor (or sponsors). Providing a link to the outside world, corporate sponsors, resources, and mentors will help make each student's work engaging, relevant, and motivating.

As a school of choice within a district that has nine comprehensive high schools, the Academy School will focus on the core and related programs it requires for its academies and graduation, but it will not offer athletic or performing arts programs. It will include a physical education space and a digital graphic arts program closely tied to its academies.

We propose to organize schooling into five advisory areas: one on the first floor and two each on the second and third floors. Figure 15.7, figure 15.8, and figure 15.9 illustrate our minimal changes to the existing floor plan.

Each group will include approximately five or six teacher advisors, each from a different discipline. Teacher advisors will have open workstations dispersed about each floor to ensure close daily contact with students. The school's focus on interdisciplinary, project-based instruction will ensure collaboration between teacher advisors and their corresponding disciplines.

Each advisory will have a vertical assortment of students, each assortment in different stages of its studies. Students and teachers in the advisory will come to know each other well and will support, advise, and collaborate on every aspect of their schooling. Each student will have a personal digital device and a personal workstation through which

The Academy School

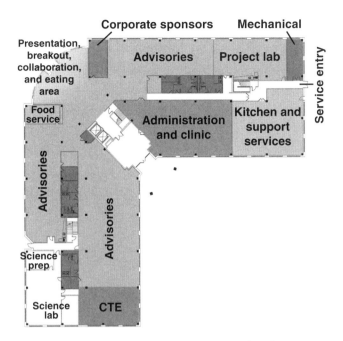

Figure 15.7: Our modified floor plan for the Academy School first floor.

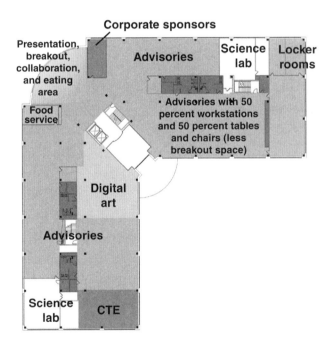

Figure 15.8: Our modified floor plan for the Academy School second floor.

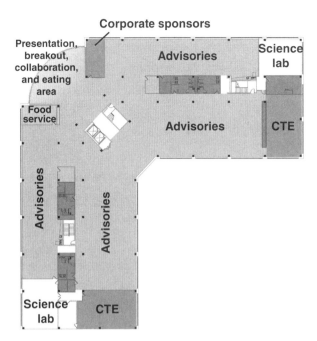

Figure 15.9: Our modified floor plan for the Academy School third floor.

Each teacher-advisor group will include a science teacher and a science lab. The science teacher will have an open workstation close to students with aides staffing the science lab, which students will access whenever they need to.

Each advisory area will include breakout collaboration spaces where students and teacher advisors may gather to work together on projects. These will vary in character, with loose tables and chairs that teachers and students may rearrange. There will be a few acoustically enclosed conference spaces (with four to ten seats) for meetings where acoustical privacy is necessary, but the vast majority of all teaching and learning spaces will be open to encourage communication and collaboration.

With students working at their own pace, there will be no bells and no quarters or semesters—no starting or stopping of studies. Graduation occurs for each student when he or she achieves the learning outcomes his or her path dictates. With the school open year-round, students may complete their studies in more than or less than the customary four years.

they can access digital content for the duration of their time at the school. Students will be able to store and secure their personal items at their workstation while working at their own pace with the supervision and support of a teacher advisor who will digitally monitor their progress. Students and teacher advisors will meet when they need to.

On each floor, there will be a small office area to provide the related corporate sponsors a base on the campus. Sponsors' representatives will come to the campus for student discussions, presentations, and reviews, and students will frequently visit the sponsors' places of business as well.

The school will have a very small library collection and a librarian to support students' research efforts. The students may access other libraries and materials in the district or access online library services to which the district subscribes.

In the center of each floor, there will be a presentation and exhibition space in which teachers and students will gather for student presentations and to review projects. The school will display projects in this area and throughout the rest of the school in both digital and paper forms. The presentations and reviews will require students to present and defend their work, which is an essential part of project-based learning. Project exhibitions will help all students see the work their peers are doing at the school, allowing students to learn from and inspire each other and thereby stimulate work and learning within the school.

We envision a central kitchen on the first level with access to the loading area. The kitchen will prepare foods and beverages for distribution via a serving counter on each of the three floors. Students and teachers may acquire food and drinks for consumption in the presentation and exhibition spaces, or they may take their food back to their workstations. The serving counters will be open most of the day. Students and teachers, like workers in corporate offices, will be responsible for keeping their workstations clean and functional.

Immediately adjacent to the advisories on each level of the building, there will be specialized spaces for science, career technology, art, and project work. Each will house a teacher advisor's workstation and specialized furnishings and equipment. To the extent possible (pending noise and safety issues), these spaces will be visibly and functionally open to adjacent areas to facilitate the integration of the core and specialized studies in the academies. The art space will house specialized computers, scanners, printers, and plotters through which students may learn visual art and graphics skills they will employ in making presentations related to their studies and in maintaining their individual portfolios. On the first floor, near the service entrance, there will be a project space with work counters, 3-D printers, sinks, and other equipment to permit students to prepare models and display their projects.

Figure 15.10 describes the full second floor with all the furnishings and equipment in the advisories and specialized supporting spaces. Notice how very different the Academy School will feel from a conventional school organized around classrooms.

Except for the core spaces, most of the floor will be open with natural light all the way around the perimeter. Although each teacher advisor and student will be part of an advisory group, they will be open to and in visual contact with others. Compared to typical high schools, the floor will be very small (not quite thirty-six-thousand square feet). As students and teachers move about the floor to meet with other students and teachers to access specialized spaces, serving pantry, or sponsor offices, they will have a real sense of community that is often lacking in schools where the typical floor may exceed one-hundred-thousand square feet with long double-loaded corridors.

The teacher-advisor workstations in figure 15.10 are intentionally tall, rising well over the student workstations and breakout areas. Our intent is for these stations to function as visual anchors for the spaces and help students and teachers find each other as they work together over time. The exhibition and presentation area is clearly visible in the center of the building near the elevators.

Cost and Time Implications

The fact that the Academy School already exists within a converted office building has a huge impact on the cost and time implications for our proposal.

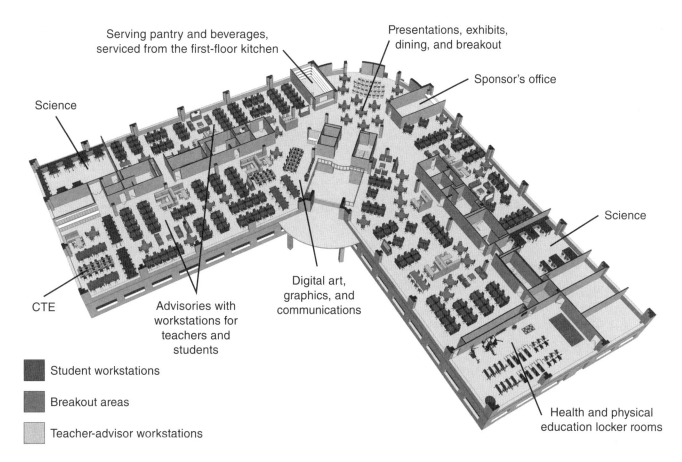

Figure 15.10: A detailed illustration of the second-floor arrangement.

For generations, districts have tried to make school buildings that are durable and permanent, buildings that can resist the wear and tear of schooling and students for many years. Unfortunately, they've been very good at that. Schools built with concrete block or glazed tile walls and terrazzo floors look and function exactly as they did generations earlier, while the world these schools serve has changed enormously and continues to change at an accelerating pace. Architects design office and retail buildings to provide durable shells with highly flexible interiors that are likely to change many times over the life of the building. Conventional middle and high schools would be well-served in adopting a similar focus on flexibility.

Our Academy School is within an existing suburban office building that crews built in a period of four-and-a-half months from the start of construction to occupancy. Crews could just as easily accomplish this in an existing retail structure. Although there are cost and time advantages to using such structures for school spaces, there are also advantages related to the context in which these buildings typically appear. Office and retail buildings are almost always in areas near major roadways and other similar structures. Schools located in this context, rather than residential areas, would link to a much more diverse and lively environment that can benefit learning for secondary school students. Area businesses can provide resources on which the school can draw, such as having students go to such businesses for mentorships and work experiences.

Although school districts almost always build and own their facilities, there could be real advantages to leasing space. It affords the district and school the flexibility to change the location, quantity, or nature of their spaces over time. Should enrollment grow or shrink, the school can relocate or lease more space. This is precisely why many businesses lease rather than buy their own spaces. Over time, the populations of most school districts shift and evolve, and some school districts find themselves with spaces and sites they cannot fill with students nor readily repurpose. Flexibility and the ability to respond to changing instructional methods and different enrollments have huge cost implications.

One other element of flexibility is important to the Academy School's costs. The cost for the buildout of its interior spaces will be relatively low because the amount of construction for partitions, finishes, and so on is relatively low compared to typical school classroom areas. However, the cost of the furnishings for the advisories will be higher. The big benefits come over time, as students and staff can quickly and economically change spaces and arrange furniture to adapt to changing needs. The easier and more economical changes are to make, the more likely a school is to realize them to better support and enhance teaching and learning.

Observation

What is truly important about the Academy School is that it breaks the mold that schooling must happen in spaces specially constructed for education. If schooling can happen here, it can also happen in other venues, and we could offer students more diverse schools that better serve diverse needs. The Academy School's total cost per square foot is remarkable relative to the cost of creating new spaces on a new site. This handsomely benefits both students and taxpayers.

Essential Questions

As you reflect on this chapter, consider the following questions.

- Reflect on the existing Academy School and its setting within a former office building: How do its nonschool spaces constrain or help realize the elements of schooling's intent? What structures already exist within your district that might effectively and economically support 21st century learning?

- The Academy School's purchase and transformation of an existing building and site to serve high school programs took four months at a total cost of $11.7 million ($109.51 per square foot): How does that cost compare to what your district or school spends on new construction projects?

- The Academy School is near homes on one side and shopping and office areas on the opposite side: How might its integration of educational, residential, and commercial activities benefit teaching and learning?

- The Academy School provides every course that students need to graduate, but does not have athletics or performing arts: Provided that students can choose the school that they attend, why is it OK to have schools that have clear academic focuses, but no or limited extracurricular activities?

Epilogue
CONCLUDING THOUGHTS
by Frank Kelly and Ted McCain

You never change things by fighting existing reality. To change something, build a new model that makes the existing model obsolete.

—Buckminster Fuller

Our collective failure to recognize the nature of schooling—what we illustrate in our elements of schooling figure—explains why we've known for decades that our schools serve many students poorly, yet we've persisted with practices we know don't work. Our failure to recognize the nature of schooling has allowed us to ignore great ideas for transforming schools in ways that could produce different and better results. Yet, the wider education community widely ignores these ideas, let alone attempts to replicate them.

It's this kind of thinking that explains why the wider education community views the open-plan concept as a giant boondoggle, without realizing that it's our collective failure to coordinate instruction, time, facilities, and technology to improve school-based education that doomed it. This cognitive momentum is also why people still raise the specter of the open-plan school despite the fact that modern technology and a clear need for individualized instruction make the idea much more valid and useful for the 21st century than it was in the mid-20th century. Indeed, modern technology makes our traditional method of stand-and-deliver, park-and-bark instruction—a format we already know is not an effective way for students to learn—all the more obsolete.

Powerful new forces are rapidly entering education (Whittle, 2012), and public schools face the very real possibility of becoming the 21st century Kodak or the *Encyclopædia Britannica*. What we propose in this book is not an incremental school improvement process that unfolds in a series of steps over a period of years or decades. Rather, it is a transformation that can and must occur in a relatively short period as a cohesive, coherent, and concerted effort. Consider what time means in the life of a student and the millions of students our schools serve every year.

We must recognize that there are powerful forces external to education that are trying to realize sweeping changes with or without the participation of public schools. We must be mindful of this epilogue's epigraph and understand that we don't change existing models by fighting existing reality, but by building a new model to make the existing one obsolete. We believe our advisory-school concepts, with their ability to change with the times, are that model.

Do not mistake what we say about public schools. We passionately believe in the broad spirit and noble intent of our public schools and everyone who works within them. We also truly believe in the vital role U.S. public schools play in the U.S. democracy and economy. But the way these schools operate does not now, nor will it in the future, sustain that role. We cannot ignore the clear and present danger. We cannot let our public schools travel down a slow road to collapse, with all the terrible implications this would have for their communities. We must transform our schools, creating from within new schooling models that reflect the needs of students both for today and tomorrow.

So, in this concluding epilogue, we examine seven real-world schools that have successfully offered the kinds of schooling we envision and wrap it all up with some final thoughts on the path forward.

Schools That Break the Mold

Before we close *Learning Without Classrooms*, we need to acknowledge one final educational conundrum—creating a new type of schooling, even one that continually demonstrates its value, does not mean that other educators, even in the same school district, will recognize it or learn from it or try to duplicate it. Schools that practice the ideals inherent in our elements of schooling do already exist, and we highlight several of them in this chapter. As you read about these schools, some of which have been around since the 1960s, reflect on how many students walk through their doors to learn and benefit from them versus those who attend traditional industrial age schools.

Westside High School

Location: Omaha, Nebraska

Website: http://whs.westside66.org

Opened in 1967, Westside High School is based on J. Lloyd Trump's (1959) *Images of the Future*. In 2014–2015, it served 1,942 students in grades 9–12 and boasted a graduation rate of 93.5 percent. The U.S. Department of Education twice recognized it with a National Blue Ribbon School Award of Excellence.

The school has a separate West Campus (formerly known as Westside High School Career Center) to provide a smaller learning environment to aid students in graduating. It divides semesters into five units of study, which allows students to earn credits immediately, and if they lose credits, they can start earning them during the next grading period—they do not have to wait until the next semester.

The school offers four modes of instruction: (1) large-group instruction for efficient content delivery allowing teachers more time for work with students, (2) small-group instruction with fifteen to twenty students for discussions and developing communication skills, (3) laboratory and hands-on instruction in which students learn by doing, and (4) independent study time during which students decide how to best use their time and may work in instructional materials centers that include integrated student and teacher workstations.

Westside uses modular scheduling with school days divided into twenty-minute increments to allow maximum flexibility in scheduling. The school also features a traditional competitive athletic programs.

Reflecting on the elements of schooling, Westside uses varied modes of instruction without conventional classrooms, and realizes real flexibility in time via modular scheduling and flexible semesters.

Kerr High School

Location: Alief, Texas

Website: www.aliefisd.net/kerr

Established in 1994, Kerr High School is a magnet school based on J. Lloyd Trump's (1977) *A School for Everyone*. It serves eight hundred students in grades 9–12, and the U.S. Department of Education awarded it a Blue Ribbon School Award of Excellence for 2010–2011. Kerr had the highest academic ranking (*exemplary*) from the Texas Education Agency for 2009, 2010, and 2011 and has very high local and state rankings from CHILDREN AT RISK (www.childrenatrisk.org), a research and advocacy organization that promotes children's quality of life ("Alief Kerr High School," n.d.).

Unlike most magnet schools and schools of choice, Kerr distinguishes itself through its approach to teaching and learning and not by the subjects it offers. Admissions are based on grades, student behavior, and attendance records.

The school does not separate students into individual classes with an assigned teacher. In lieu of traditional assignments, students receive personal activity kits (PAKS) that include all work for the learning unit. Seminars and large groups provide opportunities for teacher direction and group learning. Students may seek out a variety of peer and teacher input while working at their own pace. After a student submits his or her PAK, he or she takes a test over the material. Students may complete courses and move on in less than a semester but must complete courses by the end of each semester. Once admitted, students proceed through their courses on their own pace. They may complete courses faster but must still complete the course by the end of each term.

In lieu of classrooms, the school has large centers for each core subject, including centers for art, business, English language arts, foreign languages, journalism, mathematics, science, and social studies. It does not have competitive athletic programs.

Kerr touches on most of our elements of schooling. It has no classroom group instruction that responds to individual students, rather students may work at their own pace, providing for a highly flexible environment. Its exemplary student outcomes are the ultimate measure of the school's approach to teaching and learning.

School of Environmental Studies

Location: Minneapolis, Minnesota

Website: http://sesmn.org

Opened in 1995, the School of Environmental Studies in Minneapolis, Minnesota, is a partnership between Independent School District 196 (www.district196.org), the City of Apple Valley, and the State of Minnesota (the Minnesota Zoo) to create smaller, more effective learning communities that provide authentic learning experiences. Located on the grounds of the Minnesota Zoo (community residents often identify it as the *Zoo School*), it resides near Lebanon Hills Regional Park and is part of Independent School District 196.

The school immerses its four hundred junior- and senior-year students in the study of environmental topics and issues while they work with and alongside professionals in the field. The district has four other high schools whose students may elect to attend the School of Environmental Studies under Minnesota's open-enrollment option. Most students come from the greater Minneapolis–St. Paul areas to fill available slots.

The Zoo School's two-year program culminates with a series of senior capstone activities. Its program requires students to initiate sustainable service experiences, proclaim their evolving environmental ethic, and present an environment issue of choice at a forum that the general public, family, and significant individuals in the student's life attend.

There was a special design process for the school. A committee, charged with the planning, conducted two years of research to define the interdisciplinary, project-based, and real-world experiences they hoped to provide. The central idea was to provide student workstations in groups of ten to form pods. Ten pods together form a *house*. The school has four houses, each with three teachers. Each house has a large, central, flexible, and common workspace, and each overlooks a forum that contains the library and cafeteria. These workspaces serve multiple purposes.

The school organizes its days and weeks in large blocks that afford students the kind of flexibility that is more often associated with universities rather than high schools. It does not have competitive athletics.

While the Zoo School was not originally created with modern technology in mind, it realized most of the other aspirations of our elements of schooling. It has no classrooms and no stand-and-deliver instruction. Students and teachers work together in families which we've dubbed advisories. Every teacher and student has their own workstation, and the school uses project-based learning. Its beautiful context on the grounds of the Minnesota Zoo makes it a special place for students and teachers.

New Technology High School

Location: Napa, California

Website: www.newtechhigh.org

Established in 1997, the New Technology High School is a product of the New Tech Network (https://newtechnetwork.org), a leading design partner for comprehensive school change. New Tech Network does not operate schools, rather it works with districts and communities throughout the United States to transform schools into innovative learning environments. In 2017, it partnered with 126 high schools, forty-one middle schools, and twenty-three elementary schools with a total of 71,280 students in 113 districts. Across all high schools, the average four-year graduation rate is 91 percent, enrollment in college is 70 percent, and persistence in college is 83 percent. The New

Technology High School enrolls four hundred students in grades 9–12.

The New Technology High School's instruction is grounded in project-based learning, so learning is contextual, creative, and shared. Students collaborate on meaningful projects that require critical thinking, creativity, and communication so they can answer challenging questions or solve complex problems. By making learning relevant to them in this way, students see a purpose for mastering state-required skills and content concepts.

New Tech doesn't just assess students on their understanding of academic content, but on their ability to successfully apply that content when solving authentic problems. Through this process, project-based learning gives students the opportunity to develop the real-life skills they need for 21st century success.

At all participating New Tech Network schools, students and teachers alike have ownership over the learning experience and their school environment. Educators collaborate in integrated interdisciplinary and team-taught classes, use collaborative protocols to provide constructive feedback, and share the leadership of the learning community. In this way, professional culture at the schools mirrors the culture students need for life after graduation.

Although the high schools have classrooms, these serve two teachers and classes from different disciplines to encourage interdisciplinary thinking on projects spanning subjects. The same process allows teachers and students flexibility to work with larger increments of time as they require. These schools will benefit greatly implementing the level of technology we propose in our elements of schooling.

The Met High School

Location: Providence, Rhode Island

Website: www.themethighschool.org

Established in 1996, the Metropolitan Regional Career and Technical Center (the Met) in Providence, Rhode Island, is a big-picture learning school comprised of six small school facilities on three separate campuses serving 690 students. The Met is consistently ranked among the state's top high schools for attendance, graduation rates, parental involvement, school climate, and quality of instruction. Specifically, 98 percent of Met students are accepted to college, 75 percent enroll in college (the U.S. average is 47 percent), and 75 percent are the first in their families to go to college.

The school is based on the belief that students must be actively engaged in their education. At the core of the curriculum is its *learning through interests* (LTI) program, which helps students find opportunities to learn in real-world settings and through meaningful projects. The Met pairs students with adult mentors in the community who share their career interests and passions. Two days each week, students intern at these worksites and contribute projects that benefit that organization. Back at school, students work with their advisors to build and reinforce the skills and knowledge they need to complete those projects. The school provides physical health programs, but no athletics.

Relative to our elements of schooling, the Met is remarkable for planning its teaching and learning around each individual student's interests and drawing upon the surrounding community to expand the school's resources. On the campus, the students work closely with a teacher advisor part of each week and then go off campus to work with their mentors. The rich environment is good for learning and for developing each student's personal skills to relate with the world beyond their school. The multiple very small campuses also help knit the school into the community.

Cristo Rey Jesuit High School

Location: Minneapolis, Minnesota

Website: www.cristoreytc.org

Established in 2007, the Cristo Rey Jesuit High School is a private, coeducational Roman Catholic school. It serves 455 students in grades 9–12 and is part of the Cristo Rey Network of high schools first established in Chicago, Illinois, in 2000 (www.cristoreynetwork.org). The network includes thirty-five Catholic work-study preparatory schools in the United States and admits students of all faiths and cultures. An objective of the schools is to help students from underserved, low-income communities prepare for college. On average, 40 percent of Cristo Rey students are not Catholic.

Schools within the Cristo Rey Network integrate four years of college-preparatory academics with continuous professional work experience that pays most of the cost of a student's education. Students work five full days a month in local businesses through each school's corporate work study program to fund over half the cost of their education. Four students share one full-time job, with each student working five full days per month. The school transports him or her to and from work each day, and the student works standard daily business hours.

The school's students enroll in college at rates more commonly associated with high-income students and have completed their college studies at a rate considerably higher than that of other low-income high school graduates ("Cristo Rey Network," n.d.). The school year extends for approximately ten months from the middle of August to the middle of June, and the typical school days are approximately eight hours. The school has several athletic programs (no football) and competes with other Catholic schools. Spatially, the school is organized around small families of teachers and students that share a common breakout area which includes food services. The space ensures very close and regular contacts between students and teachers and enhances the small scale of the overall campus.

Relative to our elements of schooling, the school's very small size ensures close individual student-teacher relationships, and its work programs ensure real-world experiences in the community which help students learn, grow, and mature. Although time is not flexible in terms of the school year or even the day, between each student's school and work days, it has diversity and richness that are an important part of the schooling process.

Carl Wunsche Senior High School

Location: Spring, Texas

Website: www.springisd.org/wunsche2

Established in 2006, the Carl Wunsche Senior High School is part of the Spring Independent School District, and it serves 1,500 students in grades 9–12. In 2007, the school received the James D. MacConnell Award, an international design award, from the Council of Educational Facility Planners International (now the Association for Learning Environments).

Academically and spatially, the school has five academies, and each includes integrated core and CTE programs. The academies are: health sciences, technology, legal studies, business and finance, and childhood studies and teacher preparation. Core, CTE, and academy studies are closely related to support student engagement. Typically, each academy focuses on an open, highly flexible space surrounded by classrooms for core subjects and specialized classrooms, labs, and shops for CTE studies. There are extensive walls of glass throughout the school so that, as students move about the building each day, they may see what is happening in the diverse areas of study. In establishing the school, the district sought input from businesses in the community and continues to draw upon them to support its programs. The school provides students with 1:1 digital devices, but does not offer athletic or performing arts programs; however, students interested in these programs may return to their zoned school to participate in them. With its close links to its other district comprehensive high schools, Wunsche adheres to a conventional bell schedule and school year.

The basic thinking in the elements of schooling (with regard to the integral relationships between the elements) is really important here. There are no departments in which various disciplines or subjects are isolated, but rather the academies very purposefully expose what both teachers and students do for all to see and share. The intent is to help students to discover areas of study with which they may not be familiar.

The Path Forward

We believe there is an urgent need for significant change in our schools; and that the need is much bigger than most parents, educators, and other taxpayers realize. Could public schools fail? Could other learning organizations replace or bypass public schools? Could new educational approaches render public schools irrelevant? How will emerging technology continue to disrupt education in public schools as it has in private industry? Most students do not have the same choice in schools as they might when deciding what to buy or where to eat, but that could quickly change if education does not respond to a changing world.

Too often, those of us within education and outside it have a misguided sense that we have done the right thing by simply building and funding our schools, despite the fact that 17 percent of students who start first grade don't complete high school (U.S. Department of Education, 2014), and a large percentage of those who do graduate are incapable of doing college-level work in core subjects (Bidwell, 2013). These things don't even consider the debate as to whether graduation requirements have any relationship to what skills students will need to succeed in life beyond school.

We live in a time of unrelenting change. It's evident all around us every day. Yet many of our students attend schools that have not markedly changed conceptually or spatially for generations. Do we stick with tradition and continue to do things we already know do not work?

Perhaps the most powerful idea we outline throughout *Learning Without Classrooms* is that society should see schooling as an ongoing, continuous service that proceeds at each student's individual pace rather than a seasonal event that inhibits the student from keeping up or allows him or her to fall behind. We set a minimum age for driving, and then require young drivers to learn the rules and take a test to demonstrate their competence. In schools, you can fail and fail and fail, but when you reach age sixteen, seventeen, or eighteen, you can drop out and enter the world ill-prepared for what it holds in store. Is driving more important than graduating? Is failing to learn or graduate less dangerous or costly for our society than failing to have a driver's license? Could we focus more attention on creating schools that students *want* to attend rather than *must* attend? Consider the financial implications these decisions hold.

Do parents, taxpayers, teachers, administrators, board members, or politicians really understand how school districts spend their funds? Do they know on a campus-by-campus basis how much districts spend for teachers, staff, technology, learning materials, and facilities? Do they know how much districts spend for core instruction? CTE courses? Visual and performing arts? Extracurricular activities and athletics? Facilities? Maintenance and utilities? Instructional staff? Administrative staff? Central administrative staff? Transportation? Construction? Debt financing? Most important, do community stakeholders understand how these expenditures reflect the community's priorities?

Do community stakeholders really understand how inefficiently most communities use their school facilities over the course of a calendar year? Do they understand what percentage of the school day educators and students use instructional spaces for teaching and learning? Do they understand what percentage of the year teachers actually work with students? Do they understand what the operating and maintenance costs for facilities are when they're using them relative to when they sit empty? Do they understand what the interest on school debt is regardless of whether the facilities are open or closed?

We can't afford to let our schools fail. We have responsibility for the lives of millions of students who are preparing to enter society. Across the United States, we invest trillions of dollars in staffing, teacher development, learning materials, facilities, infrastructure, and so on. Consider the seven schools we explored in chapters 9–15. Physically, we could modify over a summer or school year most of these facilities so that they provide an advisory format that facilitates continuous, individualized learning. Over that same span, teachers are quite capable of transforming themselves for the teacher-advisor role we envision so that they tailor instruction to the communities and students they serve. One size does not have to fit all. Education must be the constant, with time as the variable, so that we can achieve parity of learning between individual students rather than parity of teachers, courses, facilities, or funding.

In our vision for advisory-based schooling, flexible time to accommodate diverse learners and learning styles will emerge as students work and complete learning objectives. Districts can modify and reduce school costs while still helping more students succeed even as both facilities and teachers serve more students. Students will complete learning objectives in their own time using independent schedules. Some might take less time and some more, but none would fail.

Our vision ensures that the public can see more clearly what various parts of schooling cost, allowing all stakeholders to make more informed decisions about how to prioritize school funding while still giving parents, students, and all manner of businesses increased flexibility. Students can take vacations, pursue personal interests, and find employment all year round.

Education is big business. The World Bank (n.d.) reports that education comprises 5.5 percent of the U.S. gross domestic product. The future does not ensure the virtual monopoly customarily afforded public schools. Education is attracting huge interests from large business enterprises. Higher education is searching for ways to make schooling more widely available with more choices and lower costs via all manner of free online resources ("The log-on degree," 2015). Will public schools recognize the opportunities and collaborate with these enterprises, or will public schools resist until these very same enterprises assume the role public schools have occupied for generations? Public education has both the potential and opportunity for large-scale investment (Leventhal & Tang, 2013).

Now is the time to transform our schools. This is not just about tinkering with our existing industrial age schooling models. Schools must evolve along with the communities they serve. Education must provide a structure that allows schools to constantly reassess their effectiveness and adapt to ever-changing circumstances. We must move beyond making schools durable and permanent and focus more on making them flexible and adaptable, so they can support changing perspectives on teaching and learning for decades to come.

As part of that process, it is important to understand that we need not construe facilities from the past as constraints on the future. Concrete blocks, gypsum boards, carpeting, lights, ducts, tablet arm desks, and so on are much easier and less costly to change than old mindsets about how we teach, the relationship between teachers and students, the school year, passing and failing classes, libraries, and all the other considerations we wrote about in this book.

We should also not raise funding as a constraint. It is the very clear intention of the concepts we outline in this book to affirm that by using facilities year-round; by giving staff members an opportunity to choose to teach year-round; by using digital technology for teaching, learning, and instructional materials; by not allowing students to fail; and by increasing our graduation rates, we can make better schooling at a lower cost per graduate. This will have a huge cost benefit to everyone involved. But in the very same breath, we must acknowledge that the costs of failing to change our schools could be disastrous, not just for our schools, but for our nation.

REFERENCES AND RESOURCES

Adams, C. J. (2015, March 25). Employers are integral to career-tech programs. *Education Week.* Accessed at www.edweek.org/ew/articles/2015/03/25/employers-are-integral-to-career-tech-programs.html on December 15, 2017.

Alief Kerr High School. (n.d.). In *Wikipedia.* Accessed at http://en.wikipedia.org/wiki/Alief_Kerr_ High _School on May 1, 2018.

Alliance for Excellent Education. (2010). *Prioritizing the nation's lowest-performing high schools.* Accessed at https://all4ed.org/reports-factsheets/prioritizing-the-nations-lowest-performing-high-schools on December 15, 2017.

Amazon.com. (n.d.). *What are customer analytics?* Accessed at https://aws.amazon.com/pinpoint/customer-engagement/customer-analytics on February 12, 2018.

Anderson, L. W., & Krathwohl, D. (Eds.). (2001). *A taxonomy for learning, teaching, and assessing: A revision of Bloom's taxonomy of educational objectives.* Boston: Allyn & Bacon.

Andrade, H., & Valtcheva, A. (2009). Promoting learning and achievement through self-assessment. *Theory Into Practice, 48*(1), 12–19.

Andrews, E. (2016). *8 legendary ancient libraries.* Accessed at www.history.com/news/history-lists/8-impressive-ancient-libraries on February 12, 2018.

Baller, S., Dutta, S., & Lanvin, B. (Eds.). (2016). *The global information technology report 2016: Innovating in the digital economy—Insight report.* Accessed at http://online.wsj.com/public/resources/documents/GITR2016.pdf on February 12, 2018.

Battro, A. M., Fischer, K. W., & Léna, P. J. (Eds.). (2008). *The educated brain: Essays in neuroeducation.* Cambridge, England: Cambridge University Press.

Bergsagel, V., Best, T., Cushman, K., McConachie, L., Sauer, W., & Stephen, D. (2007). *Architecture for achievement: Building patterns for small school learning.* Mercer Island, WA: Eagle Chatter Press.

Berman, A. E., & Dorrier, J. (2016, March 22). *Technology feels like it's accelerating—because it actually is.* Accessed at https://singularityhub.com/2016/03/22/technology-feels-like-its-accelerating-because-it-actually-is on April 24, 2018.

Berra, Y. (2002). *When you come to a fork in the road, take it! Inspiration and wisdom from one of baseball's greatest heroes.* New York: Hyperion Books.

Bidwell, A. (2013, August 21). High school graduates still struggle with college readiness. *U.S. News & World Report*. Accessed at www.usnews.com/news/articles/2013/08/21/high-school-graduates-still-struggle-with-college-readiness on December 15, 2017.

Big data. (n.d.). In *Wikipedia*. Accessed at https://en.wikipedia.org/wiki/Big_data on February 9, 2018.

Bloom, B. S., Engelhart, M. D., Furst, E. J., Hill, W. H., & Krathwohl, D. R. (1956). *Taxonomy of educational objectives: The classification of education goals. Handbook I: Cognitive domain.* New York: Longmans, Green.

Booker, C., as cited in Moe, M. T., Hanson, M. P., Jiang, L., & Pampoulov, L. (2012, July 4). *American Revolution 2.0: How education innovation is going to revitalize America and transform the U.S. economy.* Accessed at www.asugsvsummit.com/files/American_Revolution_2.0.pdf on April 5, 2018.

Bowman, S. (2017, May 22). *"How technology rewires the brain" revisited (and what to do about it)* [Blog post]. Accessed at http://bowperson.com/2017/05/how-technology-rewires-the-brain-revisited-and-what-to-do-about-it on February 12, 2018.

Boynton, M., & Boynton, C. (2005). *The educator's guide to preventing and solving discipline problems.* Alexandria, VA: Association for Supervision and Curriculum Development.

Bransford, J. D., Brown, A. L., & Cocking, R. R. (Eds.). (2000). *How people learn: Brain, mind, experience, and school.* Washington, DC: National Academies Press.

Bryant, J. (2015, April 20). *We learn from failure, not from success—Bram Stoker.* Accessed at http://selfmadesuccess.com/we-learn-from-failure-not-from-success-bram-stoker on April 15, 2018.

Cameron, G. (2015). *The engineer at large: The essential guide to structured problem solving and creative innovation.* Charleston, S.C.: CreateSpace.

Cannon Design, VS Furniture, & Bruce Mau Design. (2010). *The third teacher: 79 ways you can use design to transform teaching & learning.* New York: Abrams.

Carey, B. (2013, December 6). 'iLabs' offer a new way to add science experiments to online education. *Stanford Report*. Accessed at http://news.stanford.edu/news/2013/december/lab-ina-box-120613.html on December 15, 2017.

Cavanagh, S. (2014, January 14). U.S. learning registry aims to tailor online content for educators. *Education Week*. Accessed at www.edweek.org/ew/articles/2014/01/15/17registry.h33.html on December 15, 2017.

Center for Public Education. (2010). *Cutting to the bone: How the economic crisis affects schools.* Accessed at www.centerforpubliceducation.org/Main-Menu/Public-education/Cutting-to-the-bone-At-a-glance/Cutting-to-the-bone-How-the-economic-crisis-affects-schools.html on February 12, 2018.

Cohen, R. D. (2002). *Children of the mill: Schooling and society in Gary, Indiana, 1906–1960.* New York: Routledge.

Cristo Rey Network. (n.d.). In *Wikipedia*. Accessed at https://en.wikipedia.org/wiki/Cristo_Rey_Network on May 1, 2018.

Cuban, L. (2013). *Inside the black box of classroom practice: Change without reform in American education.* Cambridge, MA: Harvard Education Press.

Davis, J. (2013, October 15). A radical way of unleashing a generation of geniuses. *Wired*. Accessed at www.wired.com/2013/10/free-thinkers on February 15, 2018.

Dewey, J. (1916). *Democracy and education: An introduction to the philosophy of education*. New York: Macmillan.

DeZyre. (2015). *5 big data use cases—How companies use big data*. Accessed at www.dezyre.com/article/5-big-data-use-cases-how-companies-use-big-data/155 on February 12, 2018.

Doorley, S., & Witthoft, S. (2012). *Make space: How to set the stage for creative collaboration*. Hoboken, NJ: Wiley.

Dvorkin, M. (2016, January 4). *Jobs involving routine tasks aren't growing* [Blog post]. Accessed at www.stlouisfed.org/on-the-economy/2016/january/jobs-involving-routine-tasks-arent-growing on February 12, 2018.

Dweck, C. (2015, September 22). Carol Dweck revisits the 'growth mindset'. *Education Week*. Accessed at www.edweek.org/ew/articles/2015/09/23/carol-dweck-revisits-the-growth-mindset.html on February 13, 2018.

E and S Consulting. (n.d.). *Case studies*. Accessed at www.e-and-s.com/full_screen_movie.htm on December 14, 2017.

Educational Facilities Laboratories. (1973). *Five open plan high schools: A report*. New York: Author. Accessed at https://eric.ed.gov/?id=ED083690 on April 25, 2018.

Elias, M. (2013). *The school-to-prison pipeline: Policies and practices that favor incarceration over education do us all grave injustice*. Accessed at www.tolerance.org/magazine/spring-2013/the-schooltoprison-pipeline on April 25, 2018.

Elmore, R. F. (2006). *Leadership as the practice of improvement*. Accessed at www.oecd.org/edu/school/37133264.pdf on December 15, 2017.

Florida, R. (2002). *The rise of the creative class: And how it's transforming work, leisure, community, and everyday life*. New York: Basic Books.

Flynn, D. (2014, June 17). Managing a team across 5 time zones. *Harvard Business Review*. Accessed at https://hbr.org/2014/06/managing-a-team-across-5-time-zones on April 13, 2018.

Gardner, H. (2011). *Frames of mind: The theory of multiple intelligences*. New York: Basic Books.

Gates, B. (2005, March 1). What's wrong with American high schools: The approaches of 50 years ago cannot work today, Bill Gates says. *Los Angeles Times*. Accessed at http://articles.latimes.com/2005/mar/01/opinion/oe-gates1 on December 15, 2017.

Gates, B. (2016, August 22). *I love this cutting-edge school design*. Accessed at www.gatesnotes.com/Education/Why-I-Love-This-Cutting-Edge-School-Design on June 5, 2018.

Gillies, T. (2017, July 9). *Get smart: How artificial intelligence is changing our lives*. Accessed at www.cnbc.com/2017/07/09/get-smart-how-artificial-intelligence-is-changing-our-lives.html on February 12, 2018.

Glasser, W. (1993). *The quality school teacher: A companion volume to the quality school*. New York: HarperCollins.

Gonzalez, J. W. (2014, February 9). Bexar County's cloud-based library system spans digital divide. *Houston Chronicle*. Accessed at www.houstonchronicle.com/news/houston-texas/houston/article/Bexar-County-s-cloud-based-library-system-spans-5219826.php on December 15, 2017.

Gonzales, R. (2012). *School district owes $1 billion on $100 million loan*. Accessed at www.npr.org/2012/12/07/166745290/school-district-owes-1-billion-on-100-million-loan on February 15, 2018.

Graduate Management Admission Council. (2014, August 7). *Employers want communication skills in new hires* [Blog post]. Accessed at www.mba.com/us/the-gmat-blog-hub/the-official-gmat-blog/2014/aug/employers-want-communication-skills-in-new-hires.aspx on April 14, 2018.

Harris, P., Smith, B. M., & Harris, J. (2011). *The myths of standardized tests: Why they don't tell you what you think they do*. Lanham, MD: Rowan & Littlefield.

Hasak, J. (2015, January 20). Make K–12 skills relevant to students. *Education Week*. Accessed at www.edweek.org/ew/articles/2015/01/21/make-k-12-skills-relevant-to-students.html on December 15, 2017.

Henderson, T. (2017, May 8). Why innovation is crucial to your organization's long-term success. *Forbes*. Accessed at www.forbes.com/sites/forbescoachescouncil/2017/05/08/why-innovation-is-crucial-to-your-organizations-long-term-success/#278778bc3098 on February 12, 2018.

Herold, B. (2016, January 11). The future of big data and analytics in K–12 education. *Education Week*. Accessed at www.edweek.org/ew/articles/2016/01/13/the-future-of-big-data-and-analytics.html on February 12, 2018.

IBM. (n.d.). *How conversation (with context) will usher in the AI future*. Accessed at www.ibm.com/watson/advantage-reports/future-of-artificial-intelligence/ai-conversation.html on March 29, 2018.

Jaschik, S. (2015, September 29). *Admissions revolution*. Accessed at www.insidehighered.com/news/2015/09/29/80-colleges-and-universities-announce-plan-new-application-and-new-approach on June 25, 2018.

Jensen, E. (2005). *Teaching with the brain in mind*. Alexandria, VA: Association for Supervision and Curriculum Development.

Jukes, I., McCain, T., & Crockett, L. (2010). *Understanding the digital generation: Teaching and learning in the new digital landscape*. Thousand Oaks, CA: Corwin Press.

Kelly, F. S., McCain, T., & Jukes, I. (2009). *Teaching the digital generation: No more cookie-cutter high schools*. Thousand Oaks, CA: Corwin Press.

Kelly, K. (2016). *The inevitable: Understanding the 12 technological forces that will shape our future*. New York: Penguin Books.

Kuang, C. (2011). *The 6 pillars of Steve Job's design philosophy*. Accessed at www.fastcodesign.com/1665375/the-6-pillars-of-steve-jobss-design-philosophy on February 12, 2018.

Latif, A., Choudhary, A. I., & Hammayun, A. A. (2015, April 15). Economic effects of student dropouts: A comparative study. *Journal of Global Economics, 3*(2). Accessed at www.omicsonline.org/open-access/economic-effects-of-student-dropouts-a-comparative-study-2375-4389-1000137.php?aid=57059 on March 25, 2018.

Lee, H. (1960). *To kill a mockingbird*. Philadelphia: Lippincott.

Lengel, L. (n.d.). *The information economy and the internet.* Accessed at http://docplayer.net/14293721-Journalism-and-mass-communication-vol-ii-the-information-economy-and-the-internet-laura-lengel-the-information-economy-and-the-internet.html on June 25, 2018.

Leventhal, M., & Tang, I. (2013, September 3). *Specialized Eduspace investors: "The twelve"* [Blog post]. Accessed at http://equityforeducation.wordpress.com/2013/09/03/specialized-eduspace-investors-the-twelve on December 15, 2017.

Levine, A. E. (2011, May 25). *The school of one: The school of tomorrow.* Accessed at www.huffingtonpost.com/arthur-e-levine/the-school-of-one-the-sch_b_288695.html on March 25, 2018.

The log-on degree: College in America is ruinously expensive—Some digital cures are emerging. (2015, March 12). *The Economist.* Accessed at www.economist.com/news/united-states/21646219-college-america-ruinously-expensive-some-digital-cures-are-emerging-log on December 15, 2017.

Madsen, P. M., & Desai, V. (2010). Failing to learn? The effects of failure and success on organizational learning in the global orbital launch vehicle industry. *Academy of Management Journal, 53*(3), 451–476.

Mahdawi, A. (2017, June 26). What jobs will still be around in 20 years? Read this to prepare your future. *The Guardian.* Accessed at www.theguardian.com/us-news/2017/jun/26/jobs-future-automation-robots-skills-creative-health on April 13, 2018.

Mallett, C. A. (2016, April 19). The school-to-prison pipeline: Disproportionate impact on vulnerable children and adolescents. *Education and Urban Society, 49*(6), 563–592.

Massachusetts Department of Elementary and Secondary Education. (2014). *The impact of dropping out: Summary of research findings and references.* Malden, MA: Author.

McCain, T. (in press). *Teaching with the future in mind.* Manuscript submitted for publication.

McCain, T. (2005). *Teaching for tomorrow: Teaching content and problem-solving skills.* Thousand Oaks, CA: Corwin Press.

McIntosh, S. (2002, December 16). The changing demand for skills. *European Journal of Education, 37*(3), 229–242. Accessed at https://onlinelibrary.wiley.com/doi/abs/10.1111/1467-3435.00106#citedby-section on April 13, 2018.

Medina, J. (2014). *Brain rules: 12 principles for surviving and thriving at work, home, and school.* Seattle, WA: Pear Press.

de Melker, S., & Weber, S. (2014, September 7). *Agrarian roots? Think again. Debunking the myth of summer vacation's origins.* Accessed at www.pbs.org/newshour/education/debunking-myth-summer-vacation on February 12, 2018.

The Mind Tools Content Team. (n.d.). *Coping with change: How to make the best of a stressful situation.* Accessed at www.mindtools.com/pages/article/coping-with-change.htm on April 24, 2018.

Mitra, S. (2013, June 15). Advent of Google means we must rethink our approach to education. *The Guardian.* Accessed at http://m.guardian.co.uk/education/2013/jun/15/schools-teaching-curriculum-education-google on December 15, 2017.

Naiman, L. (2014, June 6). *Can creativity be taught? Results from research studies.* Accessed at www.creativityatwork.com/2012/03/23/can-creativity-be-taught on April 13, 2018.

Nair, P., Fielding, R., & Lackney, J. (2005). *The language of school design: Design patterns for 21st century schools*. Minneapolis, MN: DesignShare.

National Association of Secondary School Principals. (1996). *Breaking Ranks: Changing an American institution*. Reston, VA: Author.

National Association of Secondary School Principals. (2004). *Breaking Ranks II: Strategies for leading high school reform*. Reston, VA: Author.

National Education Commission on Time and Learning. (2005). *Prisoners of time: Reprint of the 1994 report of the National Education Commission on Time and Learning*. Accessed at www.ecs.org/clearinghouse/64/52/6452.pdf on December 15, 2017.

Opportunity Network. (n.d.). *Top 10 employability skills*. Accessed at www.opportunityjobnetwork.com/job-resources/help/top-10-skills.html on June 5, 2018.

Organisation for Economic Co-operation and Development. (n.d.). *PISA 2009 key findings: PISA 2009 database*. Accessed at www.oecd.org/pisa/pisaproducts/pisa2009keyfindings.htm on December 15, 2017.

Orwell, G. (1949). *1984*. Bronx, NY: Ishi Press International.

Ostdick, N. (2016, December 15). *Teach me: Automation's role in education* [Blog post]. Accessed at www.uipath.com/blog/teach-me-automations-role-in-education on February 12, 2018.

Palfrey, J., & Gasser, U. (2010). *Born digital: Understanding the first generation of digital natives*. New York: Basic Books.

Palfrey, J., & Gasser, U. (2016). *Born digital: How children grow up in a digital age*. New York: Basic Books.

Physicist: U.S. losing edge in science. (2013, October 24). *Houston Chronicle*. Accessed at www.houstonchronicle.com/news/nation-world/article/Physicist-U-S-losing-edge-in-science-4923988.php on December 15, 2017.

Puccio, G., & Szalay, P. (2014, June 17). *Creativity can be taught*. Accessed at www.td.org/insights/creativity-can-be-taught on April 16, 2018.

Rasiel, E. M., & Friga, P. N. (2002). *The McKinsey mind: Understanding and implementing the problem-solving tools and management techniques of the world's top strategic consulting firm*. New York: McGraw-Hill.

Richmond, E. (2015). *High school reform: Learning more outside of the classroom than in*. Accessed at http://hechingerreport.org/learning-more-outside-of-the-classroom-than-in on February 12, 2018.

Robinson, K. (2001). *Out of our minds: Learning to be creative*. Oxford, England: Capstone.

Robinson, K., & Aronica, L. (2015). *Creative schools: The grassroots revolution that's transforming education*. New York: Penguin Books.

Rosen, L. D. (2010). *Rewired: Understanding the iGeneration and the way they learn*. New York: St. Martin's Griffin.

Rothstein, D., & Santana, L. (2011). *Make just one change: Teach students to ask their own questions*. Cambridge, MA: Harvard Education Press.

Roza, M. (2010). *Educational economics: Where do school funds go?* Washington, DC: Urban Institute Press.

Schlechty, P. C. (1997). *Working on the work: An action plan for teachers, principals, and superintendents.* San Francisco: Jossey-Bass.

Seiter, C. (2015, January 21). *Working across multiple time zones: Tools and strategies that help connect.* Accessed at https://open.buffer.com/working-across-multiple-time-zones-tools-strategies-help-us-connect on April 13, 2018.

Steinbeck, J. (1939). *The grapes of wrath.* New York: Viking Press.

Sousa, D. A. (2011). *How the brain learns* (4th ed.). Thousand Oaks, CA: Corwin Press.

Tapscott, D. (2000). *Growing up digital: The rise of the Net generation.* New York: McGraw-Hill Education.

Tapscott, D. (2008). *Grown up digital: How the Net generation is changing your world.* New York: McGraw-Hill Education.

Texas Comptroller of Public Accounts. (n.d.). *DAAG—Independent school districts.* Accessed at https://comptroller.texas.gov/transparency/local/debt/isds.php on April 13, 2018.

Texas Education Agency. (n.d.). *Texas Accountability Rating System.* Accessed at https://rptsvr1.tea.texas.gov/perfreport/account/index.html on April 30, 2018.

Thiede, R. H. (n.d.). Gary plan: Education. In *Encyclopædia Britannica.* Accessed at www.britannica.com/topic/Gary-Plan on February 12, 2018.

Thornburg, D. (2014). *From the campfire to the holodeck: Creating engaging and powerful 21st century environments.* San Francisco: Jossey-Bass.

Thornhill, J. (2013, November 22). Bill Strickland's education revolution. *Financial Times.* Accessed at www.ft.com/content/fa27388e-523f-11e3-8c42-00144feabdc0 on December 15, 2017.

Tokuhama-Espinosa, T. (2010). *Mind, brain, and education science: A comprehensive guide to the new brain-based teaching.* New York: W. W. Norton.

Torpey, E., & Hogan, A. (2016). *Working in a gig economy.* Accessed at www.bls.gov/careeroutlook/2016/article/what-is-the-gig-economy.htm on February 12, 2018.

Towler, L. (2014, November 25). *Deeper learning: Moving students beyond memorization.* Accessed at http://neatoday.org/2014/11/25/deeper-learning-moving-students-beyond-memorization-2 on April 12, 2018.

Trump, J. L. (1959). *Images of the future: A new approach to the secondary school.* Reston, VA: National Association of Secondary School Principals.

Trump, J. L. (1977). *A school for everyone: Design for a middle, junior, or senior high school that combines the old and the new.* Reston, VA: National Association of Secondary School Principals.

UBS. (n.d.). *AI's coming of age.* Accessed at www.ubs.com/microsites/artificial-intelligence/en/ai-coming-age.html on March 29, 2018.

U.S. Department of Education. (2014). *SY 2012–2013 consolidated state performance reports part I.* Accessed at www2.ed.gov/admins/lead/account/consolidated/sy12–13part1/index.html on December 15, 2017.

VanGundy, A. B. (1988). *Techniques of structured problem solving* (2nd ed.). Rotterdam, the Netherlands: Springer.

Vygotsky, L. S. (1978). *Mind in society: The development of higher psychological processes.* Cambridge, MA: Harvard University Press.

Wagner, T. (2012). *Creating innovators: The making of young people who will change the world.* New York: Scribner.

Whittle, C. (2012, July 4). We can pay teachers more. *Washington Post.* Accessed at www.washingtonpost.com/wp-dyn/content/article/2005/09/14/AR2005091402193.html on February 1, 2018.

The World Bank. (n.d.). *Government expenditure on education, total (% of GDP).* Accessed at http://data.worldbank.org/indicator/SE.XPD.TOTL.GD.ZS?end=2014&locations=US&start=1986&view=chart on December 15, 2017.

Wurman, R. S. (1989). *Information anxiety.* New York: Doubleday.

Yamamoto, W. K. (2011, December 19). *We don't understand exponentials* [Blog post]. Accessed at www.kazabyte.com/2011/12/we-dont-understand-exponential-functions.html on April 24, 2018.

Zhao, Y. (2009). *Catching up or leading the way: American education in the age of globalization.* Alexandria, VA: Association for Supervision and Curriculum Development.

Zubrzycki, J. (2013, September 24). Missouri districts verge on bankruptcy after ruling. *Education Week.* Accessed at www.edweek.org/ew/articles/2013/09/25/05missouri_ep.h33.html on December 15, 2017.

INDEX

A

Academy School, 117, 171–179
    cost and time, 176–178
    existing school, 172–174
    spatial modifications, 174–176
Adams, C. J., 84
advisory schools, 41-43
    academy high schools, 102, 104–105, 108
    challenges, 114–116
    community context, 84, 87, 125–126, 148
    components, 71–75
    comprehensive high school, 102–104
    core vision, 61–87
    cultural/community concerns, 115–116, 118
    effecting change, 89–99
    effective instruction thresholds, 112–114, 118
    examples of, 101–108, 117, 119–179
    funding resources, 82–83, 96
    identities, 70–71
    instructional approach, 66–75
    middle schools, 102, 106–107, 127–140
    minimum thresholds for instruction, 112–114
    monitoring student progress, 115
    project-based learning, 44–45, 102, 104–106, 113–114
    repurposing traditional schools, 112, 116–179
    resources on, 71
    spatial environments, 68–75, 83, 94–95, 97–98, 119–179
    staff development, 85–86, 90, 94, 96, 98–99, 114–115, 118
    technology resources, 75–77, 87, 94–95, 113
    transition from elementary schools, 84–85
    transition to advisory format, 111–117
    use of time, 70, 77–82, 87, 112–114
agrarian calendar, 6, 13, 78–79, 87, 139, 149
Alieff, Kerr High School, 183
Amazon, 23
    Alexa, 20
Anderson, L. W., 20, 26, 30
Andrade, H., 3
Andrews, E., 20
Apple, 35
    "Knowledge Navigator, The," 50
    Siri, 20
Aronica, L., 3
assembly-line approach. *See* factory school model
assessment
    educational adequacy, 91
    school, 67–68
    student, 67, 115
    technology, 91–92

B

Battro, A. M., 22
Bergsagel, V., 71
Berman, A. E., 19
Berra, Y., 39–40
Best, T., 71
Bidwell, A., 187
big data, 23–24, 115
Bloom, B. S., 3
Booker, C., 89
Born Digital (Palfrey & Gasser), 21
Bowman, S., 21
Boynton, C., 24

Boynton, M., 24
Brain Rules (Medina), 23
Bransford, J. D., 23, 36
Breaking Ranks (NAASP), 64, 146, 164
Breaking Ranks II (NAASP), 64, 146
Bretford, 71
Brown, A. L., 23, 36
Bruce Mau Design, 71
Bryant, J., 36
building flexibility, 18, 24, 28, 41–43

C

Cameron, G., 33
Cannon Design, 71
Canvas, 76
Capital School, 116, 119–126
    cost and time, 125
    existing school, 120–122
    spatial modifications, 122–124
career fairs, 42–43
Carey, B., 70
Carl Wunsche Senior High School (Spring, TX), 185–187
Cavanagh, S., 75
Center for Public Education, 5
challenges, 111–118
    creating new environments, 114–116
    cultural and community concerns, 115–116
    effective instruction thresholds, 112–114, 118
    instructional resources, 114–115
    repurposing traditional schools, 112, 116–179
    student progress, 115
Choudhary, A. I., 5
Cocking, R. R., 23, 36
Cohen, R. D., 12
collaboration skills, 31, 33, 38, 44–45, 64
communication skills, 31–32, 34, 104, 136, 183
community context, 3, 4, 12, 84, 91, 98
comprehensive advisory high schools, 102–104
Connected School, 116, 135–140
    cost and time, 139
    existing school, 136–137
    spatial modifications, 137–138
content-focused approaches, 24

convergent thinking, 36, 38
Council of Educational Facilities Planners International, 186
Coursera, 75
creativity skills, 27, 38
    imagination, 31, 34–35
    innovation, 31, 35–36
Cristo Rey Jesuit High School (Minneapolis, MN), 185–186
Cristo Rey Network, 186
Crockett, L., 21
Cushman, K., 71
cyberbullying, 36–37

D

Darling-Hammond, L., 26
data and vision, 91–95
Davis, J., 26
Desai, V., 36
Dewey, J., 101
DeZyre, 23
digital portfolios, 66, 105
District School, 117, 151–162
    cost and time, 160–161
    existing school, 152–157
    spatial modifications, 157–160
divergent thinking, 36
Doorley, S., 71
Dorrier, J., 19
Drupal, 76

E

E and S Consulting, 35
eBooks, 76
EdSurge, 75
Education Commission of the States, 17
Education Elements, 76
Education Week, 75
Educational Facilities Laboratories, 62–63
EdX, 75
effecting change, 89–99
    budgets, 90, 95–96
    construction, 90, 97

construction documents, 90, 96
elementary schools, 84–85
funding resources, 90, 92, 96
planning, 90, 95–96
spatial elements, 90, 97–98
staff development, 90, 98
vision, 90–95
elements of schooling, 3–6, 108, 133, 140, 149, 162, 170, 179, 182
Elias, M., 66
Encyclopædia Britannica, 182
Engelhart, M. D., 3
essential skills. *See* process skills
extracurricular activities, 80, 103–104, 149, 162, 179

F

factory school model, 12–13, 15, 22–23
Fielding, R., 71
Fischer, K. W., 22
Five Open Plan High Schools (Educational Facilities Laboratories), 62
Florida, R., 78
Flynn, D., 33
focus on individuals, 18, 22–24, 28, 41–42, 114, 118
Ford Motor Company, 35
forward-focused schools
construction, 90, 97
construction documents, 90, 96
data and vision, 90–95
funds, 90, 96
materials, 90, 97–98
occupy and operate, 90, 98
schedules and budgets, 90, 95–96
staff development, 90, 98
Friga, P. N., 33
Fuller, B., 181
funding resources, 3, 5, 82–83, 90, 92, 95–96
furnishings. *See* workstations
Furst, E. J., 3

G

Gardner, H., 3
Gasser, U., 21

Gates, B., 11, 29
Gillies, T., 20
global networking, 52–57
Global Student Connect, 54
Gonzales, R., 112
Gonzalez, J. W., 76
Google Books, 76–77, 104
Google Home, 20
Graduate Management Admission Council, 32
Green School, 116, 127–133
cost and time, 131–132
existing school, 128–129
spatial modifications, 129–131
Growing Up Digital (Tapscott), 21
Grown Up Digital (Tapscott), 21

H

Hammayun, A. A., 5
Harris, J., 26
Harris, P., 26
Hasak, J., 84
Haworth, 71
Henderson, T., 35
Herman Miller, 71
Herold, B., 24
higher-level-thinking skills, 18, 20, 26–27, 87, 94, 114
Hill, W. H., 3
Hogan, A., 32
Honda, 50
hyperinformation, 19–20, 28, 30, 33–34

I

IBM, 20
Images of the Future (Trump), 183
Inevitable, The (Kelly), 50
Information Anxiety (Wurman), 34
information investigation skills, 31, 33–34, 38
information presentation skills, 31, 34
instructional approach, 3–4, 66–74
instructional resources, 114–115
Instructure, 75
International Baccalaureate program, 164, 173
internet citizenship skills, 31, 36–37, 38

interpersonal skills, 31–32
intrapersonal skills, 31–32
Izzy+, 71

J

James D. MacConnell Award, 185
Jaschik, S., 66
Jensen, E., 23
Jukes, I., 21, 62

K

Kaku, M., 1
Kelly, F. S., 62
Kelly, K., 18–19, 50
Kerr High School (Alief, TX), 183–184
Khan Academy, 75
Knewton, 75
Kodak, 182
Krathwohl, D., 20, 26, 30
Kuang, C., 35

L

Lackney, J. A., 71
Latif, A., 5
Learning Registry, 75–76
Learning Policy Institute, 26
Lee, H., 46–47
Léna, P. J., 22
Leventhal, M., 188
Levine, A., 15
libraries, 65, 76, 103–104, 113–114, 131, 139, 152, 168–169, 176
literacy skills, 30–31

M

Madsen, P. M., 36
Mahdawi, A., 32
Mallett, C. A., 5
Massachusetts Department of Elementary and Secondary Education, 5
McCain, T., 21, 33, 62, 114
McConachie, L., 71
McIntosh, S., 32

Medina, J., 4, 23
Melker, S. de, 78
Met High School, The (Providence, RI), 185
metacognition, 36
middle schools, 102, 106–108, 163–170
Mind Tools Content Team, The, 19
Minneapolis (MN) Independent School District 184
Minneapolis Zoo, 184
Mitra, S., 61, 64, 86
mobile technology, 19–20
modern schooling principles
    building flexibility, 18, 24
    focus on individuals, 18, 22–24
    higher-level-thinking skills, 18, 26–27
    technology, impact of, 18–20
    use of time, 18, 25–26
Moodle, 75

N

Naiman, L., 35
Nair, P., 71
National Association of Secondary School Principals, 64, 74, 146, 164, 183
National Education Commission on Time and Learning, 4
New Tech Network, 136–137, 153–156, 184–195
New Tech School, 152, 156–157, 160–162
New Technology High School (Napa, CA), 184–185
Newcastle University, 64
1984 (Orwell), 26
North Face, 35

O

Open School, 116, 141–149
    existing school, 142–144
    spatial modifications, 144–148
    cost and time, 148
open-plan schools, 62–64, 83, 182
    repurposing, 141–149
Opportunity Network, 26–27
Organisation for Economic Co-operation and Development, 79
Orwell, G., 26
Ostdick, N., 20

P

Palfrey, J., 21
problem-solving skills, 27, 31–33, 87, 114
process skills, 24, 27 (*See also individual skills*)
    obsolete vs. necessary, 30–31
project-based learning, 44–45, 94, 102, 104–106, 113–114
Puccio, G., 35

Q

Questia, 76–77, 104

R

Rasiel, E. M., 33
Rewired (Rosen), 21
Richmond, E., 20
Robinson, K., 3, 30
Rosen, L. D., 21
Rothstein, D., 36
Roza, M., 83

S

Santana, L., 36
Sauer, W., 71
Schlechty, P. C., 67
School for Everyone, A (Trump), 64, 183
School of Environmental Studies (Minneapolis, MN), 184
Schoology, 75
Seiter, C., 33
SimArt Center, 53–54
Simon Fraser University, 33
smart technology, 19–20, 48–52, 57
Smith, B. M., 26
Solution Tree, 71, 75, 96, 102, 120, 128, 136, 143, 153, 164, 173
social networking, 21, 36–37
    global, 52–57
Sousa, D. A., 23
spatial environment, 3–5, 12–14, 64–66, 68–74, 83, 94–95
    Academy School, 171–179
    attachment to classrooms, 14–15
    Capital School, 119–126
    Connected School, 135–140
    District School, 151–162
    Green School, 127–133
    Open School, 141–149
    Tech School, 163–170
Spontaneous ad hocism, 15
Spring (TX) Independent School District, 186–187
staff development, 85–86, 90, 94, 96, 98–99, 114–115, 118
Stanford Graduate School of Education, 26
STEAM schools, 173
Steelcase, 71
Stephen, D., 71
student learning
    elements of, 3–5
Szalay, P., 35

T

Tang, I., 188
Tapscott, D., 21
teacher's role, 19–20, 25–26, 64–67, 85–86, 112–114, 118
Teaching for Tomorrow (McCain), 114
Teaching the Digital Generation (Kelly, et al.), 62
Teaching With the Future in Mind (McCain), 114
Tech School, 117, 163–170
    cost and time, 169
    existing school, 164–166
    spatial modifications, 166–169
technological changes, 2–4, 12 39–58, 75–77, 87, 94–95
    accelerating, 19
    advisory schools, 41–42
    career fairs, 42–43
    global networking, 52–57
    hyperinformation, 19–20, 28, 30, 33–34
    mobile technology, 19–20
    project-based learning, 44–45, 94, 102, 104–106, 113–114
    smart technology, 19–20, 48–52, 57
    social networking, 21, 51–57
    to how students learn, 21–22
    transforming lives, 18–20
    virtual learning environments, 45–47, 76
technology resources, 75–77, 87, 94–95, 113
Texas Comptroller of Public Accounts, 112
Texas Education Agency, 128, 156–157, 164
Thiede, R. H., 12

Thornburg, D., 3
time management. *See* use of time
To Kill a Mockingbird (Lee), 46–47
Todd, A., 36
Tokuhama-Espinosa, T., 22
Tommy Hilfiger, 35
Torpey, E., 32
Towler, L., 26
traditional classrooms
    common assumptions, 13–14
    limits of, 2–3, 12–13
    moving beyond attachment, 14–15
    repurposing, 112, 116–179
    technology changing, 12–16
Trump, J. L., 63–64, 183

U

UBS, 20
Udemy, 75
U.S. Department of Defense, 75
U.S. Department of Education, 75, 183, 187
Understanding the Digital Generation (Jukes, McCain, & Crockett), 21
use of time, 3–4, 18, 25–26, 41–42, 70, 77–82, 87, 95, 112–114

V

Valtcheva, A., 3
VanGundy, A. B., 33
virtual learning environments, 45–47, 76
VS Furniture, 71
Vygotsky, L. S., 3

W

Wagner, T., 3
Weber, S., 78
Westside High School (Omaha, NE), 183
Whitthoft, S., 71
Whittle, C., 182
Wired magazine, 18
Wirt, W., 12, 24
Witthoft, S., 71
workstations, 65, 68–71, 71–75
    Academy School, 174–176
    breakout space, 74
    Capital School, 122,
    Connected School, 139
    flexible, 73–74
    Green School, 130
    Open School, 147
    student, 73
    teacher-advisory, 72–73, 104
    Tech School, 169–170
World Bank, 188
Wurman, R. S., 34

Y

Yamamoto, W. K., 19
YouTube, 23, 36

Z

Zhao, Y., 3
Zoo School. *See* School of Environmental Sciences
Zubrzycki, J., 66

Different Schools for a Different World
Scott McLeod and Dean Shareski
This resource details six key arguments for why educators must approach schooling differently in the 21st century: (1) information literacy, (2) the economy, (3) learning, (4) boredom, (5) innovation, and (6) equity. Learn how schools are tackling these six arguments head-on in order to help students grow into globally aware citizens, risk-takers, innovators, and literate content consumers.
BKF729

Creating the Anywhere, Anytime Classroom
Casey Reason, Lisa Reason, and Crystal Guiler
Discover how to enhance student learning in online and blended classrooms. This user-friendly resource offers direct guidance on the steps K–12 educators must take to facilitate online learning and maximize student growth using digital tools. Each chapter includes suggestions, tips, and examples tied to pedagogical practices associated with learning online, so you can confidently engage in the best practices with your students.
BKF772

NOW Classrooms Series
Meg Ormiston
This practical series presents classroom-tested lessons that teachers and instructional coaches can rely on to engage students in active learning and problem solving. Use these lessons, which are grounded in the essential four C skills (communication, collaboration, critical thinking, and creativity) to connect technology to key learning outcomes and prepare learners to succeed in the 21st century.
BKF797, BKF798, BKF799, BKF800, BKF801

The End of School as We Know It
Bruce Dixon
Reimagine school practices to meet the needs of modern learners. With today's digitally rich classrooms and highly connected world, the context on which traditional schools are built must shift dramatically. The author challenges school administrators and leaders to let go of their assumptions about the relevance of traditional schooling in learners' lives and deeply reevaluate the effectiveness of their current methods.
BKF692

Freedom to Learn
Will Richardson
Give students control over the learning process. The 21st century has seen vast advances in technology—which can connect students and teachers to more information, knowledge, and experts than ever before. Investigate why the traditional education system isn't working, uncover why the meanings of *education* and *success* should be redefined, and understand the teacher's role in a free learning environment.
BKF688

Solution Tree | Press

Visit solution-tree.com or call 800.733.6786 to order.

Wait! Your professional development journey doesn't have to end with the last pages of this book.

We realize improving student learning doesn't happen overnight. And your school or district shouldn't be left to puzzle out all the details of this process alone.

No matter where you are on the journey, we're committed to helping you get to the next stage.

Take advantage of everything from **custom workshops** to **keynote presentations** and **interactive web and video conferencing**. We can even help you develop an action plan tailored to fit your specific needs.

Let's get the conversation started.

Call 888.763.9045 today.

SolutionTree.com